Frontiers of the Reformation

Frontiers of the Reformation

Dissidence and Orthodoxy in
Sixteenth-Century Europe

AUKE JELSMA

Ashgate

Aldershot • Brookfield USA • Singapore • Sydney

Published by
Ashgate Publishing Limited
Gower House
Croft Road
Aldershot
Hants
GU11 3HR
England

Ashgate Publishing Company
Old Post Road
Brookfield
Vermont 05036–9704
USA

British Library Cataloguing in Publication Data

Jelsma, Auke
　Frontiers of the Reformation: Dissidence and Orthodoxy in
　Sixteenth-Century Europe.
　(St Andrews Studies in Reformation History)
　1. Reformation—Europe.　2. Counter-Reformation—Europe.
　3. Reformation—Social aspects—Europe.
　I. Title.
　274'.06

Library of Congress Cataloging-in-Publication Data

Jelsma, Auke, 1933–
　　Frontiers of the Reformation: dissidence and orthodoxy in
　sixteenth-century Europe/Auke Jelsma.
　　　p.　cm. (St Andrews Studies in Reformation History)
　　Includes bibliographical references and index.
　　ISBN 1-84014-280-4 (hb: alk. paper)
　　1. Reformation.　2. Christianity and culture—Europe—
　History—16th century.　I. Title.　II. Series.
　BR309.J44　1998
　274'.06—dc21   98–18566
                                                                           CIP

ISBN 1 84014 280 4

This book is printed on acid free paper

Typeset in Sabon by Manton Typesetters, 5–7 Eastfield Road, Louth, Lincolnshire, LN11 7AJ and printed in Great Britain by

Printed in Great Britain by The Ipswich Book Company, Suffolk.

Contents

Contents

St Andrews Studies in Reformation History

*The Shaping of a Community: The Rise and Reformation of the
English Parish c. 1400–1560*
Beat Kümin

*Seminary or University? The Genevan Academy and
Reformed Higher Education, 1560–1620*
Karin Maag

Marian Protestantism: Six Studies
Andrew Pettegree

Protestant History and Identity in Sixteenth-Century Europe
(2 volumes) edited by Bruce Gordon

*Antifraternalism and Anticlericalism in the German Reformation:
Johann Eberlin von Günzburg and the Campaign against the Friars*
Geoffrey Dipple

*Reformations Old and New: Essays on the Socio-Economic
Impact of Religious Change c. 1470–1630*
edited by Beat Kümin

Piety and the People: Religious Printing in French, 1511–1551
Francis M. Higman

The Reformation in Eastern and Central Europe
edited by Karin Maag

John Foxe and the English Reformation
edited by David Loades

The Reformation and the Book
Jean-François Gilmont,
edited and translated by Karin Maag

Preface

The religious break that occurred in the sixteenth century has had an impact which can best be compared with that of a large comet colliding with earth. As a result the climate changes. The Roman Catholic Church took on a different appearance to what it had been before the break. Protestantism in various forms put its stamp on large parts of Europe. In this period, partly because they were hounded by religious wars, the European peoples began their triumphal march over the world.

This was not without its consequences. Everyone who grows up in a country where the mentality, the outlook, the culture has been shaped by Roman Catholicism or Protestantism, bears in his or her soul seeds that were sown in the sixteenth century. Therefore, those who want to confront themselves do well to study the sixteenth century. The origin of what we carry in our souls is to be found there.

Thus it is important that this century is accessible. We must not limit ourselves to what some great figures have thought and written, however significant and influential their ideas might have been. The time of the Reformation should be regarded from various viewpoints – from top to bottom and side to side, and from the perspective of the 'victors' as well as that of the 'losers' (although in my opinion, in a quarrel about the truth there can only be losers).

Therefore, in this volume the phenomenon of the Reformation is approached from rather unusual angles. It features people who have experienced the Protestant Reformation as a failure. Attention is paid to others who have tried to lift the Christian religion above all contradictions and differences in opinion. We investigate how church leaders attempted to alter popular mentality, even the national character. Men and women who without any education began to read the Bible, as if only then had this book fallen from the sky, are also included. As a consequence, it is inevitable that we often find ourselves bordering upon heresy. During the sixteenth century, this was where many people, deliberately or reluctantly, also found themselves.

The intention of this reflection on the clash between Roman Catholicism and Protestantism is not to resurrect the differences but, rather, to enhance the dialogue. Besides, it is important to assess what, even now, can be the value of traditions and feelings that influence our behaviour and mentality almost unconsciously. These are the reasons for this volume.

Auke Jelsma

Acknowledgements

These chapters have appeared in earlier publications, but I have modified them for this volume. The original titles in which they were published are as follows:

Chapter 1: 'Terughoudende afwijzing. De Windesheimse congregatie en het protestantisme', in *Windesheim 1395. Kloosters, teksten, invloeden*, eds A. J. Hendrikman, P. Bange, R. Th. M. van Dijk, A. J. Jelsma and G. E. P. Vrielink (Nijmegen, 1996), pp. 154–69.

Chapter 2: 'De duivel in het protestantisme', in *Duivelsbeelden*, eds G. Rooyakkers, L. Dresen-Coenders and M. Geerdes (Baarn, 1994), pp. 198–215.

Chapter 3: 'A 'Messiah for Women'; Religious Commotion in the North-East of Switzerland, 1525–1526', in *Studies in Church History*, 27, *Women in the Church*, eds W. J. Sheils and D. Wood (Oxford, 1990), pp. 295–306.

Chapter 4: 'De koning en de vrouwen; Münster 1534–1535', *Gereformeerd Theologisch Tijdschrift*, 75 (1975), pp. 82–107.

Chapter 5: 'Women Martyrs in a Revolutionary Age. A Comparison of Books of Martyrs', in *Church, Change and Revolution*, eds J. van den Berg and P. G. Hoftijzer (Leiden, 1991), pp. 41–56.

Chapter 6: *Waarom de Reformatie mislukte*, Kamper Oraties, 2 (Kampen, 1993).

Chapter 7: 'Mentaliteitsbeïnvloeding door Meerdere Vergaderingen in de Noordelijke Nederlanden', in *Kerk in beraad, opstellen aangeboden aan prof. dr. J.C.P.A. van Laarhoven*, eds G. Ackermans, A. Davids and P. J. A. Nissen (Nijmegen, 1991), pp. 159–76.

Chapter 8: 'Waartoe een mans bestemd is. Over huwelijk en gezin in de reformatietijd', in *Vrouw, man, kind. Lijnen van vroeger naar nu*, ed. L. Dresen-Coenders (Baarn, 1978), pp. 79–88.

Chapter 9: 'In het donker geloven', in *Nacht die gelukkig maakt. Ervaringen met de mystiek van Johannes van het Kruis*, ed. M. Schuurmans (Zoetermeer, 1991), pp. 101–11.

Chapter 10: 'De receptie van Juan de la Cruz in het protestantisme', in *Taal van verlangen. Overwegingen bij de mystiek van Juan de la Cruz*, ed. W. G. Tillmans (Haarlem, 1992), pp. 50–62.

Chapter 11: 'Zonder een dak boven het hoofd', in *Als de hemel de aarde raakt. Spiritualiteit, mystiek, ervaringen*, ed. J. Beumer (Kampen, 1989), pp. 64–77.

I wish to thank, as I have also acknowledged in the Dutch edition, Professor Andrew Pettegree, director of St Andrews Reformation Studies Institute, for his encouragement to prepare an edition of some of my essays about the Reformation for the *St Andrews Studies in Reformation History*. I am proud that one of my books could gain a place in this splendid series. I thank him also for the opportunity to spend part of my sabbatical year in St Andrews, where I had the opportunity to study in the impressive library of that university, and for the valuable discussions with colleagues and students which he made possible.

I am very grateful to Mr J. C. van Loon and Mrs Norma Taylor for the translation of the greater part of these essays into English and to Caroline Cornish at Ashgate for her advice.

I have also very much appreciated the help of staff in all the libraries where I was able to work, especially at my own university at Kampen, the support of the Board of Trustees of this university and, not least, the contributions of my assistants Drs J. van den Berg and A. W. Aarnoutse.

I trust, they are all satisfied with this result. The subject is an important one, and I will always remain fascinated by the effects religious conflicts exercise on society, and how people have reacted to the spiritual, cultural and material confusion of their own time.

Introduction: competing concepts of reformation

It is characteristic of liberation movements that a variety of motives operate within them. Participants are united in the realization that far-reaching changes are necessary and that the repressive regime constitutes an obstruction of the future goal. However, as soon as they attempt to put into words what minimal changes should be carried out or what is the desired form of government, differences in opinion arise. Repressive authorities understand these conditions. Without exception they apply the mechanisms of 'divide and rule'. Therefore, no two groups are repressed in the same way. There is always an élite which profits if the existing order is retained and which therefore opposes all changes, but even among the people who do suffer from repression there is a fear of losing what privileges they still have. There is usually only a minority that has nothing to lose. The commonly experienced repression has many faces.

I believe it is no exaggeration if I call the Catholicism of the beginning of the sixteenth century an all-encompassing power. In the late Middle Ages the church had grown to be a system from which no one could withdraw, which determined the life of everyone to a high degree, a bureaucracy which controlled the social, judicial, economic, cultural, political and, of course, religious life in Europe:

- social: consider the ranks and classes in which it divided society; recall the works of charity which it controlled
- judicial: reflect on the church's control of civil registration, marital law and a significant part of criminal law
- economic: pause over the incredible amount of land the monasteries possessed, of the money one had to pay to gain a position in the church, also indulgences
- cultural: consider the control of the mass media and art; comprehend the influence of religious orders at the universities
- political: think of the secular power that the pope and many bishops could wield
- religious: think of the exclusive control of the means of grace.

No one could escape the church.

Resistance grew. As R. W. Scribner wrote:

> What seems to have aroused most lay anger was three things:
> clerical claims to exercise a monopoly of sacred power; their de-
> mand that this be provided only in return for payment; and their
> readiness to deny their priestley services, often for light causes and
> often because of the inability of lay folk to pay ... perhaps the
> greatest source of outrage.[1]

'You laymen hate us priests, and it is an old hatred between you and
us,' Johann Geiler von Kaysersberg (1445–1510) told the community at
Strasburg in one of his sermons.[2]

The more autonomous and knowledgeable lay people became, the
more they realized that there was something fundamentally wrong with
the institutional church, that the church had removed itself too far from
its origins, that the clergy had too much to say on too many matters and
that a thorough reformation was needed. As soon as the critics tried to
determine what had to be changed, the differences came to light. This
was inevitable.

For example, the repression in the area north of the Alps contained
elements which were absent in Southern Europe. In the German Empire
and in England the secular powers, too, were eager to rid themselves of
the monasteries. In Spain and Italy this was less of an issue; the monasteries here did not possess the huge areas of land which had been
acquired elsewhere. Throughout Europe the bourgeoisie had different
problems with the church from those of the nobility. The highest positions in the church were to a large extent in the hands of noblemen. The
lower clergy was often irritated by the greed and lack of spiritual life
they observed in their superiors; they desired that the sacraments be
taken seriously, that absolution was not for the people who had more
money but that it was linked to sincere repentance. For the lay people,
on the other hand, it was increasingly difficult to accept their sacramental dependence. They themselves wanted control of the sources of salvation, they themselves wanted to read Holy Scripture, they themselves
wanted to determine what and how to believe.

---

[1] R. W. Scribner, *Popular Culture and Popular Movements in Reformation Germany*
(London and Roncevente, 1987), p. 250. Scribner also enumerated six different types of
power wielded by the clergy: political, economic, legal, social, sexual and sacred; p. 244.
See for the complex relations: *Anticlericalism in Late Medieval and Early Modern
Europe*, eds Peter A. Dykema and Heiko A. Oberman (Leiden, New York and Cologne,
1993).

[2] Thomas A. Brady jr, '"You hate us priests": Anticlericalism, Communalism, and the
Control of Women at Strasbourg in the Age of the Reformation', in *Anticlericalism in
Late Medieval and Early Modern Europe*, eds P. A. Dykema and H. A. Oberman
(Leiden, New York and Cologne, 1993), p. 167.

Reformation

One does injustice to the diversity of motives and impulses if one suggests that only Protestantism as it developed in the wake of Luther's appearance, may be properly called reformation. The concept itself, *reformatio*, was used regularly in the late Middle Ages, and its presupposition was that the original form contained the real meaning. Divergences in later times were regarded as a distortion which had to be restored. In common parlance reformation meant nothing other than the restoration of the original intention, a return to the very beginning.[3] At the close of the fifteenth and the beginning of the sixteenth centuries there was a common realization that the church as a whole was suffering from a serious deformation, and that reformation had to be regarded as inevitable.

Consequently, we have a clear idea of the history of the sixteenth-century reformation only if we acknowledge from the outset that reformation was looked for in many different ways. The various reform movements not only opposed the repressive institution, were not only a correction of the observed deformation, but also manifested themselves as a reaction and a threat to one another. The sixteenth-century reformation was an avalanche which fell from the top of the mountain along different slopes.

Precisely the multitude and diversity of the reform movements at the end of the fifteenth and the first half of the sixteenth centuries correct the view which developed in later times, that religious life in Europe at that time was at a low ebb. Equally valid is the opinion that Christianity was doing remarkably well during that period. That is why criticism emerged from all quarters against the way in which the institutional church represented Christianity. The abuses certainly existed, but they were no longer accepted. As Steven E. Ozment wrote: 'On the eve of the Reformation we find a piety characterized by criticism of manifest religious abuses, skepticism about long-accepted clerical privileges and revered ecclesiastical practices, and a willingness to experiment with new religious forms.'[4] But that testifies rather to a growing involvement with the church than to indifference or superficiality.

---

[3] See Euan Cameron, *The European Reformation* (Oxford, 1991), p. 38.

[4] Steven E. Ozment, *The Reformation in the Cities. The Appeal of Protestantism to Sixteenth-Century Germany and Switzerland* (New Haven and London, 1975), pp. 42, 43.

Reacting to one another

In the introduction of this volume it is important to realize and acknowl-edge the diversity of reform movements. This makes it possible to reckon from the outset with the fact that these movements received their identity to a large extent from their struggle with one another. They sharpened each other. They each caused one another. They emphasized certain doctrines because of this confrontation with each other in a way which would have been impossible otherwise. Therefore, in a certain sense they also corrupted one another. They blocked each other's development.

For example, the Counter-Reformation embraced anew elements of popular religion which the Catholic Reformation had combated at first, mainly because Protestantism had taken the attack on popular piety as the spearhead of its policy. As is well known, movements such as Germanistic mysticism and Dutch Modern Devotion tried to teach Chris-tians the way of perfection through following Christ's example. Authors of devotional works such as Thomas a Kempis (c. 1380–1471) criti-cized the exaggerated passion for pilgrimages and the adoration of holy relics. But all these elements of popular piety returned during the period of the Baroque.

The struggle within Protestantism gives us another example. The Lu-theran Reformation developed its almost docile subjection to the secular authorities especially in order to be able to distinguish itself from Re-formed Protestantism which was much more open to opposition against the state.[5] The history of the sixteenth-century reformation can only be understood against the background of these mutual influences.

We do have to realize that a categorization is, in a sense, a construc-tion with hindsight, although in the sixteenth century also there were attempts to sort the various views according to certain categories. At the beginning, especially, the borders remained fluid, and there were many border crossings. People often changed position if they came to the conclusion that the reformation they had in mind was not suffi-ciently, or on the other hand was in an exaggerated way, dealt with by the movement they had initially joined, or if they felt that the movement underwent a development which they regarded as undesirable. Some-times people did not realize until later what the consequences of their choice were. There were many who left with regrets not only under the

---

[5] See an example of this in the tensions between the Lutherans and the Reformed in Antwerp. In 1566 both had acquired the right to preach within the city. Later on, however, the Lutherans chose the side of the Roman Catholic majority and turned against the Reformed. See Guido Marnef, *Antwerp in the Age of Reformation* (Balti-more, 1996), pp. 141–6.

pressure of persecutions, but also as a result of their experiences. Many held the view that the reformation they had chosen had become a failure, as Sebastian Castellio (1515–63) wrote: 'Posterity will not be able to understand this, that once again we have to live in such a thick darkness, while the light had risen.'[6] But other Protestants remained of the opinion that it had been God himself who had delivered them from the oppressing power of the Antichrist in Rome.

Reformation and Protestantism

Despite the great variety of movements during the sixteenth century, there must be a reason why in literature the term 'Reformation' usually designates only Protestantism. What distinguishes these Protestant movements from the Catholic Reformation and the Counter-Reformation? What was their surplus value? Why does the reforming character of the Catholic Reformation pale into insignificance in comparison with the movement which people like Luther and Zwingli set in motion? Why is the reforming character of the Catholic Reformation so seldom recognized?

This black and white picture is, of course, to be seen when Protestant theologians assess the Protestant Reformation exclusively on the basis of its best motives but the Catholic one on its daily praxis. In a recent volume of essays the deepest and still-existing gulf between Rome and the Reformation is regarded as a matter of authority. The Reformation is bound only by the truth of the Scriptures, and it seeks to subject the church to that authority, 'while Rome wants to bind the people to the truth of the church, to which also the Scriptures are subject'.[7] Therefore, the Catholic Reformation is void. It is undoubtedly true that the principle of *sola Scriptura* has played an important role in the polemics between Rome and the Reformation, but factually this is a rather complicated issue, especially for those in the circles of the Catholic Reformation who also wanted to call on Holy Scripture as the highest source of truth. Even in the sixteenth century several staunch champions of *sola Scriptura* experienced to their regret that, in reality, confessionalism prevailed within Protestantism. Therefore, here too the Scriptures were explained on the basis of tradition, as Chapter 6 in this volume shows. Those who do not apologetically compare the ideal of their own group with the approximate reality of their opponents, will be less inclined to discover an unbridgeable gulf on this issue.

---

[6] See Chapter 6 in this volume.
[7] W. Balke, *Omgang met de reformatoren* (Kampen, 1992), p. 14.

The principle of *sola fide* has also been regarded as characteristic of the Protestant Reformation – and at an early stage. This indeed had been Luther's great discovery, that man is justified by God for faith alone and not for works. And yet, here too the views of Catholic and Protestant reformers were not irreconcilable, as is clear from the Colloquy at Regensburg (1538–41).[8] At any rate, it can be ascertained that these differences in doctrine came into being mainly as a result of the mutual polemics, the growing estrangement and the necessity to establish one's own identity, by which one could unequivocally distinguish oneself from one's opponents.

The main reason why, in common speech, the term Reformation is used for the Protestant Reformation and not for the Catholic one, must therefore be found elsewhere. The reason why the Catholic Reformation sincerely believed for several decades that it could realize the renewal of the church from within, without having to break away, can be found in its acceptance of the clerical structure. In spite of the criticism and all attempts to come to renewal, the distinction between laity and clergy was never contested. The principle of the priesthood of all believers was the real crowbar with which the existing church was broken open. In my opinion, this is the crucial point of difference between attempts at reform from within the church and attempts that resulted in the existence of a different type of church. This explains why the Protestant Reformation could succeed only in those parts of Europe where anticlericalism was at its height and where the hate between priests and lay people, of which Johann Geiler von Kaysersberg had spoken in his sermon, had been the strongest.

A chaotic picture

The picture we have of the sixteenth century is, thanks to all these complex developments in Europe, a chaotic one. The choices people made were dependent on the position they held, on the economic, cultural and political influence they could exert or had to endure. Everybody was forced to take a position. Despite the diversity and the eruptions of agitation within the monasteries, most monks and nuns came to conclusions that conflicted with the rest of the population. The

---

[8] See especially C. Augustijn, *De godsdienstgesprekken tussen rooms-katholieken en protestanten van 1538 tot 1541* (Haarlem, 1967). In Benedictine monasteries in Italy the doctrine of *sola fide* was more than once both accepted and debated, as elucidated by Barry Collett in *Italian Benedictine Scholars and the Reformation* (Oxford 1985), pp. 68–71.

socially affluent were inclined to take a different stand than those at the lower end of society. Those who had had the opportunity to study at a university were more careful in dealing with the Scriptures and with the writings of the church fathers than the people who had just learned to read and who could do so only clumsily. This does not mean that the rifts coincided with the differences in social position. Some of the nobility chose the side of one of the Protestant positions; the majority did not. Amongst intellectuals there was great interest in the new theology which the reformers took to the market, but to many of them the new doctrines of, for example, Luther, Calvin or Menno Simons were only a source of indignation. Those who were depicted as heretics by the leaders of the Roman Catholic Church sometimes also accused one another of heresy.

In this volume we discuss the diversity of these positions. We look at this many coloured tapestry as it were from the bottom up. We will discuss the following subjects: how one responded to Protestantism in the circles of the Modern Devotion (the Congregation of Windesheim); what women in the environment of the Swiss town Appenzell experienced, who in their discussion groups had, for the first time in their lives, the opportunity to think independently about the significance of Christ; by what varying motives the adherents to the Anabaptist movement were driven; how men and women responded to persecution; the disappointment many experienced when, after fleeing from their home country, they were subjected to another yoke elsewhere; if and how the image of the Devil was subject to changes in the melting pot of new ideas; what the consequences of all these reforming activities were for the spiritual and social life; and how mysticism was sometimes the only outlet for reformed feelings.

Thus, explicit theological principles define the perspective of this volume only to a limited degree. This is by choice. The conviction behind it is that the theological justification is to a great extent a rationalization of a position already held. People choose first. Then they legitimate their choice. Intuition leads, rationalization follows. It is circumstance and character which lead people to their decisions, for which afterwards they render account to themselves.

This sequence is obvious from the U-turns even the main spokesmen of the Protestant Reformation have made. A few examples can clarify this. Luther spoke as positively about the Jews initially as he did negatively later on.[9] In the mean time the Lutheran Reformation had devel-

---

[9] For the change of Luther in his attitude towards the Jews see Heiko A. Oberman, *The Impact of the Reformation* (Grand Rapids, MI, 1994), pp. 81–140. See also H. A. Oberman, *The Roots of Antisemitism* (Philadelphia, 1984).

oped from a repressed minority into a state church. Anabaptist leaders like Jan Matthijs, who had recommended non-violence in The Netherlands, changed their outlook when they took control of a town such as Münster.[10] In the first edition of his *Institutes* Calvin had rejected the use of violence by the authorities against dissenters, but he left out this passage in later editions, when he had the opportunity to make Geneva into a City of God.[11] When circumstances change, points of view are adapted accordingly. Therefore, it is sensible for a church historian to approach the history of the Reformation from viewpoints other than merely theological ones.

The sense of the history of the Reformation

The sixteenth century was, for those involved, a confusing time. The people were confronted with new ideas for which their frame of mind, their parents, their education and their pattern of life had not prepared them. There was a general uneasiness about the way the institutional church kept life in Europe in its grip. At the same time people were looking for stability to cope with the threats on the political and social scene.

People in the twentieth century live in a similar situation. The faith of our ancestors is buried. The mass media bring us into contact with new ideas, other religions, great cultural diversity. People feel insecure, uncertain. At the same time a new autonomy is emerging. People are invited to choose from a host of possibilities in the areas of health care, systems of ultimate meaning, religion, and the old ecclesiastical institutes react as adequately as possible, albeit in very different ways, to the far-reaching changes. Preachers condemn or recommend. Some try to re-anchor the traditional teaching, others open up to different ideas with a sense of relief.

At such a stage it is worth investigating how people in an earlier time reacted to changes for which life had not prepared them. This is why this volume has come into being.

[10] See Chapter 4 in this volume.
[11] See Chapter 6 in this volume.

CHAPTER ONE

Reluctant rejection: the Congregation of Windesheim and the Protestant Reformation

I

In 1938 Adrianus Jan Bemolt van Loghum Slaterus received his doctor-ate from the University of Amsterdam on the basis of a dissertation entitled *Het klooster Frenswegen*. In accordance with common Dutch practice he had added several formal theses to the conclusive part of his dissertation. The first thesis is worth quoting: 'The opinion that the Modern Devotion prepared the way for Protestantism is totally correct with respect to the Brethren of the Common Life, but incorrect with regard to the Congregation of Windesheim.'[1] This thesis satisfies the traditional academic condition that it should be contestable. It evokes a number of questions. Is it right to characterize the Brotherhood of the Common Life as having prepared the way for Protestantism? Is it possible to speak of a total opposition between the Congregation of Windesheim and Protestantism? Was the mentality of the brothers and sisters of the common life really so different from the Windesheim congregation?

To support his thesis Van Loghum Slaterus refers to the well-known study by W. J. Kühler on the history of the Mennonites.[2] The latter indeed notes remarkable similarities between the brothers and sisters of the common life and the Mennonites. According to him, both move-ments are characterized by an aversion to dogmatic Christianity, an emphasis on evangelical commandments, training in the imitation of Christ, reform of the religious and moral life, and by the restrictions of spiritual pride wrapped in humility, spiritual drills 'which suffocate much sound life' and forms of exaltation. Even in details like the

---

[1] Adrianus Jan Bemolt van Loghum Slaterus, *Het klooster Frenswegen* (Amsterdam, 1938), thesis no. 1: 'De meening dat de Moderne Devotie wegbereidster is geweest voor het Protestantisme, is volkomen juist ten opzichte van de Broederschap des Gemeenen Levens, doch niet wat betreft de Windesheimer Congregatie.'

[2] W. J. Kühler, *Geschiedenis der Nederlandsche Doopsgezinden in de zestiende eeuw*, 2nd edn (Haarlem, 1961), pp. 24–35.

aversion to the swearing of oaths and the refusal to accept positions of public service the resemblance would be visible.

The brothers and sisters of the common life were aware of this kinship, according to Kühler. When the Protestant Reformation manifested itself, many are supposed to have left the brother- and sisterhouses. 'In numerous houses the Reformation had adherents.'[3] However, according to Kühler, this did not hold true for the Windesheim congregation: 'Windesheim remained a bulwark of Catholicism until the end.'[4]

In light of the kinship between the various branches of the Modern Devotion, the suggestion that such a difference in reaction towards the Protestant Reformation would have existed between the monasteries of the congregation on the one hand and the brother- and sister-houses on the other, requires further evidence.

In this respect, however, Kühler is found lacking. He restricts himself to the assumption that the emergence of the Windesheim congregation will have attracted the more traditional people within the brother- and sister-houses: 'Windesheim attracted the more monastic elements from the brotherhood and thus helped it maintain the more liberal spirit among its members. The congregation itself moved ever more toward severity.' So he tries to prove what van Loghum Slaterus put into words in his thesis, namely, that there indeed was a kinship between the Modern Devotion and certain currents within Protestantism but that the Windesheim congregation stubbornly and consistently took a Counter-Reformation stand.[5] Therefore further reflection on the relation between the Windesheim congregation in particular and Protestantism is certainly important.

---

[3] Kühler, *Geschiedenis Doopsgezinden*, pp. 26–9.

[4] Ibid., p. 28.

[5] See the Introduction of John van Engen in *Devotio Moderna. Basic Writings* (New York, 1988), p. 21: 'In recent years historians have emphasized the difference between canons and brothers.' In their contributions to the volume *De doorwerking van de Moderne Devotie. Windesheim 1387–1987*, eds P. Bange, C. Graafland, A. J. Jelsma and A. G. Weiler (Hilversum, 1988), based on a symposium, C. Augustijn ('Erasmus en de Moderne Devotie', pp. 71–80), Peter J. A. Nissen ('De Moderne Devotie en het Nederlands-Westfaalse Doperdom: op zoek naar relaties en invloeden', pp. 95–118) and S. Voolstra ('Hetzelfde, maar anders. Het verlangen naar volkomen vroomheid als drijfveer van de Moderne Devotie en van de doperse reformatie', pp. 119–34) have convincingly demonstrated the weakness of Kühler's argument. Kühler composed an ideal image of the Anabaptist movement, which was based less on historical reality than on his own assumptions. Hardly a trace can be found of a historical relationship between participants of the Modern Devotion and of the emerging Protestantism. They have not dealt with the question whether Kühler rightly distinguishes between the brother- and sister-houses and the monasteries of the Windesheim congregation, characterizing the first as more liberal and the latter as more conservative. In my opinion, there is no evidence for this at all.

There is reason to suppose that there must have been a mutual feeling of kinship, because they have several things in common. Both are a reaction to phenomena of decay in ecclesiastical and religious life. Both strove for reform. The situation of the monastic life was seen as one of the main causes of the decline of the spiritual life, of the general degeneration. Monasteries had become too rich. They possessed power, land, money. As a result they attracted characters who were not at all inclined toward the imitation of Christ.

The brothers and sisters of the common life attempted to prove in their houses that things could be different. The rise of this movement, called by the participants themselves *Devotio Moderna*, had already begun in the second half of the fourteenth century, as a consequence of the stimulating preaching of the deacon Geert Grote (*c.* 1340–84). One of his disciples, Florens Radewijns (*c.*1350–1400), decided to convert his house in Deventer into a community of men, following the monastic rules of poverty, chastity and obedience, but without the obligation of a formal vow. They became known as the 'Brethren of the Common Life'. In a short time all over the northern parts of The Netherlands, but also in Germany, brother- and sister-houses came into existence. In order to support themselves, they became active in every aspect of book production: writing, copying manuscripts, binding and marketing volumes, in later times, after the invention of printing, also operating their own press. A second source of income was the housing and coaching of young boys, studying at Latin schools, as in Deventer, Zwolle and Groningen.

These brothers and sisters of the common life resembled the Beguines and Beghards who several decades earlier had aroused so much suspicion in the ecclesiastical leaders. To avoid complications, soon after the death of Geert Grote, Florens Radewijns decided to set up a monastery which could offer protection, spiritual support and leadership to the houses of the adherents of the *Devotio Moderna*, and which could form a model for monasteries, which were suffering from decay. The monastery was founded in 1387 at Windesheim, between Zwolle and Deventer. The small group of former brothers of common life had chosen the rule of the Augustinian canons. Their constitutions were approved in 1395. Other monasteries accepted Windesheim as mother-house or *domus superior*; together they formed the Congregation of Windesheim. In the beginning of the sixteenth century over one hundred monasteries, in The Netherlands, Germany and Switzerland, were connected or associated with this congregation. The leadership of the congregation was held by the general chapter, with the prior superior of Windesheim as chairman. Twelve *definitores* were appointed to lead the deliberations during the meetings of the chapter and the examination of the reports of the *visitatores*.[6]

The Congregation of Windesheim was also instituted to link those monasteries which were willing to be involved in thorough reorientation and reform. Entreaties to reform went out to many other monasteries from the congregation. Abuses were dealt with thoroughly. Moreover, both the congregation and the leaders of Lutheran and Reformed Protestantism soon discovered how important the support of secular authorities was for their attempts to realize reform. Both movements did not shrink from violence, if need be, to force the people to accept the allegedly necessary reform.[7]

Although the Windesheim reform was mainly restricted to monastic life, it is not irrational to imagine that the congregation would at least have known some sympathy and a feeling of kinship with the Protestant Reformation, which aimed at a renewal of ecclesiastical life also outside the monastic realm. And yet the thesis that the Congregation of Windesheim behaved extremely negatively toward Protestantism has never really been challenged.

Of course, this relationship has been investigated before. J. G. R. Acquoy discusses it in his extensive study and concludes that 'the congregation never showed any leaning toward Protestantism'.[8] R. R. Post, too, gives a negative answer to the question whether there was any relationship between the ideas and the piety of the Windesheimers and those of Protestantism: 'There was rather a contrast between the spirituality of the Windesheimers and that of Luther.'[9]

In the analysis of the data, however, it seems important to me to distinguish between the attitude of the general chapter of the congregation and the possibilities within the various monasteries. The monasteries were certainly not identical, although they were part of this one union. Attention should also be given to the diversity of the factors

---

[6] See for the general history: R. R. Post, *The Modern Devotion* (Leiden 1968), pp. 197–313.

[7] One of the most influencial 'reformers' of monasteries was Iohannes Busch (1399/1400–79), canon of Windesheim, who has described his own experiences with the reformation of monasteries elsewhere and who has written a history of Windesheim itself. See K. Grube (ed.), *Des Augustinerpropstes Iohannes Busch Chronicon Windeshemense und Liber de reformatione monasteriorum* (Halle, 1886).

[8] J. G. R. Acquoy, *Het klooster te Windesheim en zijn invloed*, 3 vols. (Utrecht, 1875, 1876, 1880). See in the index 'Kerkhervorming' and 'Kerkhervorming in betrekking tot de Windesheimers'. The quote is from vol. II, p. 268.

[9] Post, *The Modern Devotion*, p. 655.

which formed a threat to the monasteries associated with the chapter; there were other reasons besides the influence of Protestantism why some monasteries were doomed to disappear. Only in this way can we obtain a reliable picture of the relationship between these two reform movements.

II

The general chapter did not hesitate to resist any form of Protestantization. This is not really remarkable. For Protestantism was a serious threat to monastic life. From the outset it was clear that the spokesmen of the Protestant Reformation would not ignore monastic life, for medieval monasticism had become too entangled with Catholic tradition.

Protestantism was opposed to the hierarchical structure of the Catholic Church, pleaded for the priesthood of all believers, appreciated ordinary life in marriage, family and work as the best and, in fact, only possibility to put the Christian faith into practice, rejected obligatory celibacy of the clergy and, finally, negatively assessed that which it regarded as idolatry. With monastic pilgrimages to holy places, prayer to the saints, prayer and masses for the dead and the liturgy of holy mass, Protestantism regarded the monastery as a threat, even more, regarded it as the source of all degeneration.

It was precisely from this monastic tradition that the obligation of celibacy had spread to the whole clergy, including the secular priesthood, within Latin Christendom, as distinct from Eastern Orthodoxy. Monasteries had been founded along the way to the holy sites in order to give shelter to the pilgrims. Others served as burial grounds for the nobility who in this way hoped to receive a guarantee of daily prayers and masses. The mendicant orders had come into being to sustain the papal authority and thus the whole hierarchical structure. A real transformation of the church, as the Protestant spokesmen envisaged, could only be brought about by undermining monasticism. The Windesheim congregation, which sought to improve the monastic life of which Protestantism wished to rid itself, was therefore obliged to oppose this Protestantism.

From the acts of the general chapter it is obvious how alert the Windesheim congregation was to Protestantizing tendencies within the monasteries.[10] There was reason for the leadership of the congregation

---

[10] *Acta capituli Windeshemensis*, ed. S. van der Woude (The Hague, 1953). Cited hereafter as *Acta*.

to be worried. After it had flourished in the second half of the fifteenth century, a process of decline began around 1515. A dwindling number of people appeared willing to take the lifetime vows, partly because of the influence of critical humanistic writings. Initially some monasteries lowered the requirements for admission, despite the negative consequences for the quality of the monastic life, with the result that, as early as 1518, a number of monasteries were forbidden to accept admission of novices.[11]

These were also the years in which a growing number of monastics regretted their former vows. It is important to realize that within the Congregation of Windesheim those vows varied according to the class to which one belonged. Reflection on the Bible and the writings of the ancient church fathers raised doubts in many circles as to whether ecclesiastical authorities had the right to interfere to such a high degree in the lives of believers.

The core of the congregation consisted of canons and canonesses who generally came from more prosperous families and who, therefore, were scholars, the men of whom were usually ordained priests. Their main duty was to pray the hours. Besides this they devoted most of their time to copying books. They were the only members of the community who had a seat on the chapter. Although they were a minority within the community it was they more than others who determined the character of the Windesheim monastery.

From the lay brothers or *conversi* there were different requirements. They too took vows for life, but they had more supporting tasks – in the kitchen, in the fields, in the smithy or brewery. In most monasteries there were also a number of so-called *donati*, people who, usually towards the end of their active life, in view of their preparation for death, donated their possessions to the monastery and in exchange received food and shelter. They also had to submit to certain rules, but they did not take vows. This held true for the *laici familiares* as well, lay brothers who associated themselves with the monastery, sometimes for temporary service. They promised to be obedient to the prior, but they did not take vows. They had the right to leave the monastery if they wished to do so. Finally, certain people were engaged for a longer or shorter term, to perform specific tasks in return for a salary.[12]

During the first decades, among the people who took lifetime vows there undoubtedly grew a sense of dissatisfaction. Increasingly, monastics

---

[11] *Acta*, p. 116.

[12] For an overview of the various classes see Karl Grube's introduction to *Chronicon Windeshemense und Liber dereformatione monasteriorum*, pp. 11–14. For a more extended description see Acquoy, *Het klooster te Windesheim*, vol. I, pp. 108–28.

tried to flee secretly from the monasteries to start a new life, if need be with another name. In 1519 the general chapter ordered all the monasteries to work harder at tracing and arresting former monastics. It is not clear whether this pertained to canons in particular, or to *conversi*. The latter is most likely as, in light of the new relationships, it will have been increasingly difficult for them to accept their humble existence in the shadow of the canons, to which they had bound themselves.[13]

The decrease in the number of canons soon caused problems. If in the second half of the fifteenth century the number of canons can be estimated at 1 500 to 2 000, fifty years later only half of them remained. As early as 1522 it is noted that the hours can no longer be prayed properly in all the monasteries. The general chapter tried to reduce the number of tasks for the canons. In several monasteries it was common practice that the canons preached in parish churches and sometimes fulfilled pastoral duties. This, however, was no longer a task for the canons, the chapter decided. Monasteries of the Windesheim congregation were to be closed off from the rest of society. They were to observe the enclosure.

The brothers were urged to be on their guard against unusual and deviating teachings and to strictly follow the rules of the 'holy Roman and Catholic Church of God'.[14] The gentlemen of the chapter regarded these as unhappy times for the congregation. That is why they forbade all monasteries to accept young people in the present situation, until better times arrived.

This prohibition was repeated a year later, in 1523, which was the first time that the appeal that Luther's teachings had for the monasteries of the Windesheim congregation were mentioned. There were explicit references to the regulations from Rome and to the imperial decree, probably from 1521, in which Luther's doctrine was rejected. The chapter noted that the doctrine resulted in a weakening of discipline in several monasteries. Therefore, all visitors were exhorted to pay attention to the books present when they inspected the monasteries entrusted to their care. Reading Dr Luther's writings was strictly forbidden and was to be punished severely. The prior in whose monastery such books were found, was to be corrected and punished as well. After all, he had not attended well enough to his duties.

---

[13] *Acta*, p. 117. One argument why during the first phase (till 1550) they will have been mainly lay brothers and sisters, is that no names are mentioned. In the second half of the sixteenth century we do encounter several names of canons who fled the monastery.

[14] *Acta*, p. 123: 'Ex quo nostri status non est publice docere populum Dei, monentur omnes obedientiarii ut caveant a variis et peregrinis doctrinis hominum atque se submittant determinationi sanctae Romanae atque catholicae ecclesiae Dei.'

Also, more rigorous action was to be taken against those monastics who were found outside the monastery for illegal reasons, in the chapter's view. If need be, the aid of the secular authorities was to be invoked in order to force such wandering apostates back to their monastery.[15]

The general chapter of the congregation had not hesitated. From the outset Luther's ideas were regarded as heretical, sinful and, therefore, unacceptable. Even before it was fully clear how negative the attitude of the Protestant Reformation was to the monastic life, the congregation had taken its stand. However, it is also clear from the severity and the emphasis with which this rejection was put into words that not all Windesheim monasteries took the same rigid stand.

In 1524 the regulations against Luther and his companions became even stricter. The tempting character of these teachings was mentioned. It was described as a shame that it had resulted in some having second thoughts about the severity of the discipline. Again visitors were ordered to examine carefully whether there were any Protestant writings in the monasteries. The monastics were to be compelled to listen to sermons in which the shameful character of this teaching was thoroughly explained. The visitors were not to be hindered in their work in any way. As representatives of the general chapter, they and not the prior had the highest authority.

A year later the chapter expressed itself yet more fiercely. The Protestant doctrine was compared with the plague, and what the latter could bring about in a monastic community was known to all monastics. In that period plague epidemics occurred sporadically. In Windesheim monasteries there had been several occasions when virtually the whole population had died of the disease.[16] Protestantism was as dangerous as that, in the chapter's view. Therefore, thorough supervision by priors and visitors was regarded as necessary. As soon as someone was detected as being infected with the disease, he must immediately be locked up and isolated. And when a prior appears to have been negligent or too kind-hearted, the visitors are to dismiss him from his position.

The gentlemen of the chapter then also indicated why they regarded this teaching as so harmful. Remarkably, their sole argument was that it damaged the unity of Christendom. Keeping the unity of the church had priority, in their opinion. If monastics who had run away and were infected with Lutheran ideas returned of their own accord, their prior and the monastic community might only admit them again if the prior

---

[15] *Acta*, p. 124.
[16] See, for example, van Loghum Slaterus, *Het klooster Frenswegen*, p. 55.

superior – in other words, the prior of the leading monastery, at Windesheim – had given his permission.[17]

During the following years these regulations were constantly repeated. In 1527 several priors received a specific order to seek out adherents of the Lutheran teachings and, if need be with the aid of the secular authorities, to arrest them. All the measures were no longer published. A year later a decision was made not to read aloud several regulations regarding the punishment of rebellious brothers from monasteries in Friesland, Holland and Flanders, who had been infected by the *secta lutherana*, or even to mention them in the minutes. Did this decision concern the handing over of heretics to the secular court? Did the members of the chapter fear even more rebellion if these regulations were made public?

In the following year the priors were ordered to act with impunity, to thoroughly isolate infected or apostate monastics, and even to build special cells in the monasteries from which escape was impossible. Release was allowed only after abjuration of the error, after a long process of humiliation, and with permission from the prior superior or the visitors.[18]

But the measures were not efficacious. In 1532 it was decided that brothers who had run away or were apostate were no longer permitted to undergo imprisonment and penance in their own monastery, but had to be moved to another. In 1534 it was agreed that priors had to pray privately and in public that God 'will root out all heresies and sects and

---

[17] *Acta*, pp. 126, 127.

[18] *Acta*, pp. 128–30. This punishment was still mild in comparison with those for heresy mentioned in the edicts. Incarceration in the monasteries could, however, take extreme forms, if we believe the reports. See the story in *De kroniek van Godevaert van Haecht over de troebelen van 1565 tot 1574 te Antwerpen en elders*, ed. Rob van Roosbroeck, 2 vols (Antwerp, 1929, 1930). Having remained a Roman Catholic himself, albeit with unmistakable sympathy for the Reformation, this painter described the breaking of the images in 1566. Monasteries too were plundered:

> So also in the monastery of the Friars Minor were found five or six imprisoned monks in several deep pits. Hearing their cries, the Calvinists were seen to dig after them for almost a whole day. And the monks who were in the monastery did not know where to point; the superiors who knew and who had fed them daily, had run away. It was said that some of them had been there for five or ten years, without seeing sun or moon or hardly any light, and that they professed that the sole reason that they had been imprisoned was that they had begun to teach the Gospel properly. And some were black up to their waists, because they had sat in their own faeces. Similarly two Lady's Friars or Carmelites as they are called were found in pits of masonry. See what a tyranny over their own people! Judge for yourselves whether God needed to punish or not? (Ibid., vol. I, p. 101)

that He will thus bring together his holy Church in the unity of the true faith, love and peace'. So, they were obliged to take their stand openly in the presence of all the members of the monastic community. Again the desire to uphold unity appeared to be the most important motive for the chapter.[19]

However, the regulations of the general chapter did not always appear to provide sufficient authority. In 1544 it was explicitly stated that the chapter would not shrink from severe punishment if in a monastery certain agreed rules were not adhered to.[20] And still the measures were not efficacious. Due to political circumstances, the general chapter of 1551 was not held in Windesheim but in Groenendaal near Brussels. It was asserted that because of the number of offences and deviations, stronger measures would have to be taken. It was recommended to call on the aid of the secular authorities in order to be able to punish the rebels among the brothers more severely, so that the other brothers would be imbued with fear.[21]

Meanwhile, a large number of monasteries were closed or confiscated in those areas where the secular authorities had introduced Protestantism – Germany and Switzerland. Some monasteries had even been actively involved in Protestantizing, although this led eventually to their demise. Therefore it was all the more remarkable that, in 1527, the apostasy of the brothers mentions only monasteries in Holland, Friesland and Flanders.

There was a connection with the economic and political situation. In the 1520s there was growing social unrest, especially in Germany. Farmers were exploited and suppressed. The large, rich monasteries were some of those who were guilty of this exploitation. So, when the farmers revolted, much of their rage was directed at the monasteries. In 1525 one monastery after another was attacked and plundered. In The Netherlands relationships were more favourable, initially. Here one could reflect on the value of monastic vows without being disturbed. In any event, it was mainly Dutch monasteries that were confronted by internal rebellion.

The general chapter was therefore facing great problems. In some areas there was unity within the monasteries themselves, but the peace was disturbed by rebellious farmers or plundering army units. If in a particular region the authorities sided with Protestantism, this usually

---

[19] *Acta*, p. 141.
[20] *Acta*, p. 148.
[21] *Acta*, p. 155.

resulted in the abolition of all monasteries in that area, and the general chapter could do little other than protest powerlessly and receive the expelled canons. This situation did not arise in The Netherlands until the 1570s. Charles V had already acted severely, his son Philip II outdid him. But in this region the monasteries were troubled by internal unrest, which forced the general chapter to take ever harsher measures.

After 1559 the chapter suffered another problem which was certainly no less far-reaching. In order to execute thoroughly the stipulations of the Council of Trent it was decided in a harmonious consultation between the pope and the Spanish king that under the leadership of the Archbishop of Mechelen (Malines), Granvelle, several new dioceses would be created in The Netherlands with sees in Haarlem, Deventer, Leeuwarden, Groningen and Roermond. Money was needed for this. The government hoped to find this money by abolishing several monasteries, especially some of those in the Windesheim congregation – namely Heilo, Zwolle, Bergum, Ezinge and Roermond. The pope granted his permission. 'No enemy could have struck a more severe blow than this friend,' notes Acquoy.[22] As soon as the general chapter heard of these plans it protested.[23]

So the situation was extremely threatening. The chapter had already lost a great many Windesheim monasteries in Germany and Switzerland. In The Netherlands monasteries had been plundered during the military campaigns of commanders such as Maarten van Rossum. Other monasteries in this area had perished because of floods or economic problems.

Initially, Protestantism could barely gain a foothold owing to the tough stance of Philip II. But several monasteries were considerably troubled by internal rebellion. Fugitives with Protestant sympathies who had escaped from the monasteries threatened to discredit the Windesheim congregation again and again, despite all the severe measures the chapter put in place. In the later period they were not just *conversi*. There appeared to be apostate canons as well, who were mentioned by name in the acts of the chapter.[24] Some acted as preachers in groups that met secretly, or in open air church services.

---

[22] Acquoy, *Het klooster te Windesheim*, vol. II, p. 152.

[23] *Acta*, pp. 172, 174.

[24] *Acta*, p. 132: Johan Geyns and Petrus Titulus, 1530; p. 140: br. Haerlingen, 1533; p. 180: Jasper Buren, Adriaan van Deventer, 1564; p. 181: Arnold Ghestel, 1565; p. 198: Gerard Vulpes van Hasselt, Frans Philippi de Thenis, 1571; p. 201: Christiaan Dosborch, Reinier van Tongeren, 1572; p. 206: Gerard van Raamsdonck, Petrus Lomel, Martinus Lomel, Johannes Leonardi, 1573; p. 207: Jacobus Oosterwyck, 1573. Names known from elsewhere: Johannes Meurs, see Acquoy, *Het klooster te Windesheim*, vol. II, p. 155; vol. III, p. 18; Johannes Sartorius, see Acquoy, *Het klooster te Windesheim*, vol. II, p. 155.

It is not unthinkable that, as a result, the Spanish government and the Pope had little faith in the possibilities of the Windesheim congregation contributing effectively to the execution of the Counter-Reformation measures of the Council of Trent. Whether or not that was so, they attached more value to the new dioceses. As far as the pope and the king were concerned a number of monasteries could disappear.

In 1569 the Duke of Alva even presumed he had reason to directly address several priors and ordered them to execute the instructions of the general chapter as quickly and as thoroughly as possible. The duke wrote that the decrees of Trent were to be put into effect in monasteries and convents before individual members had a chance to flee and withdraw from this reform. Apparently, he found it necessary to add extra weight to the pronouncements of the chapter. Needless to say, the monasteries adhered to the regulations of the chapter.

In that same year, however, the chapter revoked the instruction of 1522 in which it was forbidden for canons to preach outside the monasteries. Despite the even fewer number of canons, they were now allowed to preach. It seems that the chapter realized that the Windesheim monasteries must oppose Protestantism more actively if they were to receive support from the state and the church.[25]

The Eighty Years War and the Protestantization of part of The Netherlands, which was the result of the war, led to the abolition of most of the remaining Windesheim monasteries. In the new republic possessions were normally assigned to the city councils. Those canons or nuns that remained usually received a reasonable pension in exchange.

We may therefore conclude that the Windesheim congregation lost its vitality and most of its monasteries mainly as a result of the Protestant Reformation and despite the general chapter having used all possible means to protect the monasteries against Protestant ideas. Acquoy's conclusion that the congregation had never shown 'any sign of a leaning towards Protestantism' is certainly legitimate.[26] In practice, however, the chapter's power was limited.[27] Time and again the priors had to be exhorted to prevent any evangelical writings being smuggled into the monasteries. Time and again they had to appeal urgently to the secular authorities to seek out absconded monastics.

---

[25] *Acta*, pp. 186–9.

[26] Acquoy, *Het klooster te Windesheim*, vol. II, p. 268.

[27] See the quote which Acquoy cites from the *Constitutiones* of 1553: 'Aangezien het heilig gezag van ons Kapittel bij zeer velen vreeselijk is verminderd' [Seeing that our chapter's holy authority has decreased terribly for a great many people]; *Het klooster te Windesheim*, vol. II, p. 148.

A typical example of the somewhat hesitant attitude, even of the general chapter, can be found in its position on the possession of an organ in the monasteries' chapels. Some monasteries had an organ, others did not. The chapter preferred that the organ not be played during services. If a monastery did possess an organ it could only be played by secular organists, not by monks. Thus the use of an organ in religious services was discouraged. It was not considered fitting for monks to waste their time on something such as playing the organ and would be better if the organ was totally abandoned. In this a certain kinship with Anabaptist and Reformed Protestantism, which also wished to refrain from playing the organ during services, becomes apparent.[28]

Ultimately, we have to conclude that the Congregation of Windesheim did not, or would not, contribute substantially to the Counter-Reformation, to the foundation of new dioceses and to a forceful functioning of the Inquisition. At the beginning of the sixteenth century the canons usually preached in parish churches, but from the 1520s onwards this was increasingly hindered and made impossible. In the most critical years, the chapter discouraged the canons from participating actively in the exchange of ideas and in the combat of Protestantism. Only in 1569 was this rule revoked. The chapter did try to protect the various monasteries from heretical ideas; several times it urged severe action against monastics with dissident opinions, but nowhere did it demand capital punishment for heresy as was common in the edicts of the secular and the ecclesiastical authorities.

III

This picture becomes even clearer when we examine the history of each monastery on its own. A few monasteries appear to have supported Protestantization with consensus or with a vast majority of votes.[29] Some German and Swiss monasteries continued to acquire Protestant writings, despite the chapter's regulations.[30] In the northern Netherlands it also appeared to be extremely difficult to execute the chapter's rules. Time and again the visitors and inquisitors came across negligence.

---

[28] *Acta*, p. 145 (1538, repeated in 1539, 1540).

[29] *Monasticon Windeshemense*, vol. II: *Deutsches Sprachgebiet*, ed. Klaus Scholz (Brussels, 1977), p. 32 (Basle), pp. 57, 58 (Blomberg), p. 135 (Frankenthal), pp. 183, 184 (Halberstadt), p. 241 (Höningen), pp. 301, 302 (Möllenbeck).

[30] Ibid., for example Volkhardinghausen, pp. 445, 446.

A remarkable example is the cautious stand of the prior of the monastery at Albergen. As early as 1521 he mentioned in his chronicles the commotion that the writings of Dr Martin Luther caused. 'I do not know what will come of him in the end,' he wrote, 'But I know for sure that he has published several well-written works.' The prior showed sincere shock when in 1523 he described the death by torture of some of Luther's followers. It was difficult for him to be appreciative of the authorities' actions. 'Undoubtedly, the position of the church was everywhere very unstable in those days, when this Martin opposed the pope, his co-workers, all the clergy and especially the monastics ... For in many places the monasteries were totally wiped out.' And yet, even then he refused 'to pass an unfavourable judgement upon this man'.[31]

Later 'unashamed rebellion' against the visitors is spoken of in the convent that had been transferred from Amsterdam to Heilo.[32] In Achlum, Arnhem, Bergum, Haske and Leiderdorp, too, the visitor thought he had reason to complain about the shortcomings in discipline and in the execution of the chapter's regulations.[33] As late as 1558, in one monastery the visitor chanced upon books by Luther, Calvin, Brenz and Menno Simons.[34]

Monasteries were destroyed in The Netherlands not just as a result of the introduction of Protestantism in certain areas, but also for strategic military reasons. Monasteries were often fortified bulwarks from which besieging troops could fire at cities. Thus the war made it necessary to remove such obstacles in the cities' neighbourhood. Spanish troops were as guilty of this as the 'Sea Beggars', the mainly Dutch Protestants who rebelled against Spain.

The resultant picture is more complicated than Bemolt van Loghum Slaterus's thesis suggested. The general chapter did not hesitate, but from the outset resisted any form of Protestantism. The monasteries associated with the Congregation of Windesheim, however, revealed a more turbulent picture. Most of them seemed willing to comply with the chapter's policies, but not all instructions and regulations were

---

[31] *1520–1525. De kroniek van Johannes van Lochem, prior te Albergen*, ed. J. B. Schildkamp, T. Hesselink-van der Riet, R. Th. M. van Dijk, B. J. Thüss and B. H. J. Lenferink (Albergen and Enschede, 1995), pp. 312, 480. The prior is also remarkably positive about Erasmus, whose translation of the New Testament 'has made Holy Scripture much more intelligible'. Young people too 'regularly took books with this new edition in their hands'.

[32] *Monasticon Windeshemense*, vol. III: *Niederlande*, eds Anton G. Weiler and Noël Geirnaert (Brussels, 1980), p. 114. See also *Acta*, p. 142.

[33] *Acta*, pp. 309, 139, 155, 261, 294.

[34] *Acta*, p. 261 (Haske).

introduced everywhere. Protestant ideas trickled in. Many canons wished to keep abreast of the thoughts and writings in Protestant circles. A number of them managed to escape the monastery. The diversity of opinions among the people did not leave the Windesheim monasteries untouched. Therefore, motivation for the Counter-Reformation, as from the Jesuits and the Dominicans, did not come from the Windesheim monasteries.

This is confirmed when we analyse not only contemporaneous Protestant, but also Catholic, reactions to monasticism. The Friars Minor and the Dominicans were especially hated and feared.[35] So, when power changed hands they simply lost their possessions. They were driven out of the cities. With the leadership of the Windesheim monasteries, however, arrangements were made which included pensions. Their canons or nuns were rarely forced to leave their town.

In Protestant polemics the tone with respect to the Windesheim monasteries was also rather mild, sometimes even positive. With great appreciation the stern Calvinist Jacobus Revius generally typified the Modern Devotion as a movement which brought about a reform, albeit a moral one and not simply a reform of doctrine, but reform in such a way that it led to the new dawn of the Gospel in Protestantism.[36]

The Arminian historian G. Brandt also referred with appreciation to the devotion and the power of conviction with which the Windesheim canons tried to oppose the degeneration and abuses of the monastic life. 'They who endeavoured to make the monks live according to a better rule were already at that time called reformers of the clergy.' He was more negative about the mendicant friars, comparing a Franciscan friar like Brugman with a Windesheim canon like Thomas a Kempis 'who has proved with his life and writings that in those evil times something

---

[35] See, for example, *De kroniek van Godevaert van Haecht*. He writes about the Friars Minor that they 'meer riepen om 't volck te persequeren, metter inquisitien en placcaten, dan eenige ander monicken, waerdoer sy meer in den haet waeren' [called for the persecution of the people with their inquisitions and placards, more than any of the other monks, so that they were more hated] (vol. I, p. 47). See also Emanuel van Meteren, *Historien der Nederlanden, en haar Naburen Oorlogen tot het jaar 1612* (Amsterdam, 1663), ff. 136v, 137r, who describes extensively the offensive behaviour of the Friars Minor. He has no such stories about the Windesheim monastics. Another important contemporaneous source comes from the monk Wouter Jacobsz, who sympathized with Windesheim: *Dagboek van broeder Wouter Jacobsz*, ed. I. H. van Eeghen (2 vols, Groningen, 1959, 1960). On the appreciation for the Windesheim monasteries see J. C. van Slee, *De kloostervereeniging van Windesheim* (Leiden, 1874), pp. 328, 329.

[36] Jacobus Revius, *Deventriae illustratae, sive Historiae Urbis Daventriensis* (Leiden, 1651), pp. 3 ff. See also A. J. Jelsma, 'Doorwerking van de Moderne Devotie', in *De doorwerking van de Moderne Devotie, Windesheim 1387–1987*, eds P. Bange, C. Graafland, A. J. Jelsma and A. G. Willer (Hilversum, 1988), pp. 11–13.

good could still come from the monastics, outside the company of the Franciscans'.[37]

So, at least on the Protestant side, there appears to have been a sense of kinship between the reform that Protestantism itself tried to accomplish and the reform of monastic life by the Windesheim congregation. It is striking that for this positive assessment only fifteenth-century writings of the Windesheimers are cited. Although the official rejection of Protestantism by the chapter was unmistakable, in many a Windesheim monastery there were traces of this same sense of kinship. That is why the Congregation of Windesheim could not act as a strong instrument in the service of the Counter-Reformation. At a time of polarization this was already more than reasonably could have been expected!

---

[37] G. Brandt, *Historie der Reformatie en andere kerkelyke Geschiedenissen, in en ontrent de Nederlanden*, 2nd edn (Amsterdam, 1677), pp. 32–49.

CHAPTER TWO

The Devil and Protestantism

I

It was characteristic of the Protestant Reformation of the sixteenth century that all parts of the Christian tradition were scrutinized for their value, their truthfulness, their usefulness and their biblical background: this applied to the sacraments, the sale of indulgences, private confession, prayer to the saints, celibacy, the image of God and Christology. It is worth investigating also to what extent the image of the Devil was subject to changes.

Protestantism had something to do with the Devil, of that its Roman Catholic opponents were convinced. They suggested that Luther especially (1483–1546) had a direct relationship with the Devil, and that he probably had been begotten by the Devil himself or by one of his subordinate demons.[1] For centuries it had been commonly accepted that this was possible. Scholars had attempted several times to construct a logically acceptable theory for it. This was not easy. Since Augustine's time it was held in Europe that the Devil did not have the power to produce life.[2] He was not creative. That power was known to God alone. What the Devil could do was imitate, awaken illusions, create confusion, destroy, coax, seduce.

And yet it was regarded as an historically proven fact that demons could beget children. It was assumed that, first, a demon in the form of a seductive woman, as *succubus*, had intercourse with a man. Enriched with the latter's seed he then tried to seduce a woman, in a male form, as *incubus*. This he could do without much difficulty – the clergy

---

[1] See Heiko A. Oberman, *Luther: Man between God and the Devil* (New Haven, 1989), pp. 1–15; H. A. Oberman, *The Impact of the Reformation* (Grand Rapids, MI, 1994), pp. 51–68.

[2] See Augustine's *De civitate Dei* for his views on the abilities of the Devil and demons, and on the illusion which makes it look as if they could create something, especially books IX, X and XI. David Knowles is correct when he writes in the introduction to this work, 'There is much deep thought in the *City of God* that has been absorbed wholly or in part by Christian tradition'. In this he includes evil's inability to create something; *Augustine: City of God*, ed. David Knowles (London, 1972), p. xxvi. See for Augustine's views also Peter Brown, *Augustine of Hippo*, 2nd edn (New York, 1986), pp. 311, 395, 396.

especially were convinced of this. In this way women could give birth to Satan's children.[3]

Of course, the question raised by intelligent antagonists of this theory was to what extent one could still speak of the Devil's offspring. The Devil might have played a mediating role in the begetting, but that was all. The final result was still a child born from male and female cells which could be cleansed from all demonic influences by baptism. On the basis of this concept the master magician and, at least during that period of his life, city lawyer of Metz, Cornelius Agrippa von Nettesheim (1486–1535) succeeded in obtaining a verdict of 'not guilty' for a woman accused of witchcraft.[4]

Despite these sporadic protests, ideas relating to the offspring of the Devil and a pact with the Devil took hold of the masses, in particular in this period of history, from the end of the fifteenth and throughout the sixteenth centuries.[5] This was connected with a general feeling of being threatened. Conspiracy theories were eagerly believed. An invasion of 'aliens' was feared, people with an origin which was partly demonic whom one should track down and eliminate with all possible means. The persecution of witches took ever more serious forms. An important question was how Satan's children were to be recognized. Concrete indicators were looked for. The way someone left this world could be such an indication. An unnatural death could point to an unnatural origin.[6] It was also regarded as an omen when certain areas of the human body appeared insensitive to pain, and hunters of witches became experts in detecting such areas.[7]

---

[3] See the elaborate reflections in the infamous work by Jakob Sprenger and Heinrich Institoris, *Der Hexenhammer*, German translation of *Malleus Maleficarum* by J. W. R. Schmidt, 3rd edn (Darmstadt, 1985), pp. 41–56. See also Norman Cohn, *Europe's Inner Demons: an Enquiry Inspired by the Great Witch-Hunt* (Bungay, Suffolk, 1975), pp. 174 ff.

[4] See H. M. Beliën and P. C. van der Eerden, *Satans trawanten. Heksen en heksenvervolging* (Haarlem, 1985), pp. 129–41; Lène Dresen-Coenders, *Het verbond van heks en duivel. Een waandenkbeeld aan het begin van de moderne tijd als symptoom van een veranderdende situatie van de vrouw en als middel tot hervorming der zeden* (Baarn, 1983), pp. 157–63. See for Agrippa, Charles G. Nautert, *Agrippa and the Crisis of Renaissance Thought* (Urbana, 1965), pp. 59, 60. Agrippa tells about the occurence in Metz in his *De incertitudine et vanitate omnium scientiarum et artium* (Leiden, 1643).

[5] For example, Jeffrey Burton Russell, in *Mephistopheles. The Devil in the Modern World* (New York, 1986), p. 30, wrote: 'For the most part it was an invention of the elite, gradually spreading down through pulpit and courtroom to the people, who accepted it greedily as an explanation for their own troubles.'

[6] That is why immediately after his death it was announced of Luther in what honourable way he had departed. Oberman, *Luther*, pp. 10–15.

[7] See the examples which Kurt Baschwitz describes in *Hexen und Hexenprozesse*, 2nd edn (Munich, 1966), pp. 161–6.

It is likely that the propaganda war between Protestant and Catholic authors strengthened this belief in the activities of the Devil and of his army of demons. While Luther was the offspring of the Devil in the eyes of his Catholic adversaries, in Protestant circles the pope was regarded as the incarnation of the Antichrist.[8] This demonization of one another was intended to justify the often far-reaching propaganda measures. If the adversary was no one less than the Devil himself, then of course all means were acceptable. Perhaps the authors of this propagandistic material were still aware that they stretched the truth by portraying the others as enemies and by the demonization of their opponents. But there was a great risk that the rest of the population did not understand the nuances and regarded the caricatures as a faithful rendering of the situation. The representation of Western Europe as a battlefield on which the satanic armies in a last attempt tried to destroy the true Christian doctrine, took on ever sharper contours as a result of the religious battle. It was an almost inevitable consequence of the ever more irreconcilable battle between Protestantism and Catholicism that people became increasingly interested in the Devil.

This growing interest did not necessarily mean that the image of the Devil in Protestant circles was essentially different from the Catholic views. Regarding the most fundamental matters of faith, the most important Protestant spokesmen remained remarkably faithful to the tradition. They certainly did not ascribe any less authority to Augustine than did their Roman Catholic colleagues, rather more. But we do encounter some figures on the reformed side who, as part of the whole reorientation, also developed a new view of the doctrine of the Trinity and of Christology. And because one's images of God and of the Devil are inevitably connected they did not shrink from a contrasting view of the Devil either. However, they were combated by reformed leaders such as Luther and Calvin as severely as by their Catholic opponents. Someone like Calvin was always aware that, with regard to his theological views, he was more akin to his Catholic colleagues than to these radical innovators. As for the most important spokesmen of Protestantism, Luther and Calvin, we may therefore assume that, just as there was no essential difference regarding the doctrine of the Trinity or the doctrine of the two natures of Christ, their image of the Devil will have been similar to the Roman Catholic ideas.[9]

---

[8] This idea is already found with Luther. 'Papa est Christi adversarius et apostolus diaboli', he wrote in a letter, *Martin Luthers Werke, Briefwechsel* (16 vols), vol. II (Weimar, 1931; reprint 1966), p. 293 (letter dated 24 March 1521). Besides, the invention of the printing-press can be mentioned as another cause why certain ideas, which previously were found only in some circles, could now become accepted by the general public.

[9] 'The diabological assumptions of the sixteenth century continued to be for the most

At most we may assume that the reformed opposition against allegorical exegesis strengthened the belief in the Devil within this movement.[10] A dialogue such as that between God and Satan in the book of Job, as well as all the Gospel narratives about the activities of evil spirits, were read and experienced as stories which had truly happened. Apparently Satan could relate to God this boldly, almost at the same level. And the evil spirits did have this power, that they could foretell the future and that they could make a whole herd of swine rush over a precipice. This is compensated by the Protestant spokesmen's critical attitude toward popular culture, with which the Roman Catholic tradition had built a much more intimate relationship.

It holds true for both parties that the mutual polemics have strengthened the assumption of an increase in demonic activity. So there is good reason to investigate what Luther and Calvin have suggested concerning the Devil and his allies, although we need not expect to find essential differences in their demonology. In order to gain a clearer picture of their views, though, it is also important to examine how more radical reformed movements regarded the Devil and his activities. Finally, we will see how the various views presented themselves within The Netherlands.

II

Martin Luther

Luther took the Devil very seriously.[11] He ended his autobiography in 1545 with an appeal to his readers to pray for 'a more penetrating preaching against Satan, for he is mighty and evil, more dangerous than ever before, since he knows that he can still rage for only a short time'.[12] As a result of this fascination he was not very critical with respect to the stories told about the Devil and his armies.

---

part essentially traditional, even medieval. Witchcraft, Luther, Calvin, the Catholic Reformation, the mystics, and pre-Faustian literature all continued the old ways of perceiving the Devil', as Russell rightly writes in *Mephistopheles*, p. 26.

[10] This is also Russell's opinion, *Mephistopheles*, p. 30: 'The Protestant Reformation itself was the most important element in the revival of the Devil. The Protestant emphasis upon *sola scriptura* – the Bible as the only source of authority – meant a due regard for the New Testament teaching on Satan.'

[11] Russell, *Mephistopheles*, p. 34: 'Luther, who devoted more of his theology and personal concern to the Devil than anyone had done since the desert fathers.'

[12] Cited by Oberman, *Luther*, p. 163. See for Luther's views on the Devil, Hans-Martin Barth, *Der Teufel und Jesus Christus in der Theologie Martin Luthers* (Göttingen, 1967).

A few times in his *Table Talk* he refers to an event in which he himself was involved. During a trip with the Prince of Anhalt he encountered a severely handicapped 12-year-old boy in Dessau. The only thing the child could do was feed, Luther wrote, 'more than four farmers could eat'. He gave the prince well-meant advice to drown the boy in the river. Mentally handicapped children he regarded as changelings. One could expect such tricks from the Devil, he thought. If an opportunity arose the Devil would take away from their cot children created by God and replace them with his own offspring. Luther thought it characteristic of the Devil to create a *massa carnis*, a lump of flesh, which on the outside looked like a human being, but which did not have a soul and therefore lacked the ordinary human abilities. Whoever destroys such a creature does not kill a creation of God but only combats the Devil and therefore does God a service, Luther maintained. The prince regarded this suggestion as too rigorous.

Then Luther advised the authorities in Dessau to take the child to church daily and to say the Lord's Prayer over him, until God drove out the demon. This counsel was followed. And with success. A year later the child had died. 'And so it should be.' During this conversation he also referred to an unnamed author who according to him had written a wise exposition on the way the Devil could beget children through *succubi* and *incubi*.[13]

This anecdote shows how much the great Reformer shared the general sentiments regarding the Devil. The latter's abilities were limited, Luther agreed with that. The Devil was not able to create something, but he could disturb, sicken, destroy, awaken illusions, suggest evil thoughts, create doubts. 'The Devil is such a magician that he is able to hide Christ in the midst of our trials, and that he wrenches the word of grace from our hearts to such a degree that we lose Christ.' According to Luther, Satan, being the 'prince of this world', could be held accountable for all that went wrong on earth: 'He is the cause of all illness and all accidents.'[14]

Luther held God and God's love for his creation in such high regard that he preferred to deem the power of darkness responsible for the darker side of life, rather than make the good God accountable for them. The advice he gave to the Prince of Anhalt shows that this belief could also have dangerous consequences.

More remarkable than the counsel itself is the prince's rejection of it. With his advice Luther appealed to the ancient custom to kill at birth

---

[13] *Martin Luthers Werke, Tischreden* (6 vols), vol. V (Weimar, 1919; reprint 1967), no. 5207, 8, 9, pp. 8–10. In his *Table Talk* he often speaks about the Devil.

[14] Ibid., no. 5207, 8. The title 'prince of this world' was taken from the Gospel of John.

children who were unmistakably invalid, against which even in the early Middle Ages missionaries had protested.[15] Factual data about the situation after the Christianization are absent, but we may assume that this custom remained in practice for a long time, especially among the poorest of society. By his counsel Luther sanctioned this custom. Life which is unworthy does not need to be maintained; the Devil has been too much involved in it. Apparently, the prince was aware of the risks of such a principle.

It goes without saying that we do not do justice to Luther's views of the Devil if we look only at the spontaneous and ill-considered remarks contained in his *Table Talk*. People express themselves differently in a domestic situation than in well-considered writings. But in his *Large Catechism*, too, Luther ascribes great power to the Devil, especially when he explains the line in the Lord's Prayer 'deliver us from evil'. From the choice of words it is clear, says Luther, 'that the whole contents of this prayer is directed against this main enemy. For it is he who wants to hinder all that we pray'. Again he holds the Devil accountable for the suffering that may befall people.

> Because the Devil is not only a liar but also a murderer, he continually threatens our lives ... That is why he breaks the neck of many, or he makes them mad, others he has drowned in water, and he induces many to commit suicide ... In fact, there is little else for us to do on this earth than continually pray against this main enemy. For if God would not protect us we would not be safe from him for one hour.[16]

Therefore, his counsel to the Prince of Anhalt to say the Lord's Prayer daily over this child of Satan was fully consistent with his views.

People may count on this protection, if indeed they pray daily, Luther thought. The Devil is too powerful and man too sinful for the latter to resist him with his own strength. So, continuous prayer is necessary, but also sufficient. Despite his fascination with the Devil's power Luther believed in God's omnipotence. God was in charge. Whoever relies on God's grace in Christ no longer needs to fear the Devil. 'A mighty fortress is our God.'[17]

---

[15] See on the Germanic law to kill new-born babies Marieke van Vlierden, *Willibrord en het begin van Nederland* (Utrecht, 1995), p. 30.

[16] *Martin Luthers Werke*, (66 vols), vol. XXX, part 1 (Weimar, 1910; reprint 1964), 'Der grosse Katechismus' (1529), pp. 123–238.

[17] In this well-known hymn of Luther's we find a summary of his views on the power of the Devil:

> Der alt böse Feind
> Mit Ernst er's izt meint,
> Gross Macht und viel List

This well-known hymn of Luther's shows up another aspect of his beliefs regarding the Devil. It is true that God's children do not need to fear the Devil and his evil powers, as long as they lead prayerful lives. And yet, it is they who have to deal with him. Their piety evokes Satan's rage, just as the coming of Christ in the flesh led to a mobilization of evil spirits.[18] Believers are troubled by the Devil more than others, especially now that the end of this earth's history is near, something of which Luther was convinced. 'The Devil does not rage against adulterers, thieves and murderers.'[19]

This view does not appear to be fully consistent. For elsewhere Luther holds the Devil accountable for all misery in this life. So, one has to distinguish between various activities of the demonic forces. By their sins, and sometimes also because they deliberately made a pact with Satan, people have given free rein to the Devil, as can be seen in disasters and calamities. That the Devil gained power in this way may result in a preferential treatment of his favourites. Therefore the true believers suffer all the more, but as long as they trust themselves to God in prayer there is no need to be too fearful. Despite his awareness of the greatness of Satan's power Luther could also speak remarkably lightly about his trials. One way he himself could resist them was by going to bed with his wife more often. This was an excellent remedy, he had noticed.[20] So, although he continued to be aware of how much the Devil could do, we also find Luther with a rationalization of his power. In fact, he regarded it as a reassuring sign that the Devil was so manifestly present; apparently Satan felt threatened by the rediscovery of the Gospel.

Sein grausam Rüstzeug ist,
Auf Erd ist nicht seines Gleichen ...
Und wenn die Welt voll Teufel wär
Und wollt uns gar verschlingen,
So fürchten wir uns nicht so sehr
Es soll uns doch gelingen.
Der Fürst dieser Welt
So saur er sich stellt,
Thut er uns doch nicht,
Das macht er ist gericht
Eind Wörtlein kann ihn fällen.

Cited in Russell, *Mephistopheles*, p. 44. For an English translation see the *Anglican Hymn Book* (Oxford, 1965), no. 402.

[18] See Barth, *Der Teufel*, pp. 17 ff.
[19] Cited by Barth, *Der Teufel*, p. 27.
[20] See Russell, *Mephistopheles*, p. 44.

III

John Calvin

Calvin's (1509–64) image of the Devil can best be understood from his *Institutes*, the work which grew with him through the years, and which he continually improved in order to put into words his views as clearly and convincingly as possible. His idea of the Devil was not essentially different from that of Luther. He also pictured Satan as the 'prince of this world', who could muster an infinite number of armies, demons who like the Devil had once belonged to the realm of the angels, but who had rebelled against God under the leadership of Satan and who had been thrown out of heaven. Thus the origin of the Devil and his helpers lay not in creation but in corruption. God could not be held responsible for their appearance or for their evil behaviour.

And yet we have the impression that Calvin speaks about the Devil in a more detached way.[21] He is less inclined than Luther to ascribe all infirmities, illnesses and accidents to satanic influences. His image of God is more sombre, more comprehensive, more diabolic.[22] He puts all the emphasis on God's omnipotence and therefore stresses that the Devil, although God's adversary, remains subject to God's leadership. The Devil could only jump as far as God allowed the rope to slacken. He could not do anything without the explicit will and permission from God. The behaviour of evil spirits, too, had been restrained by God. It was God himself who allowed them to subjugate godless people. With respect to God's elect they could aid only God; the only effect of their teasing was that they exercised the believers in their struggle against sin.[23]

With an appeal to several Old Testament texts Calvin even states that a demon can also be called spirit of God. God makes 'these evil tools which He has under his power and which He can turn wherever He

---

[21] This is also Russell's opinion, *Mephistopheles*, p. 47: 'But though Calvin granted the Devil as much theoretical power as Luther did, he did not give him nearly as much attention.'

[22] In his critical description, Oskar Pfister, *Calvins Eingreifen in die Hexer- und Hexenprozesse von Peney 1545 nach seiner Bedeutung für Geschichte und Gegenwart* (Zürich, 1947), p. 128, goes as far as to typify Calvin's image of God as 'Diabolisierung Gottes, der in seiner Verwerfungslehre an Grausamkeit von keinem Teufel übertroffen werden kann'.

[23] John Calvin, *Christianae Religionis Institutio*. The first edition appeared in 1536. Later editions prepared by himself appeared in 1539, 1543 and 1559. The quotations are taken from the last edition, *Ioannis Calvini Opera Quae Supersunt Omnia* (Brunswick, 1864), vol. II. See for the quotations in the *Institutio* especially vol. I. xiv. 14–19, col. 127–31.

wants, serve his righteousness'.[24] Calvin was aware that this train of thought could lead to an intermingling of God and the Devil. He continues to stress that yet, in a hidden way, there remains a distinction between what God does and what Satan and his army of little demons and godless people bring about.

To obtain a clearer picture of Calvin's point of view it is useful to choose a similar approach to that of Luther, when we compared his well-considered formulations from his catechism with his improvising remarks from his *Table Talk*. There is no extant 'Table Talk' from Calvin, and this does not come as a surprise. He improvised more in the sermons which at times he had to produce virtually daily.[25] Especially in a sermon on Deuteronomy 18:10–15 Calvin expresses his opinions on the Devil and the evil spirits; he gives a criterion to assess who is guilty of demonic activities.

Whoever strays away from the natural order enters the Devil's sphere of influence. To commit adultery, to behave in strange ways, to be different, to be discontent with the place man has been given by nature, all of this is satanic. That is why astrology is also demonic; people want to have the course of their lives determined by the stars, while according to the creation narrative the sun and the moon had been given to serve us only in order that we could master time. To discover things beyond that which God has allowed us, to wish to know what is unknown to us by nature, this smells of demonic influences.

In his sermon he discusses in more detail the special powers that people who have made a pact with the Devil are said to have. He does believe the stories that are told about witchcraft: that people change into wolves, that they know the future, in short, that they can interfere with the natural order of things. However, he sees a limitation: 'The Scriptures show us that the Devil does not have his own kingdom.' The Devil cannot bring about anything apart from God. He can merely create illusions, so that it only looks as if a man has been changed into a wolf. This is bad enough. More and more people, he fears, are tempted to make a pact with the Devil. That is how it has been through the centuries: 'We know that at all times and among all peoples witches have had the upper hand ... We could tell unbelievable things about witches.' That is why he calls on the authorities to act severely:

> So let us agree that it is out of the question for us to tolerate
> sorcerers or witches in our midst. If the judges and the magistrates

---

[24] Ibid., vol. II. iv. 5.

[25] See about the preaching of Calvin and his improvising Richard Stauffer, 'Un Calvin méconnu: le prédicateur de Genève', *Bulletin de la Société du Protestantisme Français* (1977), pp. 184–201.

understand their duties, they will surely not permit this, just as they
do not permit murder. And why? Because here the service of God is
turned upside down and so the natural order is interfered with.

While he thus calls for persecution of witches and sorcerers he stresses
at the same time that the evil spirits can only execute God's wrath over
people.[26]

The same inconsistency that we encountered in the *Institutes* appears
here. Calvin does not want to detract from God's superiority and omnipotence. Even the Devil cannot bring anything about unless God
allows him to. Whatever he does fits into God's plan. At the same time
he remains God's adversary, he wants to interfere with God's created
order and he does indeed succeed. At the same time one has to act
mercilessly against all who apparently co-operate with evil spirits. They
can be known by the fact that they resist the natural order.

One of the consequences of this view was that Calvin actively incited
the persecution of witches, while at the same time he did not pay much
attention to the Devil in his writings. In the end, the latter was, however
active, however inventive, however influential, however evil, a mere
angel of God himself. This difference in approach between Luther and
Calvin probably has been the reason why many Lutheran writings have
appeared in which the Devil's influence and power are expounded,
while hardly any such works exist in Calvinism.

IV

Radical movements within Protestantism

In his *Institutes* Calvin indicates that in his time there were other views
about the Devil and evil spirits. Some even denied the existence of evil
spirits. They acknowledge that the New Testament, especially, mentions
evil spirits several times, but they think this should be regarded as a
particular way of speaking. In reality evil spirits are nothing other than
bad diseases, mental disorders, possibly evil tendencies in man himself.
So, there is no reason whatsoever to persecute witches because they are
supposed to have made a pact with Satan or to have committed adultery with an evil spirit. People who say things like this talk nonsense,
according to Calvin.

---

[26] J. Calvin, 'Le troisième sermon sur le Chap. XVIII, 10–15', held 2 December 1555,
sermon CIX; *Ioannis Calvini Opera Quae Supersunt Omnia*, vol. XXVII: *Sermons sur le
Deuteronome*, vol. III (Brunswick, 1884), col. 505–16.

In this context he does not mention any names. We may assume that
he had certain spiritualists or Anabaptists in mind.[27] They shared with
him their aversion to the Catholic sacraments and ceremonies, which
they too regarded as idolatry. They were of the same infamous character as the magic after which the magicians strained. The uttering of
spells, the repetition of magic formulas, the belief that images may have
certain powers, the performance of actions which brought about changes,
all these elements of the work of magicians were also characteristic of
Catholicism, they judged. That the 'popish mass' was as much an
'accursed idolatry',[28] and therefore a demonic work, as any magic
action[29] was a view they shared with Calvin.

However, they drew a conclusion from this rejection of the magical
view of the sacraments which Calvin did not share, namely that magic
does not work. In all these actions there is nothing more than deception
in that Bible verses which seem to suggest that certain rituals do bring
something about should be understood differently, that both good and
evil reside in man himself and that, therefore, those so-called evil spirits,
just like the magical activities of the magicians and just like the Catholic
ceremonies, do not need to be taken seriously.

Besides their polemics against Roman Catholic sacramental theology,
it was especially their aversion to the ever intensifying persecution of
witches which stimulated spiritualists and Anabaptists in this direction.
One of the first opponents of the belief in the existence of a personal
Devil and of evil spirits was the glass-painter David Joris (c. 1501–56).
Other Mennonite teachers proclaimed similar views.[30] It deserves our

---

[27] Calvin may also have thought of the so-called libertines, who referred to themselves
as 'spirituelz'. In a brief essay he dealt with them: *Contre la secte phantastique et
furieuse des Libertins* in *Ioannis Calvini Opera Quae Supersunt Omnia*, vol. VII (Brunswick, 1868), col. 145–252. Concerning their view of the Devil he states that they regard
him purely as imagination. According to them, there is only one spirit, the divine, who
animates the entire creation.

[28] *Heidelberg Catechism*, question 80. This work, written by Zacharias Ursinus and
Caspar Olevianus, was published for the first time in 1563 in Heidelberg, and became
one of the three confessions of the Dutch Reformed Church.

[29] See Keith Thomas, *Religion and the Decline of Magic* (Harmondsworth, 1978), pp.
58 ff: 'From the very start, the enemies of Roman Catholicism fastened upon the magical
implications which they saw to be inherent in some fundamental aspects of the Church's
ritual.'

[30] See also the work of the Harlem Mennonite Abraham Palingh, *'t Afgerukt
Momaansight der Tooverye. Daar in het bedrogh der gewaande tooverye, naakt ontdekt
en met gezonde redenen en exempelen deze Eeuwe aangewezen wort* (Amsterdam, 1659).
See also Gary K. Waite, 'David Joris en de opkomst van de sceptische traditie jegens de
duivel in de vroegmoderne Nederlanden', in *Duivelsbeelden*, eds G. Rooijakkers, L.
Dresen-Coenders and M. Geerdes (Baarn, 1994), pp. 216–31.

attention that it was this group in particular that was critical of the current demonology. Their rejection of infant baptism apparently had a deeper cause than their conviction that people were only to be baptized after they had come to faith, just as, conversely, in the ancient church the protagonists of infant baptism also had an often hidden motive. The very belief in the presence and the power of evil spirits, who could all too easily take possession of a human soul, had incited people from the third century onwards to look for an almost magical protection of their children. Baptism at as early an age as possible meant protection, it was a sign from which demons shrank.[31]

It took courage to reject, centuries later, the divine protection which was expected from the sacrament of baptism. It was only possible to withhold this sign from young children if not only the efficacy of the sacrament was denied, but also the existence of evil spirits. Such people talk nonsense, thought Calvin. He refused to deal with their arguments. This did not mean that their influence was utterly weakened. Although these spiritualists and Anabaptists were persecuted all over Western Europe, they emerged time and again, and their criticism of the current demonology continued to surface. Because from the end of the sixteenth century they were no longer persecuted in the free provinces of The Netherlands, it was there, in particular, that they could exert their influence.

V

The Devil in the history of the Dutch Reformation

The most crushing critique of the then current belief in the Devil and demons was given by Balthasar Bekker (1634–97) in his four-volume study *De betoverde Weereld*.[32] To combat the persecution of witches and the now orthodox demonology Bekker appeals, under the influence of the teachings of René Descartes (1595–1650), to the Bible, common sense and a sober analysis of the reports on sorcery and witchcraft. One of his most important arguments against the then current views was their pagan origin and the way in which they were developed in Roman Catholicism. When one wants to free oneself from pagan idolatry and

---

[31] W. C. Friend, *The Rise of Christianity* (n.p., n.d.), pp. 676, 677, 695.

[32] Balthasar Bekker, *De betoverde Weereld, zijnde een grondig ondersoek van 't gemeen gevoelen aangaande de Geesten, derselver aart en vermogen, bewind en bedrijf, als ook 't gene de menschen door derselver kraght en gemeenschap doen*, 4 vols. I use the edition of Deventer, 1739.

'popish' superstition, one should no longer harbour such ideas, according to Bekker. The liberation of the Roman yoke can only be complete if one distances oneself from these wild fantasies as well.

The Devil does exist, in his opinion, but not in the way and with the means of power that people ascribe to him. 'And so as a result of the Devil's insignificance the realm of magic should perish.'[33] Bekker's assumption was that the Devil had been banned by God to hell immediately after his fall, and that therefore his influence should be regarded as extremely small. All those stories about evil spirits and women who have made a pact with the Devil, should be dismissed as nonsense. Of course he also pays attention to the counter-arguments, which were mainly taken from the Bible. He analyses all the verses that speak of angels, evil spirits, the Devil or Satan, and he concludes that there is no reason to believe in the existence of demons as demigods or sub-gods. The accounts of good or fallen angels contradict one another and are unclear. It is true that the New Testament mentions several times Jesus driving out evil spirits, but one needs to realize that Jesus adapted his actions and words to the views of his time.

Bekker's work, of which the first two volumes appeared in 1691, was received enthusiastically. People who were suspected or persecuted because of their alleged relationship with the Devil, experienced his work as a liberation. In a pamphlet from 1883 the Amsterdam minister J. P. Stricker tells about a visit that Bekker received in 1696 from a German widow and her two sons: 'They almost fight for his hands, while tears are flowing along their cheeks.' It appeared that the quite wealthy widow had been accused of witchcraft by someone whose proposal she had turned down. The judges 'made her endure the most terrible tortures on the rack to induce her to confess her adultery with Satan'. Her lawyer got hold of a copy of Bekker's book and appealed using his arguments with so much success that she was released.[34]

Such experiences gave encouragment to Bekker; and he needed this. The edition of 1691 evoked 170 written reactions. On 28 June 1691 the church council of Amsterdam, where Bekker was a minister, condemned his views as contrary to the teachings of the church. At meetings of the classis and the synod the case was discussed and, in the end, this led to Bekker's demise as minister. He was disciplined. However, attempts to

---

[33] Bekker, *De betoverde Weereld*, vol. III. p. 1. See for the situation in The Netherlands, Ferdinand van Hemelryck, *Heksenprocessen in de Nederlanden* (Louvain, n.d.); L. Dresen-Coenders, *Het verbond*, pp. 196–266.

[34] J. P. Stricker, *Balthazar Bekker* (Amsterdam, 1883), pp. 21–3.

block new editions of his work failed because of the support Bekker received from the Amsterdam regents.[35]

It is worth investigating the arguments his opponents used. They opposed Bekker's Cartesianism, that is, the absolute separation of spirit and matter, from which he had drawn the conclusion that a spirit without a body could not have intercourse with a human being to the degree which was assumed. Also the way in which he dealt with biblical data received severe criticism. He was accused of letting himself be influenced by David Joris and Spinoza (1632–77). The lack of power he attributed to a Satan bound by God especially called for opposition. It could make people careless if they knew that the Devil had lost his say.[36] Many of Bekker's opponents could accept that he was critical of the way in which witches were persecuted; trials against witches had become extremely rare in The Netherlands. But the power of the Devil could not be tampered with.

In his detailed and particularly popular essay about the *Redelyke Godsdienst* (reasonable service of God) Willem à Brakel (1635–1711) summarizes the orthodox point of view regarding the Devil and his evil spirits, without clearly polemizing against Bekker:

> That there are demons is obvious for pagans and Christians, for both the godly and the godless; and Scripture speaks so often and so clearly about them that no man can doubt it, unless he wants to go stubbornly against all people and against God's word. ... There are demons, and many of them at that.[37]

On the basis of Bible verses he shows in what way the Devil and evil spirits can influence people. The author does, however, acknowledge regarding all that is said about evil spirits 'that very many of those stories and tales are mere fables and decorations'. In his description of what the Devil and his allies can bring about there are no references to witchcraft and no rumours of *incubi* or *succubi*. The Devil's power over people shows rather in that they are tempted not to go to church, or if they go, in that he distracts their thoughts during the sermon.[38]

In the Dutch Reformed Protestantism of this time one no longer believes that women want to commit adultery with this cold Satan or that they fly around on brooms. But it does evoke rage in orthodox circles if biblical narratives which speak of the activities of the Devil

---

[35] W. P. C. Knuttel, *Balthasar Bekker, de bestrijder van het bijgeloof* (The Hague, 1906); Beliën and van der Eerden, *Satans trawanten*, pp. 142–52.

[36] See for a descripton of the arguments Knuttel, *Balthasar Bekker*, pp. 224 ff.

[37] W. à Brakel, *Logike Latreia, dat is Redelyke Godsdienst* (2 vols), 18th edn (Rotterdam, 1767), vol. I, p. 243.

[38] Ibid., pp. 246, 247.

himself or of evil spirits are not understood literally. Using this approach the Devil is in the background. It is God who reigns and who, at most, tolerates the Devil as the quiet shadow by his side. This was to be expected from a religious trend which was mainly orientated towards Calvin.

It is remarkable that already in the second half of the sixteenth century, while elsewhere in Europe one witch after another was compelled to confess under torture and then burnt and in the reports of the Inquisition we find several trials against witches, there is hardly any real witchcraft to be found in the minutes of the Reformed churches. People are indeed exhorted when they have visited a fortune-teller or have been involved in some kind of sorcery, but it is certainly not of great importance. And yet there are many disciplinary actions. Regularly people are barred from the Lord's Supper, not because they have participated in a witches' Sabbath, but because they are guilty of adultery, drunkenness or fights. The Devil has become the invisible power in the background. The belief in his power is not given up. It manifests itself more in the continuous influence of Catholicism and in the emergence of heresies than in sensational phenomena like a destructive thunderstorm or a sudden outbreak of death among cattle. In such setbacks the Reformed believer sees not so much an ugly trick of the Devil but, rather, the punishing hand of God. Presented in another way the accomplices of the Devil have disappeared from sight, together with their bizarre behaviour, as have the angels. But most of these Calvinists continued to believe in the Devil as the personification of evil, if only to be able to maintain the belief in a personal God.

CHAPTER THREE

A 'Messiah for women': religious commotion in north-east Switzerland 1525–26

I

On 17 January 1526 the Zurich reformer Ulrich Zwingli wrote a letter to the medical doctor Johannes Vadianus, congratulating him on his recent appointment as mayor of the Swiss city St Gallen. He also asked him for more detailed information concerning the terrible events which were reputed to have taken place in the vicinity of St Gallen, especially in nearby Appenzell. The Anabaptists in that area were reported to have intercourse with each other's women, with the approval of the women themselves. A woman of previously unimpeachable conduct was said to have taken to the streets naked, offering herself to all she met, with the words, 'I have died in the flesh and live only in the spirit; everyone may now use me as he wishes'.[1] And this was said to be but a sample of the incidents which demonstrated how severely the Anabaptists were guilty of misconduct.

In addition to their revolutionary character, the Anabaptists were accordingly charged by what George H. Williams termed 'the Magisterial Reformation' with improper sexual conduct.[2] They were politically

---

[1] *Huldrych Zwinglis Briefe*, translated into German by O. Farner, (Zürich, 1918), vol. I, pp. 168–72. See also his work *In catabaptistarum strophas elenchus*, *Corpus Reformatorum* (CR) 93, that is Zwingli, *Werke*, vol. VI, pt 1 (reprinted Munich, 1981), pp. 1–196, in which Zwingli described the sexual excesses of the Anabaptists in St Gallen and Appenzell. For the history of the Anabaptists in Switzerland and especially in the environment of St Gallen and Appenzell, cf. E. Egli, *Actensammlung zur Geschichte der Zürcher Reformation in den Jahren 1519–1533* (Zurich, 1879); *Die St. Galler Täufer*, (Zurich, 1887); E. Eglin, *Schweizerische Reformationsgeschichte* (Zurich, 1910); H. Fast, *Heinrich Bullinger und die Täufer* (Weierhof, 1959); U. Gäbler, *Huldrych Zwingli im 20. Jahrhundert; Forschungsbericht und annotierte Bibliographie 1897–1972* (Zurich, 1975) and *Huldrych Zwingli; Leben und Werk* (Munich, 1983); G. W. Locher, *Die Zwinglische Reformation im Rahmen der Europäischen Kirchengeschichte* (Göttingen and Zurich, 1979) and *Zwingli und die Schweizerische Reformation; Die Kirche in ihrer Geschichte*, vol. III (Göttingen, 1982); J. Yoder, *Täufertum und Reformation in der Schweiz 1523–1538* (Weierhof, 1959).

[2] George H. Williams, *The Radical Reformation*, 3rd edn (Kirksville, MO, 1992), pp. xxviii–xxv.

and morally suspect. And most Lutheran and Reformed authors of the sixteenth century accepted this general evaluation. 'Just when the Reformation came to a head,' wrote the preacher Walter Klarer of Appenzell in his Chronicles, 'we were overtaken by the dangerous and damaging storm of the Anabaptists'.[3] With respect to the rise of Anabaptism, Heinrich Bullinger remarked: 'They committed deeds of glaring shame and vice; they asserted in public that women to be saved must become gross sinners, since it is written: "The harlots go into the kingdom of God before you".'[4]

The most influential representatives of Anabaptism of this period were conscious of the risk that their movement would be brought into discredit by these events in north-east Switzerland. Originally they were pleased by the tremendous following in this area by people of all social classes. However, when they heard of the sexual aberrations they were quick to distance themselves. Partly for this reason they gathered for deliberation in 1527 in the vicinity of Schaffhausen, and wrote their conclusions in 'The Schleitheim Confession of Faith'. In the introduction to the seven articles they asserted:

> A very great offence has been introduced by certain false brethren among us, so that some have turned aside from their faith, in the way they intend to practice and observe the freedom of the Spirit and of Christ. But such have missed the truth and to their condemnation are given over to the lasciviousness and self-indulgence of the flesh. They think faith and love may do and permit everything, and nothing will harm them nor condemn them, since they are believers. Observe, you who are God's members in Christ Jesus, that faith in the Heavenly Father through Jesus Christ does not take such form. It does not produce and result in such things as these false brethren and sisters do and teach. Guard yourselves and be warned of such people, for they do not serve our Father, but their father, the devil. But you are not that way. For they that are Christ's have crucified the flesh with its passions and lusts. Separate yourselves from them for they are perverted.[5]

---

[3] *Quellen zur Geschichte der Täufer in der Schweiz*, ed. H. Fast (Zurich, 1973), vol. II. pp. 567, 568.

[4] Quotation by J. Horsch in 'An Inquiry into the Truth of Accusations of Fanaticism and Crime against the Early Swiss Brethren', *Mennonite Quarterly Review*, 8 (1934), p. 18.

[5] John C. Wenger, 'The Schleitheim Confession of Faith', *Mennonite Quarterly Review*, 19 (1945), pp. 243–53. See also Robert Friedmann, 'The Schleitheim Confession (1527) and Other Doctrinal Writings of the Swiss Brethren in a hitherto Unknown Edition', *Mennonite Quarterly Review*, 16 (1942), pp. 82–98. In her study 'Das Schleitheimer Täuferbekenntnis 1527', *Schaffhauser Beiträge zur vaterländischen Geschichte*, 28 (1951), pp. 5–81, Beatrice Jenny made a connection between this confession and the excesses in north-east Switzerland.

Of course this condemnation of all sexual deviations, uttered by the Anabaptist leaders themselves, did not escape the attention of the most important representatives of the Magisterial Reformation. But they viewed the internal division as yet another symptom of the movement's decay. The author of the famous French book of martyrs, Jean Crespin, a printer from Geneva, faithful follower of Calvin and reformer of similar mind, claimed to be able to discern no less than 15 different groups within the Anabaptist movement. Naturally he mentioned the revolutionary group that under the leadership of Jan Matthijs and Jan van Leiden had captured the city of Munich. Likewise, the Anabaptists in St Gallen and Appenzell he considered as a separate group. The ultimate misconduct he identified in the actions of a certain woman of Appenzell, 'who managed to convince many that she was the Christ, the Messiah for women; she chose for herself twelve disciples'. He described her conduct as 'shameful, beastly and repulsive'.[6]

Circa 1570 it was therefore clear to everyone that not all Anabaptists could be classified together. But this did not mitigate the general condemnation of this radical movement. In Calvinist and Lutheran circles the excesses continued to be viewed as typical of the movement as a whole, even if these excesses did not always surface everywhere with equal clarity. Emphasis was placed upon affinity between the groups. But this was opposed by Mennonite historians. They were of the opinion that groups which had been rejected by the official leaders of the Anabaptists should be omitted. The true Brothers had always preserved themselves from violence and sexual aberrations. Since a connection between the Anabaptists in St Gallen and Appenzell and the movement as it had begun in Zurich could not be denied, John Horsch concluded that the charges of sexual impropriety must have been invented. He called attention to comparable accusations lodged by the Catholics against Luther and Zwingli themselves.[7]

But this denial appeared to be untenable. Paul Peachey therefore attempted to demonstrate that the persons guilty of misconduct in St Gallen and Appenzell scarcely belonged to the movement.[8] Heinold

---

[6] Jean Crespin, *Histoire des vrays Tesmoins de la Verité de l'Evangile, qui de leur sang l'ont signée, depuis Jean Hus usques au temps present* (Geneva, 1570), p. 84. In the margin the words: 'Chose horrible d'une femme qui se dit estre le Messias'.

[7] John Horsch, 'An Inquiry', pp. 18–31, 73–89: 'Likewise the Mennonites and Calvinists of the Netherlands were accused of being polygamists. Of Martin Luther it was asserted that he renounced Romanism because he desired license to sin, that he lived in drunkenness and finally ended his life as a wretched suicide.'

[8] P. Peachey, *Die sociale Herkunft der Schweizer Täufer in der reformationszeit* (Karlsruhe, 1954), pp. 76–9: 'Es handelt sich also um eine Bewegung, die umfassender war, als das Täufertum.' 'Die fünf extremen Fälle ... sind psychopathische Fälle, meistens nicht einmal Täufer betreffend ... .'

Fast concluded that they were initially guilty of improper conduct only after the authorities had forced them to renounce their Anabaptist feelings. Even George Williams wished to distinguish between the behaviour of certain persons in north-east Switzerland and authentic leaders of the Anabaptist movement: 'It is hard to find anything in common between this phase of St Gallen Anabaptism and the sober fervour and evangelical zeal of Grebel, Mantz, and Blaurock.'[9]

In general the various authors demonstrate extreme reserve in their descriptions of precisely what happened. They do not give a detailed picture of the excesses. In his article Heinold Fast wrote:

> I don't wish to relate all of this in detail. To the point of absurdity, biblicism was combined with libertine fantasies. But the happenings lend themselves more to psychiatric research than historical, for the historian can merely search the reliability of the reports and investigate the affiliation with the Anabaptists themselves.[10]

Nor do I care to describe perversities in detail. But in my opinion Fast's reserved approach treats the events too lightly. Aberrations have a real social background, and this is an essential part of an historical investigation. Furthermore, his approach threatens to leave certain questions unanswered. It is worth pursuing a number of these questions. What were the accused actually guilty of? Why did the women receive such emphasis? Was there a difference between what these women did and what was done to them? Did they truly change their conduct after they were forced back into the official church? I believe that an investigation of these questions will yield insights into the manner in which men and women related to each other, as well as into the opportunities allotted to women in this period of history. It is for this reason that I first wish to summarize the reports of the most important and very reliable writer of chronicles in St Gallen, Johann Kessler.[11]

II

In his *Sabbata* (the title indicates that he wrote his diary in the hours he could manage to free for himself), the saddle-maker John Kessler de-

---

[9] Heinold Fast, 'Die Sonderstellung der Täufer in St Gallen und Appenzell', *Zwingliana*, 11 (1960), pp. 223–40. The same opinion was held by J. Yoder, *Täufertum und Reformation in der Schweiz*, vol. I (Zurich, 1962), pp. 49–54. George H. Williams, *The Radical Reformation*, p. 228.

[10] H. Fast, 'Die Sonderstellung', p. 233.

[11] J. Kessler, 'Sabbata', in H. Fast (ed.), *Quellen zur Geschichte der Täufer in der Schweiz* (Zurich, 1973), vol. II, pp. 590–638. Complete edition: E. Egli and R. Schoch, *Johannes Kesslers Sabbata* (St Gallen, 1902).

scribed the history of the Reformation in the area of St Gallen from approximately 1523 to 1539. He himself played an active role in this Reformation. When he returned to St Gallen in 1524, after a period of study in Wittenberg, he was requested to give Bible lessons to those who were interested. He was 21 or 22 years old at the time. After a while the work was taken over by the monk, Wolfgang Ulimann, who joined the Anabaptists and was baptized in the Rhine at Schaffhausen. From that moment onwards Ulliman occasionally received divine revelations. His steadily growing support became more radical, and he was forced to leave the city.[12] Kessler began to distance himself from the movement. He followed the policy of the doctor and mayor, Vadianus, who under Zwingli's influence pursued a more restrained ecclesiastical reformation.

Similarly, in nearby Appenzell there also arose a strong Anabaptist movement. Here a group formed around a goldsmith who gave particular heed to Christ's injunction to be as children.[13] Women especially listened to this call, relates Kessler. In their gatherings they danced, leaping and singing.

In St Gallen the actions of the women also attracted attention, at least that of Kessler. They cut their hair short and in response to Kessler's queries as to why they conducted themselves in such a manner, which was contrary to custom and nature, they responded that their hair in part was responsible for their attraction for men, in other words, for sins. His appeal to the words of Paul[14] they casually dismissed as irrelevant. Kessler concluded that in this conduct they did precisely what they previously accused the nuns of.

Despite the fact that the movement originally emphasized pursuit of greater knowledge of the Bible, some began – in part on the basis of a biblical citation! – to reject an appeal to Scripture as the only source of inspiration. 'The letter kills but the Spirit gives life.'[15] Whoever attempted to bring them to conversion on the basis of Bible texts was simply derided. According to Kessler this was the main reason why certain errors could grow unchecked. With the exception of one incident, in which a man murdered his brother, Kessler primarily described the activities of women.

A certain woman named Margarete Hattinger, who was originally from Zollikon, and who through her admirable conduct had earned a

---

[12] See for the banishments of Ulimann (17 July 1525 and 22 January 1526) *Quellen zur Geschichte der Täufer*, vol. II, pp. 400, 401, 405, 406.

[13] Luke 18:17.

[14] 1 Corinthians 11:6.

[15] 2 Corinthians 3:6.

good reputation, began to present herself as God. In response to criticisms of such an assertion, her supporters called attention to words of Jesus himself. He too was accused of blasphemy, because as a human being he had called himself God.[16] Some of those supporters no longer prayed in a normal manner; they spoke in a language that nobody could understand.

Perhaps it was in imitation of her that Magdelene Müller called herself 'the way, the truth and the life'.[17] She, too, was generally considered of high repute. Often she was in the company of two other women, Barbara Mürglen, and a servant-girl from Appenzell, Frena (or Verena) Bumenin. The latter attempted to increase her influence upon the others, especially by stimulating their feelings of guilt. In one of their confrontations Magdalene was so deeply affected that she lost consciousness. When she came to she demanded that they would do penance and repent of all the unnecessary chatter with which they could only dismay the Holy Spirit.

The following evening and night the three met again. Now Frena presented herself as the new Messiah, the Christ. She viewed her friends as a sort of reincarnation of Peter and Mary Magdalene. She wanted to recruit her 12 disciples. Barbara and Magdalene she sent to another woman, Wibrat. They were to tell her that the Lord had sent them to her. She was to leave her sins and follow her Master. The woman obeyed the call and joined the group. Slowly the group grew. Frena encountered a young man, Lienhardt Wirt, behind a weaver's loom. By the highest power of God she ordered him to join his Saviour. He obeyed immediately and followed her. Later, when the movement had died out, he married her. They had a child who was baptized on 8 June 1528, in accordance with the prescribed regulations.[18]

Friends and associates were invited by the members of the group to gather together at a certain place outside the city. A number of them met at this gathering, and all confessed their sins to one another. As the evening proceeded Frena became increasingly disturbed. She thought she had received a commission to give birth to the Antichrist. At her request Barbara, whom she viewed as Peter, disrobed her. When one of the men expressed his embarrassment about the matter she reproached him.

The meeting lasted the entire night. Frena neither ate nor slept. She cursed all who would not submit to God. At a certain point she became convinced that Judas too was in their midst. She ordered him to hang

---

[16] John 10:33–8.

[17] John 14:6.

[18] See a remark in the book of baptisms of St Gallen; *Quellen zur Geschichte der Täufer*, vol. II, p. 619, n. 135.

himself. One of the men thought that the instruction must apply to him, and departed to carry it out. But at the door of the barn he banged his head so severely against a beam that he came to his senses and changed his mind. Later Frena herself departed. Her absence was so prolonged that the others went in search of her. Finally, chilled to the bone, she returned. In the dark December night she had stumbled into a stream. They laid her by the fire. Once again she lost control of herself. She introduced herself as the great whore of Babylon required to bear the Antichrist.

The following day her condition became even worse. Naked, foaming at the mouth and covered in dirt, she wandered to the townhall of St Gallen to proclaim God's judgement to the councillors. The town council wished to send her to her birthplace, Appenzell, to recuperate. She refused, and finally she was chained and confined to a separate room in the *Seelhaus*, the hospital of St Gallen.

In this condition, a man who was not part of the group took advantage of her. He announced that God had sent him to have intercourse with her. She allowed it. When he returned to her the following evening she had come to her senses enough to refuse him. For six weeks she remained in the hospital. By that time she could slip the chains off of her wrists. The council sent her out of town.

Part of her following accompanied her. The group wandered through the countryside and increased rapidly. Kessler mentions a total of 1 200! When the following winter settled over the area most of them sought the shelter of their own houses and families. At this time the assemblies were officially forbidden. Only the die-hard members of the group gathered during the evenings in the barns. Their meetings took on an increasingly ecstatic character. People fell on the ground, writhed 'as if they had to cry intensely but couldn't', and fell unconscious. 'Dying' they called this phenomenon. And when they recovered again they related the heavenly messages they had received in their 'absence'. Kessler claims to have encountered numerous members of the group in such a state. Apparently one of his relatives was closely affiliated to the group. He told Kessler that this 'dying' had gripped him contrary to his will. In Appenzell it even happened to someone during a church service. When someone else emptied a kettle of water over his head he soon came to. Kessler once addressed a group about this matter. His speech was received with hand-clapping and cries of 'Mourn O mourn you scribes; mourn O mourn you hypocrites!'. Finally he simply left. Kessler compared the phenomenon to the situation of the slave girl with a spirit of divination encountered by Paul in Thyatira.[19]

---

[19] Acts 16:16–18.

Although both in St Gallen and in Appenzell the authorities were extremely reluctant to take action, finally they banned all assemblies and ecstatic scenes. A few women were imprisoned. The pressure exerted upon them was of such a nature that they changed their minds and complied with the leadership of the official church. However, they now went to the opposite extreme. Earlier they had burned their hairbands, jewellery and collars, but now they remade them. And when men and women of these circles visited one another they often committed adultery. 'They have fallen from their previous purity into whoredom,' concluded Kessler. And if they were confronted on the matter they answered, 'Why do you judge? We have passed through death. What we now do is against our will in the spirit'.[20] With obvious regret Kessler was forced to conclude that the same people who once were so spiritual had become so fleshly that the world could say, 'Mourn the Anabaptists, how they have fallen'. 'I never expected,' wrote Kessler, 'that the people who had sought divine truth so sincerely could fall into such shameless error.'[21] His final conclusion was, 'This is indeed true; the devil can for a time be an angel, but he cannot remain one forever'. Also significant is his announcement that because of these aberrations, marriage and baptismal records were subsequently kept with more precision.

III

Has it been worthwhile to recall these somewhat offensive details about which church historians have often remained silent? I believe so. It helps considerably to sharpen our perspective of the history of the Reformation in north-east Switzerland. I wish to clarify a number of points.

First, the Anabaptist movement in north-east Switzerland, in contrast to the movement in Zurich, lacked sufficiently developed leadership to be able to detect certain pitfalls. There was certainly a strong desire amongst the people for increased Bible knowledge but there arose an unresolvable tension between biblicism, which was accepted by the Anabaptists in order to justify their break with the official church, and the conviction that God continues to reveal himself to people. It was precisely biblical texts that people employed in their argument not to rely upon Bible texts. While they rejected others who attempted to warn them on the basis of Paul, they simultaneously had a desire to literally

---

[20] Kessler, 'Sabbata', p. 629.
[21] Ibid., p. 631.

heed other Biblical admonitions. Once again there was the phenomenon
of women especially appealing to the words of Jesus precisely when
they were being admonished with the words of Paul![22]

Second, upon numerous occasions Kessler relates that it was women
in particular who were attracted to this radical movement. However,
such remarks can easily lead to wrong conclusions. From other sources
we know that both in St Gallen and Appenzell it was also especially
women who defended the old Roman Catholic faith. In St Gallen the
nunnery of St Catharina formed the bastion of Catholic opposition.
Regarding Appenzell, the preacher Walter Klarer complained foremost
about the stance of the women who blocked the Reformation.[23]

It was always the opponents who complained about the participation
of women in the movement which they contested. They had reason for
this. Church leaders were in general convinced that women were easier
to mislead than men, that they were more accessible to demonical
influence, that they fell more easily into heresy.[24]

The most that we can conclude is, therefore, that in a transitional
phase, for lack of concrete guidelines, men and women at all levels of
society were forced into active participation in determining their stance.
Women were well represented in all groups, from the most radical
reformers to the most conservative members of the established church.

Third, the women who were converted under the influence of
Anabaptism wanted to do harsh penance for their previous conduct.
They cut off their hair, burned all make-up and, in short, attempted to
rid themselves of all previous means of enhancing their attractiveness.
Nor did they wish to continue to discuss senseless matters; they would
purify the topics of their conversations. Accordingly, they adopted the
customs which previously were typical only of the nuns. They drew
themselves towards the life of the cloister.

Fourth, a few women identified themselves strongly with Jesus. Such
a pretension can easily cause misunderstanding and has, in fact, done
so. Margarete Hattinger's appeal to Bible passages such as John 10 and
15 is indicative of what she must have thought. She did not view herself
as a new incarnation of God, but placed herself within the mystical
traditions of certain Beguines and German mystics, who laid such emphasis upon becoming one with God that the difference became nearly
imperceptible. Magdalene Müller also appears to have had something

---

[22] See Auke Jelsma, *Tussen heilige en helleveeg*, 2nd edn (The Hague, 1981), pp. 47,
48. [German translation: *Heilige und Hexen; Die Stellung der Frau im Christentum*
(Konstanz, 1977), pp. 60–63].
[23] Emil Egli, *Schweizerische Reformationsgeschichte*, pp. 126–31, 344–56.
[24] See Chapter 5 in this volume.

similar in mind when she announced herself as the way, the truth and the life. In her readiness to obey God she could claim for herself the promises Jesus had made with respect to living in the hearts of his followers.

The maid, Frena, apparently went a step further. In her ecstatic state she clearly viewed herself as a sort of reincarnation of Christ, as is evident in her commissioning of apostles, the names she gave to her followers and the self-conscious manner in which she drew Lienhardt from behind the loom. For a woman to identify with Christ in this manner is indeed remarkable. Ordinarily such phenomena were restricted to men.[25] Women often played an important role in such cases, but as a reincarnation of Christ's mother or of Mary Magdalene.

This variation also has a precedent. In the thirteenth century, Guglielma of Milan presented herself as the new and the last incarnation of God, basing her views upon the threefold historical division suggested by Joachim of Fiore. After God had revealed himself in the second phase as a man, it was logical to suppose that the third and final stage would be introduced with an incarnation in the form of a woman. For a period of time Guglielma managed to have a considerable following.[26]

Frena's identification was less elaborately founded, more impulsive and emotional, considering her later conviction that she was called to bear the Antichrist. Even so, spiritual aberrations have their own form of logic, and behind this incident lay hidden a particular view of history. According to the Bible the Antichrist must appear before God can bring to completion human history. She saw it as her duty as God's chosen Messiah to facilitate the arrival of the Antichrist. From Kessler's account we have the impression that Frena's adherents must have viewed her in a manner similar to the reception given to Margarete Hattinger.

Fifth, sexual misconduct appears to have played a minor part. Naturally, speculations in this area were expressed, especially when large groups of men and women left their families behind to traipse around together day and night. But the community actually lived in the immediate expectation of the end of history. In this period, in their opinion, people were called to abandon earthly possessions and natural relations to concentrate solely upon penance and preparation for the Last Judgement. Sexuality does not appear to have been a significant factor. Mass

---

[25] During the first centuries, for example, Mani. For the early Middle Ages see Gregory of Tours in *Historiae Ecclesiasticae Francorum Libri Decem*, vol. X. 25 (Migne, *Patrologia Latina* 71, cols 556, 557). In the twelfth century in The Netherlands Tanchelm, in France Eudo de la Stella.

[26] See Marjorie Reeves, *The Influence of Prophecy in the later Middle Ages: a Study in Joachimism* (Oxford, 1969), pp. 248 ff.

hysteria occurred. The people passed out and underwent visionary experiences, as was also the case in other charismatic movements such as Montanism, the American Revivalists and the Pentecostals. Speaking in tongues was a regular occurrence.

Kessler's first example of sexual misconduct was that of the abuse of Frena by someone who did not belong to the group. It was only after the authorities stepped in and put the women especially under pressure to relinquish their views that some of them indulged in sexual misconduct. The imprisonment of members of the group concerns only Magdalene Müller and Wibrat, the first followers of Frena. The accounts are not entirely clear. In another chronicle of St Gallen, written by a preacher, Hermann Miles (1464–1535), it is stated that both women were first imprisoned after they had ecstatic experiences. They were forced to walk through the city with a stone hung round their necks. Subsequently they were guilty of whoredom. They were again imprisoned and forced to carry the stone of shame.[27] Kessler mentions only one imprisonment. The account by Miles seems to be the most acceptable. Frena appears to have abstained from further affairs, and almost immediately after these happenings she married Lienhardt.

Evidently it also amazed Kessler that the women who, during their Anabaptist period, were so proper later fell into promiscuity. What caused them to do so? Degradation would have played an important role. For the sake of the Faith, in a matter of months they had lost the good name that they had previously earned. Their willingness to sacrifice, their devotion to God, their dedication to his kingdom, all of this had earned them nothing but suspicion, mockery and, finally, anything but gentle treatment during their imprisonment. They had become women who no longer needed to be treated respectfully by men. It is worth noting the comment that Kessler cites from them, 'What we do now is against our will ...'.[28] The concept of *Gelassenheit*, resignation, acquired a new meaning in this situation. Furthermore, Kessler particularly emphasizes the change of conduct in previously very proper women; and evidently there were plenty of men who were more than ready to confirm the negative self-image of these women.

Sixth, in what respect do we now have a clearer picture of this history? The manner in which the church functioned was not adequate for the general public of St Gallen and Appenzell. Men and women alike felt the urge to live in a more intense anticipation of the coming of Christ's kingdom than was permitted by the official church. Many were prepared to undertake a radical renewal of ecclesiastical and social life.

[27] See *Quellen zur Geschichte der Täufer*, vol. II, p. 705.
[28] Kessler, 'Sabbata', p. 631.

Among them were many women. They were the most conspicuous, perhaps because they were usually inconspicuous in church life. As is usual in charismatic movements, many followers had ecstatic experiences. Their conduct and their view of Scripture disturbed ecclesiastical and political leaders, who did what they could to restrain the more enthusiastic expressions. And the end result was that both Catholics and Protestants introduced more stringent regulations, as is evident from reports of visitations and consistory records of the sixteenth century. Kessler makes a direct correlation between this desire to establish order, and the excesses of the Anabaptist movement.

It is also clear that the fear of chaos expressed by the spiritual leaders has led to an unjustifiably negative impression of the Anabaptist movement. The final conclusion of Williams is striking but not entirely warranted. He wrote:

> In this degeneration of the movement one seems to see beneath the lifted weight of centuries of ecclesiastical domination a squirming, spawning, nihilistic populace on its own, confused by the new theological terms of predestination, faith alone, *Gelassenheid*, and by the new Biblical texts seized upon with an almost maniacal glare.[29]

When Anabaptists received the opportunity to develop their own ecclesiastical model, they appeared to be perfectly capable of eventually creating orderly conditions, as is evident in the later history of the Mennonites. In any event, those particular Anabaptists of north-east Switzerland are more deserving of our understanding than of a zealous superficial judgement.[30]

---

[29] G. H. Williams, *The Radical Reformation*, p. 228.

[30] I should like to thank Dr W. Koopmans for his help with the English version of this chapter.

CHAPTER FOUR

The king and the women: Münster 1534–35

I

The dream

The Anabaptist movement controlled the city of Münster for almost one and a half years. This is old news, but in view of the possibilities in that period it continues to be almost unimaginable that a city of such size could be used in this way for what was experienced as the advancing kingdom of God.

Initially, the followers of Melchior Hoffman had thought that Strasburg was the place where Jesus would return on heavenly clouds. That idea had not really been far-fetched, not if one soon expected the second coming of Christ; and the Anabaptists shared this expectation with many others. Where would have been a better place for the Lord to return to at that time? For Strasburg was a city in which many things were possible, where the city council ministers had created a climate of tolerance – not an everyday occurrence. So when an old prophet from East Friesland ordered Melchior Hoffman to go to Strasburg to wait for the Lord there, in all probability it would have scarcely surprised the former tanner. The motivation for this order was really much more remarkable. In Strasburg he would be imprisoned. He had to complete what was still lacking in regard to Jesus's afflictions.[1] His suffering would be the high road along which Jesus wished to come. The prophet predicted an imprisonment of half a year.

Of course, Melchior, being as credulous as he was, immediately hastened to Strasburg, in the spring of 1533. His arrest took its time. He had to work hard to attract attention. For that is how tolerant things were in Strasburg. When at last he was taken prisoner he was ecstatic with joy, and one of his followers, Obbe Philips, related later on:

> He beat his hat from his head, threw his shoes away, raised his fingers to heaven, and swore by the living God that he would not enjoy any other food or drink but water and bread until his stretched

---

[1] Colossians 1:24.

arm would point to the one who had sent him; this is the way in which he entered the prison, prepared, joyous and comforted.[2]

A number of his followers, mainly from The Netherlands where Hoffman had gathered most of his adherents, also travelled to this city to be part of the great events. Under the leadership of people like the prophetic couple Lienhard and Ursula Jost they prepared themselves for the second advent.

It goes without saying that they were greatly disillusioned when half a year later the Lord still had not returned. Melchior Hoffman had a serious breakdown from which he recovered only with difficulty. In The Netherlands too, there was great disappointment over the delay. In the mean time the movement had attracted the attention of the authorities. The stakes bearing the victims of the intensified persecution spread not only stench and smoke across the country, but also fear. An imminent second coming would have been welcomed by the Anabaptists, because the economic situation worsened every year. From 1531 The Netherlands was involved in the struggle for the Norwegian–Danish crown. One of the consequences was that the Sound was closed to Dutch ships which made the import of grain, as well as the export of textiles and other products, across the Baltic Sea impossible. Prices rose and in their wake followed inflation, hunger and unemployment, among the small craftsmen in particular.[3]

The disappointment over the postponement of the Endtime resulted in a radicalization of the movement. Jan Matthijs, a baker from Haarlem, tall and with a long, black beard,[4] pushed himself into the foreground as a leader. He sent out apostles who, contrary to Melchior Hoffman's continuing prohibition to baptize, were allowed to baptize new converts. They kept alive the hope for imminent salvation. No one needed to fear possible reprisals by the authorities, according to them. 'There

---

[2] 'Bekentenisse Obbe Philipsz', in *Bibliotheca Reformatoria Neerlandica*, ed. S. Cramer, (The Hague, 1910), vol. VII, p. 124. On Melchior Hoffman see P. Kawerau, *Melchior Hoffman als religiöser Denker* (Haarlem, 1954); K. Deppermann, *Melchior Hoffman. Soziale Unruhen und apokalytische Visionen im Zeitalter der Reformation* (Göttingen, 1979). For the situation in Strasbourg the work of A. Hulshof is still relevant: *Geschiedenis van de Doopsgezinden te Straatsburg van 1525 tot 1557* (Amsterdam, 1905). See especially *Quellen zur Geschichte der Täufer*, vol. VIII, *Elsass II. Stadt Strassburg 1533–1535*, eds M. Krebs and H. G. Rott (Gütersloh, 1960).

[3] For the situation in the Netherlands see A. F. Mellink, *De Wederdopers in de Noordelijke Nederlanden 1531–1544* (Groningen and Djakarta, 1953) and his *Amsterdam en de Wederdopers in de zestiende eeuw* (Nijmegen, 1978).

[4] That is how Heinrich Gresbeck describes him in 'Bericht von der Wiedertaufe in Münster', in *Die Geschichtsquellen des Bisthums Münster*, vol. II, *Berichte der Augenzeugen über das Münsterische Wiedertäuferreich*, ed. C. A. Cornelius (Münster, 1853; photographic reprint, 1965), p. 40.

was no need to be afraid,' wrote Obbe Philips in his memoirs, 'for no Christian blood would be shed; before this, God would wipe all shedders of blood, tyrants and godless from the face of the earth.'[5]

Two of the apostles arrived in Münster and discovered that in the mean time the situation there had become much more favourable than in Strasbourg. Thanks to the activities of the reformer, Bernhard Rothmann, this city had been declared evangelical by a treaty of 14 February 1533. The bishop had been forced to leave and, to the dread of many, Rothmann had become much more radical. He now also opposed infant baptism and was encouraged in this direction by a number of ministers who had been forced to find refuge in the town. The polarization increased. Lutheran patricians fraternized again with their Catholic fellow-citizens in order to form a united front against the Anabaptist elements. On 11 December 1533 Rothmann was ousted from the city. But his popularity appears to have been so great that three days later he could preach openly in one of the churches again, and no one dared to lift a finger against him. The guilds and the common people in particular supported him. Such was the situation when the apostles of Jan Matthijs entered the city. Rothmann and the other ministers were now baptized. The Anabaptist movement asserted itself more and more. Prophets and prophetesses ran shouting through the streets of the town, calling all to repentance. An atmosphere of anxiety began to rule in the city.

The bishop, Franz von Waldeck, thought he could seize this opportunity to regain control. With a small army he marched towards the town. Beyond this threat, in Anabaptist circles too the willingness to use violence grew. Jan Beukelszoon, of Leiden, and Jan Matthijs appeared in the city. At the end of February all who were unwilling to be baptized were sent out of the town. It was a cold night, Kerssenbroch, who had been part of the exodus as a boy, remembered. The unwilling were urged forward with spears. Just outside the city walls a woman had to give birth to a child in the snow. A few days later the bishop began his siege, but Münster had become Anabaptist.[6]

---

[5] 'Bekentenisse Obbe Philipsz', p. 129.

[6] For the situation in Münster see C. A. Cornelius (ed.), *Berichte der Augenzeugen*; R. van Dülmen, *Das Täuferreich zu Münster 1534–1535; Berichte und Dokumente* (Munich, 1974); K. H. Kirchhoff, 'Die Täufer im Münsterland; Verbreitung und Verfolgung des Täufertums im Stift Münster 1533–1550', *Westfälische Zeitschrift*, Band 113 (Regensberg and Münster, 1963); K. Löffler, *Die Wiedertäufer zu Münster 1534/35; Berichte, Aussagen und Aktenstücke von Augenzeugen und Zeitgenossen* (Jena, 1923); O. Rammstedt, *Sekte und soziale Bewegung; Soziologische Analyse der Täufer in Münster (1534/35)* (Cologne and Opladen, 1966); R. Stupperich, *Das Münsterische Täufertum* (Münster, 1958); *Die Wiedertäufer in Münster*, ed. Hans Galen, 2nd edn (Münster, 1982).

The Lord would not appear in Strasbourg. Wrongly, Hoffman had thought that waiting patiently was the stimulus which put the coming of Jesus in motion. Something had to be done. Only after a landing-place had been cut out in the jungle of this corrupted world, could the great occurrence take place. In Münster this condition had been met. There was at least one place now where all had been baptized, one city where the difference between state and church no longer existed. A whole town had become a church, in other words, the church had been absorbed into the new kingdom. The people knelt as easily in the streets as in the church. Sermons were preached in the church buildings but also in the squares of the town, wherever people congregated. Imagine a whole city in which all the people had this in common, where, as Rothmann later wrote in his *Restitution*, all that served selfishness had been done away with, where it was no longer possible to feast on the labour of others and where the rich could no longer eat and drink the sweat of the poor.[7] 'No one among us is too distinguished for the others, for we form a community of love' is how it was formulated in the confession which was drawn up in this initial period.[8]

As is self-evident, in reality it was not so easy to continue to comply with these high expectations but it was this ideal which the brothers and sisters of the new covenant had in mind, and a wave of excitement rolled through The Netherlands and Westphalia now that an entire city was available to realize the ideal. Even Melchior Hoffman, whose imprisonment was made more severe as a result of this course of actions, greeted the leaders of Münster as true prophets of God.[9]

Before one speaks in a derogatory way of what happened in Münster, one should allow this impression to permeate, this wave of excitement which became visible especially in the lowest strata of the Dutch population. Everything everywhere had looked so immovable. Barriers had been all around. The classes seemed to be part of creation itself, and that is how they were depicted. The church had society in its grip to such a degree that people who wished to experience their faith in a different way had no chance from the outset; and add to this the threat that inflation and unemployment caused for those on the lower rungs of the social ladder. It was an unbearable situation which moved people of its own accord in any direction where there was some hope but, because of the barriers, virtually all movement was impossible. And suddenly

---

[7] B. Rothmann, 'Restitution rechter und gesunder christlicher Lehre', in *Die Schriften Bernhard Rothmanns*, ed. R. Stupperich (Münster, 1970), p. 256.

[8] 'Bekenntnis des Glaubens und Lebens der Gemeinde Christi zu Münster (1534)', in *Die Schriften Bernhard Rothmanns*, ed. R. Stupperich (Münster, 1970), p. 203.

[9] J. M. Stayer, *Anabaptists and the Sword* (2nd edn Lawrence, KS, 1973), p. 223.

there was this breakthrough via the class distinctions, through the ecclesiastical and political system. Is it any wonder that Münster was experienced in The Netherlands as the beginning of the end, an open door to the new reality of a 'community of love'?

Because of the subsequent developments this episode has usually received a negative judgement. Opponents found plenty of arguments here to justify their fierce rejection of the whole movement. Every protagonist of believers' baptism was from now on projected against the dark background of Münster where what happens when the Anabaptists are given free rein was clear for all to see. If one wanted to prevent a repetition of these events one had to let such heretics go up in smoke.

Reacting to this, the Anabaptist movement, after Münster, of course tried to distance itself as much as possible from its past. This can be noted, for example, in the otherwise fascinating *Geschiedenis der Nederlandse Doopsgezinden in de zestiende eeuw* of W. J. Kühler, who characterizes this episode as 'the utter corruption of Anabaptism'.[10] As much as he was able to, Kühler tried to exonerate the Anabaptists in The Netherlands from this corruption. He opposed the violent actions in Münster with the non-violence of Melchior Hoffman and his followers. In Münster only a temporary derailment had taken place, in which the majority of the Dutch Anabaptists were not involved. That this depiction does not do justice to reality has been shown convincingly by A. F. Mellink in his well-documented book *De Wederdopers in de Noordelijke Nederlanden 1531–1544*.[11] All leaders of some significance were related to the kingdom of God in Münster.

And yet I think that one has to be careful with the conclusion that the whole movement can be called revolutionary. However, all those in The Netherlands who were part of this movement were captivated by this sudden, unexpected breakthrough, when a city had been liberated for the new covenant without bloodshed. Only if one keeps this fascination in mind is it possible to understand why the Anabaptists hesitated until the end with their condemnation of what happened in Münster.

The course of events

With hindsight we can say that the course of events was somewhat predictable. How else could it have happened, in view of the increasing

---

[10] 'De volslagen verbastering van het Anabaptisme': W. J. Kühler, *Geschiedenis der Nederlandse Doopsgezinden in de zestiende eeuw*, 2nd edn (Haarlem, 1961), p. 84.

[11] See note 3 in this chapter. See also A. F. Mellink, 'De beginperiode van het Nederlandse Anabaptisme in het licht van het laatste onderzoek', *Doopsgezinde Bijdragen*, n.s. 12–13 (Amsterdam, 1987), pp. 29–39.

severity of the siege, the high ratio of women to men, the identification of the church with the kingdom of God, and the rediscovery of the Old Testament?

There are many reasons to place interest in the Old Testament in the foreground. When at the time of the Reformation the Bible came within everyone's reach, many lay people discovered the Old Testament for the first time in their lives. A whole new world opened up for them. Certain words from the New Testament suddenly appeared in a new light. Those who during this exploration were not inhibited by knowledge of the tradition and a theological education lost their way quite easily, a phenomenon which also often occurred in later times. In particular, prophecies that seemed as yet unfulfilled attracted attention, now that generally the expectations of an imminent end were running high. Everywhere one was convinced of seeing signs of the end of time. Melchior Hoffman's preaching is a clear example of this.

In Münster they were defenceless against a parallel with the history of the people of Israel which included even more events. Jan Matthijs regarded himself as a second Gideon and a second Samson. With only a few faithful people he would be permitted to defeat the enemy. Cut to pieces he was sent back. Hille Feickens could not be deterred from her calling by the leaders in Münster to kill the bishop as a new Judith; God himself had instructed her to do so. She was arrested and beheaded. These disappointing experiences did not prevent Jan Beukelszoon from thinking himself the new David, called to conquer the kingdom of God which he would be allowed to offer the Prince of Peace at his coming.

This identification of church and state with the kingdom of God caused all distinction between ceremonial and civil laws to be absent, just as in ancient Israel. The ratio of women to men was so high that regulations were needed, precisely in order to avoid licentiousness. And finally, the ever more rigorous siege forced a leader like Jan of Leiden to revert to an increasingly strict discipline, especially when the hunger became worse and with it grew the chances of betrayal. To relieve the tensions and to overcome boredom, spectacles were put on stage that to outsiders looked bizarre, as a result of which the Münster movement lost more of its credibility, but which in that situation were totally acceptable to the people in the besieged city.

At the same time it remains understandable that the later events and actions in the Anabaptist kingdom in Münster were generally condemned. Not that all the stories that Kerssenbroch in particular concocted[12] are to be believed, but even then enough remains to understand

---

[12] Hermann Kerssenbroch, who became rector of the Latin School in Münster in 1550, lived through the first phase as a student, until the end of February 1534.

why the Anabaptist movement as a whole has tried to rid itself of this past. And yet, this episode cannot be dismissed by characterizing Jan of Leiden as 'a virtuoso in cheating' and the inhabitants of Münster as 'irresponsible fanatics'.[13] There has to be more than this.

In the descriptions it is mainly the introduction of the kingship and of polygamy that are criticized. But it is precisely these most spectacular facets that can elucidate what Münster was all about.

II

The kingship

It will probably forever remain a mystery what Jan Beukelszoon of Leiden's own part was in the prophetic message that induced his coronation. A suitable moment was chosen. Several weeks earlier, on 31 August 1534, a full-scale attack by the bishop's army had been repulsed under Beakelszoon's inspiring leadership. The victory had been such that the bishop's army was in total disarray. In later reflections one has to ask why Jan of Leiden did not exploit this situation more. He could easily have destroyed the few remaining factions as well. Usually it is attributed to cold calculation. He would have preferred a weak opponent, like the bishop, to princes and army commanders who undoubtedly would have intervened after a total victory.[14] My interpretation is that other factors also played a role.

The Anabaptist movement in Münster repeatedly rejected accusations that it had devised revolutionary plans or plans of conquest. Rather, the population of Münster had, just like any other free city, the right to govern itself and to defend its freedom. It was itself responsible for the way in which it was governed, for its mayor and councillors. They remained within bounds, even when they tried to defend the city against the attacks of the bishop. This had happened before. In an earlier period the city council declared Münster an evangelical city, and the bishop had tried to intervene, using violence but they had closed the gates to him. Burghers stood guard. None of the princes had accused them of revolution then. They did what was their right to do; they

Therefore, his 'Anabaptistici furoris historica narratio', which he wrote later, while rector, is an eyewitness account only for this period. In his description of the course of events after February 1534 he presents rumours as facts.

[13] 'Virtuoos in het bedriegen' and 'ontoerekenbare dwepers'. These and similar judgements in Kühler, *Geschiedenis der Nederlandse Doopsgezinden*.

[14] Kühler, *Geschiedenis der Nederlandse Doopsgezinden*, pp. 123, 124.

defended themselves. Now that the city had become Anabaptist the bishop laid siege again. The town population was indignant when all of a sudden the surrounding princes supported him.

In the pamphlets the Anabaptists distributed among the besiegers they repeated again and again that there was no reason whatsoever for the bishop to treat them as rebels, for they were free burghers in a free city!

> Since we not only want to keep the peace but also whole-heartedly want to relate to all people with brotherly love in Christ, on what grounds then can You account before pious people, let alone before God, for the fact that we are violently besieged and killed by You, contrary to the written and sealed laws of peace and without any declaration of war?

Time and again they returned to the same theme. There had not even been a declaration of war! They were treated as if they were rebels instead of free citizens who had the right to defend their city against attacks.[15]

It was this dispute which made it impossible for Jan of Leiden to leave the environs of the town after repulsing the attack and to chase the fleeing remnants of the bishop's army, for then he would not have limited himself to the defence of the city. After his arrest he, too, declared explicitly that he would never have usurped the territory and the position of the bishop, even if he had remained King of Münster. Although Jan of Leiden was convinced that he and his followers were the people destined to execute God's judgement on the world, he seems to have expected the realization of this only after the great day of God would have come. In this period of history, with this dispensation, he was never really intent on extending his territory. Though it was in his confession that he said this, when it was in his own interests to depict his actions as favourably as possible, there is still reason to take this statement seriously. Minister Bernt Krechting, who was executed with Jan of Leiden, also emphasized that even after the lifting of the siege the Anabaptists would have left the bishop and his territory untouched.[16]

Therefore, it was impossible for Jan of Leiden to exploit the great victory of 31 August 1534 if he was not to be put on a par with Thomas Müntzer or any other chief of rebels. He did, however, strengthen his position within the city itself. Fourteen days later, during an assembly

---

[15] K. Löffler, *Die Wiedertäufer zu Münster*, pp. 86, 87. In the above mentioned confession of faith too they defend their behaviour; R. Stupperich (ed.) *Die Schriften Bernhard Rothmanns* (Münster, 1970), pp. 207, 208.

[16] The text of their confessions is in Cornelius, *Berichte der Augenzeugen*, 369 ff.; Dülmen, *Das Täuferreich zu Münster*, pp. 264 ff.

of the population, the limping prophet of Warendorf, the goldsmith Johann Dusentschur, came forward, driven by the Spirit. He announced to the people that God himself had elected Jan Beukelszoon as king of the whole earth, higher than all emperors, kings and princes. All authorities would submit themselves to him.[17]

It is self-evident that the trustworthiness of this prophetic inspiration was doubted. During interrogations Jan of Leiden was asked whether he had made a secret agreement with Dusentschur. Of course, he denied it up to his death. It will probably never be known what part Jan of Leiden himself played in this heavenly inspiration. Others can have evoked such a prophecy. At any rate the kingship meant more than giving in to a prank of someone who liked to play the king. This is obvious from the way it functioned in the appeal that went out from Münster to the Anabaptists elsewhere.

If one wants to evaluate Jan of Leiden's kingship properly, one needs to compare the writings of Bernhard Rothmann with another work written at the same time.

'Bericht von der Wrake'

The most penetrating pamphlet by Rothmann which is still extant, the 'Bericht von der Wrake', summarizes the Münster view of the kingship in a remarkable way. Kühler called it a 'Marseillaise in prose'.[18] When the situation in Münster had become very critical, in December 1534, this pamphlet was given in large numbers to messengers who had to distribute it mainly in The Netherlands.

This was Rothmann's final attempt to help the Anabaptists in The Netherlands overcome their consciences, in order that they should actually come to the aid of the city of Münster. In a passionate way he declared to his readers that the children of God were now truly allowed to take up arms. In the past this was not permissible, but now it was. With all the arguments he could commandeer he attempted to show why something that used to be forbidden could now even be commanded. God's commandment can change, dependent on the moment in the history of salvation in which one lives. God's plan of salvation does not follow a straight line. It contains curves. It is life-threatening

---

[17] One needs to remember that the formulation that Dusentschur used has been transmitted to us by Kerssenbroch; K. Löffler, *Die Wiedertäufer zu Münster*, p. 126.

[18] Kühler, *Geschiedenis der Nederlandse Doopsgezinden*, p. 130. The text of the 'Bericht van der Wrake', in *Die Schriften Bernhard Rothmanns*, ed. R. Stupperich (Münster, 1970) pp. 284 ff.; H. Fast, *Der linke Flügel der Reformation*, Klassiker des Protestantismus, vol. IV (Bremen, 1962), pp. 342 ff.

not to note the transitions in God's polity. This had happened in the old Jerusalem, so that Jesus wept: 'If you, even you, had only known on this day what would bring you peace.'[19] According to Rothmann, the destruction of the ancient city of God had been the inevitable consequence of the blindness of the Jews who had not recognized the significance of Jesus's entry into Jerusalem. Unexpectedly, therefore, certain shifts may take place and a new phase in God's plan may dawn in which new laws are valid.

Rothmann did not deny that there is something permanent in God's commandments. For God himself does not change. Therefore the command to combat the Devil and his kingdom is always valid, but God did determine how long his servants have to suffer and when the moment has come to destroy the power of the evil one by force. Thus God does not always demand from man the same behaviour. The Bible is not the only norm, the history of salvation is another. In determining how to behave, man must ask himself in what time he lives and what are the specific demands of this moment in time, before he can decide what biblical instructions he now, at this instant in God's plan of salvation, has to obey.

For the apostles it meant that they had the commission to proclaim the coming of God's kingdom. One after the other was killed in doing this. None of them resisted the violence that came over them as a wave. Even God himself did not intervene. For that was the time of suffering. But the suffering reached its full measure when the persecutors of Christ started to appeal to the name of Christ, the pinnacle of evil which at the same time became the turning-point. If in the apostles' time it was only a matter of proclamation, while they were not allowed to resist the cruelty with which the messengers were treated, in Rothmann's time, now that the most holy things had been disgraced, it became a matter of revenge. Therefore, he who had an eye for God's times had to realize that the moment had come to range oneself under the banners of divine justice.

Of course, it is important to assess what evidence Rothmann had for his allegation that this change was happening precisely at this time. His first argument was a rather arbitrary way of juggling with biblical numbers, which is of little importance for this chapter.[20] More

---

[19] Luke 19:42.

[20] In Elijah's days the people of Israel were punished with drought for three and a half years. The apostasy in later times was worse, therefore the punishment likewise: the Babylonian captivity took $3\frac{1}{2} \times 20 = 70$ years. The death of the apostles was followed by an even longer period of punishment: $20 \times 70 = 1\,400$ years. According to this calculation it was now the time for the great turn.

remarkable was the argument he distilled from the situation, for everyone who used his eyes could see that the prophecies had been fulfilled in this very time! Did not Jeremiah and Ezekiel prophesy that Jerusalem would be rebuilt and that God would then give the kingdom to a new David?[21]

Rothmann realized that for a long time these scriptures had been applied to Jesus, but someone who really used his mind and his belief had to understand, he stated, that this was stretching the meaning of Scripture. An image should not be used wrongly, opposing itself. The Prince of Peace could not be identified with the king who had shed too much blood to build God's temple! With whom could Jesus be compared other than with Solomon? Upon his return to earth he would therefore receive the restored world out of the hands of the second David.

Now that the new King David had been revealed by God, at a moment when no one expected it, while even the person in question had no idea of it, the new phase had begun in which Abel at last had the right to use Cain's weapon against Cain. The true Christians were they, who during the first phase, were prepared to suffer for Jesus, but who now were willing to be God's instruments for revenge.

Rothmann approvingly cited the Strasburg prophet Lienhard Jost in that it was God's command to be obedient to the authorities. That was true, he acknowledged. Revolution, rebellion against the lawful authorities, was totally unacceptable. But now God had created a new authority, the highest one could think of, King David himself. Everybody was obliged to be subject to this authority in particular. When this highest command ordered the use of violence, one is obliged to obey, however much aversion one might naturally feel. Now the moment had arrived at which the ploughshares would have to be turned back into swords. If all God's children obeyed, the new world would soon dawn. Then, the people need no longer exist to enlarge the power of the unrighteous. Then, those in power would no longer be able to raise taxes arbitrarily for the sake of their private wars. Then, all God's creatures really would be free, for then the meek and the humble would possess the earth.

In view of this future and with God's actions in mind, all God's children now had to risk their possessions, wife, children, even their own life. The latest hesitations had to be overcome. It was no longer permissible to call sin that which was not sin. 'Therefore, beloved brothers, prepare yourselves for battle, not only with the humble weaponry of the apostles for suffering, but also with the glorious armour of David for revenge!'[22]

---

[21] Especially Jeremiah 30:8–9, 21.
[22] 'Bericht von der Wrake', p. 297.

This little work shows that the Melchiorites in The Netherlands and Westphalia could not accept the turn of events in Münster as easily as is sometimes suggested. Hoffman had instructed them to be prepared to suffer for God's kingdom. They also shared the general consciousness that it was totally unacceptable to rebel against the lawful authorities. Obeying God implied accepting the ranks and classes that he had instituted. The use of violence was only allowed in the service of the lawful authorities. Everywhere the propagandists from Münster had encountered this deep-rooted resistance. It appeared ineradicable. Although in The Netherlands they had become fascinated by the revolution in Münster, even to such a degree that they did not want to break off the relationship, most Anabaptists could not accept the thought that they themselves had to resist the lawful authorities. The words quoted from Lienhard Jost showed that this reluctance was even strengthened from within Strasburg.

Western European Christendom was prepared to do much, to kill Jews and Muslims, to burn witches and others who had an alternative lifestyle. The spiritual leaders could justify all this, but they were utterly negative about rebellion against the lawful authorities. Therefore, new authorities had to be created or put forward, if convinced Christians were to be motivated to revolution. Some twenty years later Calvinism in France and in The Netherlands would therefore foreground the lower authorities who were allegedly instituted by God to check the higher authorities. This was more in line with public opinion of those days than the solution the Münsterites sought.[23] For the sake of the nobility the Calvinists could resist the government without violating their consciences, albeit with some hesitation.[24]

In Münster the Anabaptists became aware of this reluctance. They understood that a higher authority had to be created to activate the Anabaptists in The Netherlands. Resistance against the city council and against Charles V was out of the question unless it was shown to be on the order of an even higher command. The only essential argument Bernhard Rothmann appeared to have at his disposal in the pamphlet

---

[23] Stayer, *Anabaptists and the Sword*, p. 235.

[24] See for the right to rebel D. J. de Groot, *De reformatie en de staatkunde* (Franeker, 1953); A. A. van Schelven, 'Het begin van het gewapend verzet tegen Spanje in de 16e eeuwsche Nederlanden', in *Handelingen en Mededeelingen van de Maatschappij der Nederlandsche Letterkunde te Leiden over het jaar 1914–1915* (Leiden, 1915), pp. 126–56; A. J. Jelsma, *Adriaan van Haemstede en zijn martelaarsboek* (The Hague, 1970), pp. 195, 196; 'The "weakness of conscience" in the Reformed Movement in The Netherlands: the Attitude of the Dutch Reformation to the Use of Violence between 1562 and 1574', in W. J. Sheils (ed.), *The Church and War*, Studies in Church History, 20 (Oxford, 1983), pp. 217–31.

with which he wanted to incense the covenantors in The Netherlands to resistance, was the Davidic kingship of Jan of Leiden.

This pamphlet apparently made an impression. The rebellions that in the spring of 1535 briefly blazed up like a straw fire in several places, all appeared to be linked with Jan van Geelen, the envoy from Münster who with three companions and with a thousand copies of Rothmann's appeal had left the beleaguered city on 24 December 1534. The pamphlet was quite capable of 'inducing rebellion and sedition', the Court of Holland wrote to the governers on 24 January.[25]

'Against blasphemy'

How important was the role which Jan of Leiden's kingship played in the discussions, can also be deduced from an anonymous work that was printed in 1627 but which must have been written much earlier. The edition of 1627 was attributed to Menno Simons. Later, however, his authorship has been contended, although the style and contents of the booklet could be his.[26] However, it is likely that it was written at the same time that Jan van Geelen tried to create unrest using Rothmann's pamphlet. That it was not printed earlier is not surprising. Rothmann's entire argument, and thus also its refutation, lost its basis when Münster fell and the king was imprisoned. For us, however, it remains interesting, since it sheds light on the motivation for Jan of Leiden's kingship from a different angle. The work's full title is:

> *Quite clear and lucid evidence from Holy Scripture that Jesus Christ is the real promised David in the spirit, a King of all Kings, a Lord of all Lords, and the real spiritual King over that spiritual Israel which is his Church, which he bought and acquired with his own Blood, written in the past to all Brothers and Covenantors, scattered in various places, against the abominable and great blasphemy of Jan of Leiden, who presented himself as a joyful King over all, and as the joy of all who are miserable, putting himself in God's place.*[27]

---

[25] 'Oproer en seditie te verwekken.' Quoted by Kühler, *Geschiedenis der Nederlandse Doopsgezinden*, p. 131.

[26] See for the discussion C. Bornhäuser, 'Leben und Lehre Menno Simons', *Beiträge zur Geschichte und Lehre der Reformierten Kirche*, vol. XXXV (Neukirchen, 1973). In the *Opera Omnia Theologia* by Menno Simons (Amsterdam, 1681, the pamphlett is also attributed to him, pp. 619–31. J. M. Stayer who used this edition, regards it without question as written by Menno Simons. If it is indeed his, then he must have mitigated his absolute rejection of all violence later on. I also quote from the edition of 1681.

[27] Anon., *Een gantsch duydtlyck ende klaer bewys, uyt de Heylige Schriftuure, dat Jezus Christus is de rechte beloofde David in den geest, een Koningh aller Koningen, een Heer aller Heeren, en de rechte geestelijcke Koningh over dat geestelicke Israël, dat is*

This title explains that the author especially opposed the notion that the image of David would not be applicable to Jesus. According to the author, the Bible showed irrefutably that God appointed only Jesus as 'King both over the whole earth and over his believing church'. Thus, wrongly, Jan of Leiden claimed to be the new David.

Those passages in which the author used the Scriptures to show that Christians were never allowed to take up the sword are important for the discussion, for the apostle, Paul, had clearly expounded what the armour of a Christian should be: the only sword we were to wield was the word of God. This was also the only sword Jesus himself used.[28] 'How then would we fight against our enemies with another sword?' The author created the impression that he quoted Rothmann literally, without mentioning him, however, when he wrote that the apostolic weapons had to be taken up again: 'The armour of David must be left at home.'

Of course, the author also dealt with the idea of progression in God's actions. He doubted whether the kingdom really was at hand. But if God finally wanted to punish sinful Babylon He would surely not do this through the hands of the believers. In this respect the Münsterites were to him not consistent enough in their application of the Old Testament, for the ancient Babylon was not brought down through the people of Israel but through the Medes. It would not be the church who in Revelation could destroy the great prostitute Babylon but the beast she rode. Nowhere did the Bible point to Christians as instruments of God when He wanted to take revenge on the unrighteous. This revenge should be executed in a totally different way, after the second coming of Jesus. He regarded the view that king David had to conquer the kingdom of God first and should hand it over to the Prince of Peace, as an unbiblical one. Finally, the author asked his readers: 'This only I would like to know from you, whether you have been baptized on the sword or on the cross? You are so foolish, that, after beginning in the Spirit, you want to continue in the flesh ... .'

The writer followed unmistakably the track of Melchior Hoffman. The willingness to suffer was the only hinge on which the door to the kingdom could open. But combating the views of Rothmann moved him further along this path. Rothmann's starting-point was the

---

sijn Gemeynte, die hy met sijn eyghen Bloet gekocht, ende verworven heeft, eertijts geschreven aen allen waren Broeders ende Bontgenooten, hier ende daer verstroyt, tegens de grouwelicke ende grootste blasphemie van Jan van Leyden, die hem uytgaf voor een blijde Koningh over al, ende der ellendiger vreughde geworden, hem settende in de stede Godts, (Amsterdam, 1681).

[28] See Ephesians 6:17 and Revelation 19:11–15.

generally accepted idea that a Christian was only allowed to use violence in the service of the authorities, and, therefore, the Anabaptists had the right to take up arms when the highest authority, instituted by God, commanded them to do so. In this way Rothmann tried to push the Covenantors across the threshold of their consciences. This controversy had realized the opposite point of view. Within the Anabaptist movement the idea that Christians were permitted to use violence in the service of the authorities was abandoned more and more. The only sword Christians might wield was the word of God.

From this discussion it is clear that the introduction of the kingship in Münster was not just a prank. The Anabaptists were continually looking for ways to defend themselves against the accusation of a revolution. Did not the inhabitants of the city have the right to defend themselves against attacks from the outside? When this argument appeared ineffective they sought new ones, adapted to and stemming from the vision of the movement. Did not the followers of Christ have the right to use violence in the service of the highest authority, of King David himself?

III

Polygamy

The Anabaptists of Münster evoked the strongest aversion by their introduction of polygamy in the summer of 1534. Undoubtedly abuses occurred then. After a few days the leaders felt obliged to adjust the situation. Women that had been forced to marry against their will had their freedom reinstated. Later, after his arrest, Jan of Leiden himself admitted in a conversation with two ministers that the introduction, although not sinful, was untimely and therefore incorrect. In the mean time he had become aware that one cannot stray too far from the general moral code without being punished.[29]

Therefore, however understandable it is that this ethics of marriage gave offence (and piqued curiosity), the judgement on this issue should be given more nuance than is usually the case. More factors play a role than, as Klemens Löffler states, only the giving in to sensual lusts by Jan of Leiden.[30] In this matter, too, the report of Kerssenbroch in particular needs to be regarded critically. He related that one night a deserted

---

[29] Löffler, *Die Wiedertäufer zu Münster*, p. 258.
[30] Ibid., p. 107: 'Soviel steht freilich fest, dasz die Vielweiberei ... den sinnlichen Lüsten Johanns von Leiden ihren Ursprung herleitete.'

soldier caught Jan of Leiden in the act of adultery in Knipperdolling's house. In order to avoid exposure, polygamy was quickly introduced. This, of course, is too simplistic a representation of the facts. Jan of Leiden was man enough to deal with a situation like this in another way, for example by executing the soldier in question. There is more to be said.

First, one needs to realize that from the very start the besiegers spread the wildest rumours about the moral life of the Anabaptists. Some of them were probably motivated by fear. They had left wives and children in the city, expecting that the Anabaptist rule would last only a few days, several weeks at most. It was unthinkable that a relatively small group of people with no military experience could defend a city like Münster against well-trained soldiers for a longer period.[31] Therefore, months before the introduction of polygamy, the Anabaptists had to defend themselves against rumours which reveal more about the fear of the inhabitants who had fled and about the imagination of the besiegers than about the moral life within the town itself. In pamphlets the Anabaptists called on their critics to come and investigate the alleged adultery themselves. 'Our life has been arranged before God in such a way that no one among us who is guilty of shameful conduct is left unpunished.'[32] 'We do not share our wives with one another,' Rothmann wrote in a confession of faith which also stems from the first phase of the siege, 'Neither do we abrogate the rules concerning blood ties.'[33]

It is even possible that the accusation that the Anabaptists would have appropriated women with the infamous words 'My spirit desires your flesh', was already uttered before polygamy was introduced. It cannot be ascertained with certainty when this accusation was first made. The origin of the words, however, is known. They are to be found in late medieval monastic literature, for example in Thomas a Kempis's volume of tracts *De Imitatione Christi*, 'Anima mea corpus tuum concupiscit', but here it refers to the soul's desire to receive the body of Christ during the Eucharistic celebration.[34] Anabaptist radicals did not shrink from unmannerly ridicule of Catholic practices. Even during the final stage of the siege Jan of Leiden could organize a

---

[31] Heinrich Gresbeck, 'Bericht von der Wiedertaufe in Münster', in C. A. Cornelius (ed.), *Berichte der Augenzeugen uber das Münsterische Wiedertäuferreich* (Münster, 1853; photographic reprint, 1965), pp. 62–3.

[32] Löffler, *Die Wiedertäufer zu Münster*, p. 87. In another pamphlet it is stated explicitly that the accusations about the moral conduct within Münster stem from the refugees. 'This kind of lie has been made up impudently by the refugees:' Ibid., p. 99.

[33] Stupperich, *Die Schriften Bernhard Rothmanns*, p. 205.

[34] Thomas a Kempis, *De Imitatione Christi*, ed. J. M. Horstius (Tournai, 1828), vol. IV, 3, 1, p. 191.

mocking mass, at which a real jester who in earlier times had served as prebendary, was dressed in Catholic vestments. Rats' heads, bats and bones were sacrificed. All other masses you ever attended were no more valuable than this one, Rothmann told the people afterwards.[35] So it is quite conceivable that the Münsterites mockingly applied the pious words of people like Thomas a Kempis to relations other than those that can exist between the believing soul and Christ. Their mockery now turned against them, but this does not necessarily mean that their moral decline was really this great.

Polygamy is likely to have been introduced to prevent worse. The situation was very complicated. As was mentioned, rich citizens had left their wives, expecting a speedy return. The number of nuns that had chosen the new covenant was considerable. Kerssenbroch writes with clear disdain about the eagerness with which they had left the convents. From elsewhere came men such as Jan of Leiden who had left their families at home. The men formed a minority. Their number has been estimated at 2 000. There were about three times as many women.[36]

In this community a particular view with respect to marriage soon developed, as is obvious from the already cited confession of faith. In accordance with words from Jesus himself, the bond with Him was regarded as of higher value than any other bond. When one or both partners in a marriage had not been baptized, the other was allowed to divorce. Only those marriages that had joined the new covenant as a whole, had been contracted in heaven and were thus indissoluble. All other marriages were not valid. Except for the small number of saints, the rest of the world lived in concubinages. God had nothing to do with all these other alliances. One of the consequences of this view was that women who had been left in Münster by their husbands had the right to enter into new alliances.[37] According to the general moral code, however, this was bigamy. Therefore these people had already left the common ground, which made it easier to deviate even further from the current patterns.

The defence of the city was much more successful than anticipated. Each attack could be repulsed. The situation was such that a number of the besieging army defected. One of them was the man we have already

---

[35] The story has been transmitted to us by Gresbeck; see Cornelius, *Berichte der Augenzeugen*, pp. 150 ff.

[36] The numbers given in the confessions of Anabaptists vary a great deal, but always the number of women appears to be considerably higher than the number of men. Gresbeck gives the following estimates: 2 000 men, 8 000 to 9 000 women, 1 000 to 1 200 children, in *Cornelius Berichte der Augenzeugen*, p. 107. See Ramstedt, *Sekte und soziale Bewegung*, p. 103.

[37] Stupperich *Die Schriften Bernhard Rothmanns*, pp. 204, 205.

cited several times, Heinrich Gresbeck, who left us the most lively and authentic eyewitness account of the events. The leadership of the town, therefore, had to take into account the possibility of a prolonged rule. The city had to remain inhabitable. The average age should not rise too much. It was important to increase the number of births. Every young woman that remained barren was a lost opportunity.

It is obvious from the proposition with which Rothmann and the other ministers persuaded the citizens, that this consideration played a role when polygamy was introduced. Every sermon on this subject hovered round the central text from Genesis 1: 'Be fruitful and increase in number!' Semen may not be wasted. Once a woman had become pregnant her husband had the right, indeed the obligation, to sow another field. The empty houses had to be filled; a city full of young, vivacious warriors. Jan of Leiden made a feast of each birth.[38]

It is unknown how the preachers came to this exegesis. But it is not fully inexplicable. It was generally assumed that marriage mainly served propagation. And the well-known traveller Marco Polo (1254–1324) could already tell of a Christian community which regarded it a sin if a man had intercourse with his pregnant wife.[39]

And yet this view did not go well with Anabaptist morality in which the bond with Jesus was given so much importance. There must be another reason why the thought that marriage only served propagation could become so dominant. In his *Restitution rechter und gesunder christlicher Lehre* Rothmann tried to defend the introduction of polygamy for the outside world. In Münster marriage has received its proper place again, he wrote. It was an abuse to seek something else in marriage than the begetting of children. It was part of a man's freedom to contract a marriage with several fruitful women. Of course, he appealed mainly to the Old Testament for this. But why did he regard it as so important that this freedom was restored? Without mincing his words he stated what was his most important motive.

---

[38] According to Kerssenbroch it was the king who gave each new-born child its name. He had called the days of the week after the first seven letters of the alphabet. The first letter of the name a child received corresponded with the day on which it was born. K. Löffler, *Die Wiedertäufer zu Münster*, pp. 136, 137. The report of the introduction in Gresbeck; in Cornelius, *Berichte der Augenzeugen*, pp. 59 ff. Grimly he relates:

> Then the Devil laughed. Then they got what they desired, the men who had an old wife and now were allowed to take a younger one. Other men would have wanted that too, who were not anabaptists and had an old wife, that they would be allowed to take a younger one in addition.

[39] *The Travels of Marco Polo*, English translation by R. Latham (5th edn Harmondsworth, 1972), p. 295. The people lived on two islands near Pakistan in the Arabian Sea.

> Man must reappropriate his dominion over woman with a manly attitude. Everywhere women have got the upper hand. They lead men just like a bear is led on a chain. As a result the whole world has been immersed in adultery, impurity and fornication. Almost everywhere the wife wears the breeches. But God places everyone in his order, the man under Christ, the woman under the man, *and that in full submission*. Women must be obedient in quietness.

In this respect too, Münster had to become a restoration. 'With us He has made all women to be obedient to the men, so that all of them, both young and old, have to be ruled by the man!'[40]

It is certainly no coincidence that in Münster the women sometimes had to be violently forced to be obedient to their husbands. In the description of the course of events too little attention has been given to the part that women played in the revolution of the city. Not without reason Mary Daly complains in her book *Beyond God the Father* about the falsification of history that took place for centuries, by which the role of women was practically eradicated.[41] This is certainly true for this episode. When one examines the descriptions of the kingdom at Münster one encounters mainly men, sometimes also what men did to women, but the positive role the women played remains unnoticed. In this respect the sociological investigations of recent years have clarified little. This, however, is inevitable. In the extant sources 778 names of Anabaptists have been found. Only 165 of them were names of women. A satisfying answer to the question how it came about that there were in Münster three times as many women as men, has still not been given.[42] Perhaps women saw a way of liberation in the new gospel that was proclaimed by the Anabaptists?

This is certainly true for the nuns who were often doomed to monastic life by their families, and who now saw a door opened to a new life, unexpected and unhoped for. From the very moment that Rothmann had been baptized by the envoys of Jan Matthijs and had called the population to repentance, the abbess of the convent Überwasser felt obliged to complain to the bishop about the enthusiasm of the nuns for the new teachings. One after another chose freedom. But did this not, in a different way, hold true for the wives of the distinguished patricians,

---

[40] 'Restitution rechter und gesunder christlicher Lehre', in R. Stupperich (ed.), *Die Schriften Bernhard Rothmanns* (Münster, 1970), pp. 258 ff.

[41] M. Daly, *Beyond God the Father: Toward a Philosophy of Women's Liberation* (Boston, 1973), pp. 92 ff. 'What had not received enough attention, is the silence about women's history ... We cannot believe the history books ... .'

[42] Rammstedt, *Sekte und soziale Bewegung*, p. 102. The numbers are remarkable. The names of about 35 per cent of the men have been transmitted in one way or another, but this applies to only 2 to 2.5 per cent of the women.

whose life within the existing order of the time was little else than imprisonment? Already on 11 January 1534, six days after Rothmann himself had been baptized, the wife of councillor Christian Wördemann let herself be baptized by him. How her husband regarded the conjugal relationship became quite clear. He gave her such a beating that, in Kerssenbroch's words, 'she could not even crawl anymore'. That is also what other women were said to have experienced who had visited the Anabaptist preachers in secret. And with respect to these reports I am inclined to believe Kerssenbroch's words. For then he was still in the town. As a 15-year-old he lived in these circles.[43]

It is also remarkable that during this first stage in Münster women began to preach, for example the daughter of tailor, Georg thom Berge, who addressed a huge crowd for two hours on 8 February. Another woman walked through the town shouting, until her voice gave up. Then she tied a sheep's bell to her girdle in order to continue her alarming work. Gesticulating she pointed to heaven from where the judgement would come. According to Kerssenbroch it was also a woman who already in this initial stage prophesied that the King of Sion would descend from heaven to renew Jerusalem. At that moment Jan Matthijs had not even arrived in the city.

Another reason why the men formed a minority in the Anabaptist movement of Münster might have been that it was mainly women who were attracted to these new teachings. We may not draw conclusions from this for the Anabaptist movement in general. Otthein Rammstedt's sociological research has clearly demonstrated that the motivation in The Netherlands differed from that in Münster. Regarding this town one cannot say that a social revolution by the lower strata of society created the movement.[44] The women probably played a greater role here than elsewhere. They raved like lunatics, as Kerssenbroch wrote. He called the behaviour of the women one of the main reasons why so many wealthy citizens had left the town.[45]

Once the city was fully in Anabaptist hands, apparently it was difficult for the leaders to bring the women back into line. In all the

---

[43] Cornelius, *Berichte der Augenzeugen*, p. 8.

[44] From the statistical appendices in Rammstedt, *Sekte und soziale Bewegung*, pp. 122 ff., it is clear that the Anabaptist movement in Münster received its support from all strata of the population. But most of all the movement in this town was supported by women. According to Kühler, *Geschiedenis der Nederlandse Doopsgezinden*, p. 83, 300 men and 2 000 women were baptized on 27 February 1534. After this, all who had not been baptized were sent out of the town. At that moment there were only 700 men in the city, a number which doubled in the following months. Rammstedt, *Sekte und soziale Bewegung*, p. 72.

[45] Löffler, *Die Wiedertäufer zu Münster*, p. 27.

regulations it was emphasized that women were to be subject to their husbands. They even had to call them 'lord'. The women agreed with each other to fulfil this rule in such an exaggerated way, as a sort of work-to-rule, that it was revoked. According to Gresbeck, numerous women were executed merely on the grounds that they had been insubordinate to their husbands.[46]

Thus Jan of Leiden's lust was not the main motive for the introduction of polygamy. There were several reasons for it. The city had to be filled again. Was not the number of the chosen ones 144 000? Besides, something had to be arranged for the women that were left behind in Münster and for the defected soldiers and others who had found their way to the new Jerusalem, an arrangement which left the holiness of the pious untouched. 'It is better for me to have many wives than harlots,' Jan of Leiden once said.[47] And, finally, about 6 000 women had to be kept in check by 2 000 men at the most. Which of these motives was the more important is difficult to ascertain. But whoever wanted to realize all this at a time when the Old Testament came to life again, was inclined to reintroduce polygamy.

IV

Jan of Leiden

So there was more behind the two most contended issues, Jan Beukelszoon's kingship and polygamy, more than the vanity and the lust of a former tailor and innkeeper. What then does this mean for our assessment of Jan of Leiden?

We are not done with him when we characterize him as a virtuoso in cheating or a cunning demagogue. A wrong impression is also conveyed when his need for theatrical performances is stressed.[48] Undoubtedly, he entered into his role as king quite easily and quite devotedly, but he was not just a skilful actor; he believed in his divine election.

This becomes obvious when Hendrik Graes, one of the 27 apostles that were sent out at the end of 1534, turned traitor after his arrest. He promised the bishop to return to Münster in order to gather informa-

---

[46] Cornelius, *Berichte der Augenzeugen*, pp. 65, 72.

[47] Quoted by Rammstedt, *Sekte und soziale Bewegung*, p. 100.

[48] G.H. Williams, *The Radical Reformation*, 3rd edn (Kirksville, MO, 1992), p. 554: 'the whole of the Münsterite action was a comic–tragic morality play, brought out into the open from the chambers of rhetoric'. See also Kühler, *Geschiedenis der Nederlandse Doopsgezinden*, p. 80.

tion about the situation there and about the Anabaptist groups in Westphalia and The Netherlands. He had himself placed near the city wall, fettered. The guards took him to the king. He told him how an angel of the Lord dropped him there, and this absurd story was taken completely seriously by Jan of Leiden.[49]

Reacting to the course of events, he interpreted prophecies in his own favour and called forth certain phenomena, but this does not necessarily mean that he was insincere. It is remarkable that the two ministers of Philip of Hesse who had several conversations with him after his arrest, were milder in their judgement of him than of the other two prisoners, Knipperdolling and Bernt Krechting. His sincerity was also clear from his faithfulness to the Anabaptist vision, even in the face of the most barbaric death one can imagine. In some respects, however, he did acknowledge that he was wrong. He admitted that it was wrong to resist the bishop, that Münster had not become what he expected of it, namely the new Jerusalem. But regarding infant baptism he still maintained that it was unbiblical. He was, however, prepared to persuade fellow believers, in order that in this respect they would conform to the general view, until the authorities would come to a better insight as well. In this connection he suggested sending Melchior Hoffman with him, for earlier on, the latter had forbidden adult baptism in view of the dangerous situation. But to the most peculiar of the latter's teachings, namely that Jesus had received nothing from Mary's flesh, but had gone through her like sunlight breaks through a window pane, he remained faithful till death.

He took a step back concerning the Lord's Supper, but this too testifies to his autonomous reflection. He acknowledged that most Anabaptists took the Zwinglian view of the Supper. But he himself, in between tortures and interrogations, had come to a better understanding. He did not want to go as far as Luther, who in his opinion stayed too close to the Catholic view, but he did not want to weaken the power of the Lord's Supper as was done by the Zwinglians. He now saw 'that the believer receives in the bread the true body of Christ and in the wine the true blood, but not in a visible but in an invisible way'. He rejected the idea that an unbeliever, too, could receive the true body and blood of Christ.

This consciously chosen middle way between the Lutheran and the Zwinglian teaching on the Lord's Supper, this formulation of receiving the true body and blood of the Lord invisibly by faith, will not be unknown to Calvinists. It is surprising, however, that Jan of Leiden voiced this view before Calvin made it public.[50]

---

[49] Löffler, *Die Wiedertäufer zu Münster*, p. 191.

[50] For the conversations with Anton Corvinus and Johann Rymeus see Löffler, *Die Wiedertäufer zu Münster*, pp. 253 ff. These conversations will have stimulated him in the

This discussion proves that Jan of Leiden considered the contents of the Anabaptist teachings seriously. He was not merely an adventurer, an actor who in this movement saw an opportunity to appropriate a role more important than any other he would ever have received. The last reports the Hessian minister Corvinus wrote, also testified to his character. In the face of death Jan of Leiden expressed his great appreciation for the count, Philip of Hesse, who had gone to the trouble of polemizing, even in writing, with the Münsterites.[51] Had the count been present he would have asked him for forgiveness. And when he was taken to the place of the execution he knelt down and prayed, 'Father, into your hands I commit my spirit'. Without uttering a cry he underwent the tortures that resulted in his death.

Of course, a more lenient judgement on Jan of Leiden does not wish to conceal the crimes he committed. He could only maintain his position in a starved town for such a lengthy time because he mercilessly liquidated all opposition. But that does not alter the fact that behind all his actions was hidden the consciousness that God had elected him to realize the kingdom of God. And as far as we know, in Münster no one was tortured and killed in such a horrible way as he himself experienced. Richard van Dülmen is correct in stating in the preface to a collection of documents on *Das Täuferreich zu Münster van 1534– 1535*[52] that the known occurrences of terror and cruelty are less characteristic of this episode than a strictly ordered life.

---

direction of this new view. It is known that Philip of Hesse sought a third way on which Lutherans and Zwinglians could find one another.

[51] The text of this work can be found in *Urkundliche Quellen zur hessischen Reformationsgeschichte*, vol. IV, *Wiedertäuferakten 1527–1628*, (Marburg, 1951).

[52] Dülmen, *Das Täuferreich zu Münster*, p. 22.

CHAPTER FIVE

Women martyrs in a revolutionary age: a comparison of books of martyrs

I

A comparison of books of martyrs is useful, as I hope to prove with the following example. On 16 July 1546 Anna Askewe, 'that most Christian martyr', was burned alive with three other martyrs at Smithfield in London, leaving behind her – as John Foxe wrote – 'a singular example of Christian constancy for all men to follow'. She had in fact left behind even more than that. Because she wanted to prevent distorted and misleading information about her trial, she had drafted a personal report of her examinations. These accounts were sent to Protestant exiles in Europe. In November 1546, John Bale published his report of the first examination, amplified with a circumstantial comment in his own hand. Three months later the second examination also appeared, again interspersed with the comments of Bale, and expanded with an eyewitness account by some Dutch merchants concerning her death. Of these original editions only a few copies remained. In the copies of the second examination some lines were excised. Nobody knows the reason. The editor of the selected works of John Bale, Henry Christmas, has made the suggestion that this had been done to spare the reputation of King Henry's minister, William Paget. There is, however, another possibility.

Without the personal remarks by Bale, the material of both examinations was reiterated in the great martyrologies of John Crespin, John Foxe and Adriaan van Haemstede. At the same place where the work of John Bale was mutilated, we find a gap in the books of Crespin and Foxe. Only van Haemstede offers an addition. This is the more remarkable since he was the only martyrologist who had the habit of abridging his material. His addition concerns the second examination, at the moment of Anne Askewe's interrogation by the Bishop of Winchester, Stephen Gardiner, who criticized her because she, as a woman, had made a study of the Holy Scripture. This had made her lose her head, he supposed. 'Everybody should behave himself in accordance with his destination,' he said. 'No more than a pig should be saddled, a woman had to concern herself with the word of God.' Anne laughed. 'Sir,' she said, 'why should not a pig bear a saddle, now even an ass bears a bishops mitre!' The bishop was not amused. It is at this point that the other martyrologists also continue their story. Gardiner threatened her with the death by fire. Her response had a close connection with the discussion about the reading of the Bible by a woman. She said: 'I have searched the whole Scripture, yet I have nowhere found that either Christ or the apostles put someone to death.'[1]

It is still not clear why this dialogue has been curtailed in most martyrologies. The reason cannot be that this passage was too embarrassing for the memory of William Paget, nor even of Bishop Gardiner. The Bishop of Winchester was not highly esteemed in Protestant circles. In the opinion of Calvin – and Crespin was a loyal adherent of the reformer of Geneva – 'he surpassed all the devils in that kingdom'.[2] Helen C. White called Gardiner 'Foxe's favourite villain'.[3] I suppose, therefore, that it must have been the sharp-witted comment of Anne Askewe which was considered not fitting for a pious woman. Did her remark perhaps evoke too much the suggestion of radical Anabaptism?[4] However that may be, the example makes clear that there is reason for a careful comparison of the books of martyrs.

II

Of course, such a comparison cannot be made in all regards. In this chapter I have confined myself to the image of women martyrs in the

---

[1] For the martyrdom of Anne Askewe, see *Select Works of John Bale*, ed. Henry Christmas (Cambridge 1849), pp. 137–248; Jean Crespin, *Historie des vrays Tesmoins de la verité de l'Evangile, qui de leur sang l'ont signée, depuis Jean Hus jusques au temps present* (Geneva 1570), fol. 164; John Foxe, *Acts and Monuments of Matters Most Special and Memorable, Happening in the Church, with an Universal History of the Same*, 3 vols (London 1684), vol. II, pp. 483 ff.; Adriaan van Haemstede, *De Geschiedenisse ende den doodt der vromer Martelaren, die om het ghetughenisse des Evangeliums haer bloedt ghestort hebben, van den tijden Christi af, totten Jare MDLIX toe, bijeen vergadert op het kortste* (n.p., probably Embden, 1559), pp. 155–65; Ludwig Rabus, *Historien der Heyligen Ausserwolten Gottes Zeugen, Bekennern und Martyrern* ... , 8 vols (Strasburg, 1554–58), vol. III, pp. 184–6.

[2] Patrick Collinson, *Archbishop Grindal; 1519–1583; the Struggle for a Reformed Church* (London, 1979), p. 90.

[3] Helen C. White, *Tudor Books of Saints and Martyrs* (Madison, 1963), pp. 152, 153. Foxe himself called Stephen Gardiner when he died: 'A man hated to God and all good men'.

[4] Irvin Buckwalter Horst, *The Radical Brethren; Anabaptism and the English Reformation to 1558* (Nieuwkoop, 1972), pp. 93, 94. John Bale was known for his kind opinion even of Anabaptists.

Protestant martyrologies of the sixteenth century, and especially the earlier editions of these books. The choice of this subject must be justified. Such an investigation could give the impression that it should be possible to speak about women in general categories. The same principle applies to female martyrs as to male martyrs: there are no two equal. But there are some reasons for this special inquiry:

1. The authors of the martyrologies were all men as were the judges and the executioners. In their description of women martyrs they permitted themselves general judgements about the female gender. The martyrologies therefore offer us useful material for an investigation into the image men had formed of women in the sixteenth century.

2. Several authors have recently studied this question. In 1968 Roland H. Bainton published an article entitled 'John Foxe and the Ladies', which later became a chapter in his tripartite study *Women of the Reformation*. A more profound investigation into the conviction of the women martyrs has been made by Ellen Macek in her article 'The Emergence of a Feminine Spirituality in "The Book of Martyrs"', published in 1988. She confined herself to the book of John Foxe. In 1985 van 't Spijker described for the Dutch situation the position of women in Mennonite martyrologies.[5] It seemed to me an interesting challenge to analyse this material on a broader scale, especially to avoid one-sided conclusions.

For our investigation it will be necessary first, without too many details, to enumerate the relevant martyrologies. In 1552 the orthodox Lutheran minister Ludwig Rabus published in Latin a study concerning the martyrs of the Old Testament and the early church. Between 1554 and 1558 he produced eight volumes of martyr stories in the German language. The first two volumes deal with the same material as his book of 1552.

In 1554 the first French edition of a book of martyrs appeared in Geneva, composed by the Calvinist printer Jean Crespin; a translation of this work in Latin was brought out in 1556.[6]

---

[5] Roland H. Bainton, 'John Foxe and the Ladies', in Lawrence P. Buck and Jonathan W. Zophy, *The Social History of the Reformatio* (Columbus, OH, 1972), pp. 208–22; R. H. Bainton, *Women of the Reformation; in France and England* (2nd edn, Boston, 1975), pp. 211–99; Ellen Macek, 'The Emergence of a Feminine Spirituality in "The Book of Martyr"', *Sixteenth Century Journal*, 19, no. 1 (1988), pp. 63–80; I. van 't Spijker, '"Mijn beminde huysvrouwe in de Heere"; Doperse vrouwen in de vroege Reformatie in de Nederlanden', *Doopsgezinde Bijdragen*, 11 (1985), pp. 99–108.

[6] J. Crespin, *Acta Martyrum, eorum videlicet, qui hoc seculo in Gallia, Germania, Anglia, Flandria, Italia, constans dederunt nomen Evangelio, idque sanguine suo*

John Foxe, like John Bale an exile on the Continent during the reign of Queen Mary, in 1554 published at Strasburg, the 'liber primus' of his *Rerum in Ecclesia Gestarum Commentarii* ... , the beginning of an enterprise which Patrick Collinson, in his study on Archbishop Grindal, characterized as 'the most important of all fruits of the exile'.[7]

The Dutch minister Adriaan van Haemstede wrote his martyrology, while at the same time the magistrates of Antwerp had put the substantial prize of 300 Carolusguilders on his head. His work was published in 1559.

Three years later the first Mennonite book of martyrs appeared under the title *The Sacrifice of the Lord*. This collection of martyr acts was later incorporated by T. J. van Braght in his expanded work *The Bloody Theatre; Or, Martyrs' Mirror of the Mennonite or Defenceless Christian* ... .[8]

These books did not all have the same construction. Foxe and Crespin began with the days of John Wycliff. Ludwig Rabus wished to demonstrate how strongly the Protestant Reformation corresponded with the early church; following his description of the martyrs during the first centuries, he leapt to the days of John Hus. Adriaan van Haemstede was the first who attempted to draft a complete history of persecution, obsessed as he was by the idea, which in another context he more than once expressed, that the true church would always be persecuted. Van Braght later followed van Haemstede's example.

With the exception of the Mennonite martyrologies, all of these authors borrowed their material from each other. Almost all the stories of Crespin were repeated in van Haemstede's book; van Haemstede also

---

obsignarunt: ab Wicleffo & Husso ad hunc usque diem (Geneva, 1556). See for Crespin, Jean-François Gilmont, *Jean Crespin. Un éditeur réformé du XVIe siècle* (Geneva, 1981); David Watson, 'Jean Crespin and the Writing of History in the French Reformation', in Bruce Gordon (ed.), *Protestant History and Identity in Sixteenth-Century Europe*, vol. II, *The Later Reformation*, St Andrews Studies in Reformation History (Aldershot and Brookfield, 1996), pp. 39–58.

[7] Collinson, *Archbishop Grindal*, pp. 79, 80. I have used the Latin edition of John Foxe: *Rerum in Ecclesia Gestarum, quae postremis et periculosis his temporibus evenerunt, maximarumque per Europam persecutionum, ac Sanctorum, Dei Martyrum, caeterarumque rerum si quae insignioris exempli sint, digesti per Regna en Nationes Commentarii* (Basle, 1559). In contrast with the edition of 1554 this edition especially regards the victims under Queen Mary.

[8] S. Cramer (ed.), *Het offer des Heeren*, Bibliotheca Reformatoria Neerlandica, II (The Hague, 1904); T. J. van Braght, *Het Bloedig Tooneel, of Martelaersspiegel der Doopsgezinde of Weereloose Christenen, die om 't getuygenis van Jesus haren Salighmaker geleden hebben ende gedood zijn van Christi tijd af tot desen tijd toe*, 2nd edn (Amsterdam, 1685). See for the edicts against heresy in The Netherlands J. Meyhoffer, *Le Martyrologe Protestante des Pays-Bas 1523–1597* (The Hague, 1907), pp. 5–25.

used some volumes of Rabus and the works of John Bale.[9] In the further elaborated English version of his work, John Foxe not only tried to assemble as many martyr stories as was possible, but also to compose, just as van Haemstede had done, a complete ecclesiastical history, but now especially for England.[10]

In this superficial survey I have intentionally emphasized the date of publication. This is of the greatest importance for understanding the motivation behind these works. Reprints in later times, and under other circumstances, were in some regards motivated by another impulse. This becomes clear by comparing the prefaces and comments in the successive editions. The negative remarks of John Foxe concerning the institutional church and the bishop's office are more in keeping with his experiences under King Henry VIII and Queen Mary than with those under the reign of Queen Elizabeth I.[11] It was also not by accident that the first editions of Rabus and Foxe, and the second edition of Crespin, were written in Latin, while reprints in later times, without exception, appeared in the vernacular.

What was the strongest motive behind the first editions of these works? Another question has to be answered first. Why especially did they appear in the period between 1552 and 1562? For the Lutheran territories in Germany this was the humiliating phase of the Interim. After some severe military defeats, Lutheran leaders such as Melanchthon were forced to make excessive concessions, which had evoked vehement indignation amongst the so-called Gnesio-Lutherans, to which group Ludwig Rabus also belonged. In France the position of Protestantism had deteriorated after the death of King Francis I in 1547. His successor King Henry II promised at his accession not only to banish but even to root out Protestant heresy. He did his utmost to fulfil his promise. In The Netherlands the persecution of Sacramentarians and Anabaptists had always been very severe; during the 1550s the Calvinists were also

---

[9] A. J. Jelsma, *Adriaan van Haemstede en zijn martelaarsboek* (The Hague, 1970), pp. 257–78. See also Andrew Pettegree, 'Adriaan van Haemstede: the Heretic as Historian', in *Protestant History and Identity in Sixteenth-Century Europe*, vol. II, *The Later Reformation*, St Andrews Studies in Reformation History, ed. Bruce Gorden (Aldershot and Brookfield, 1996), pp. 59–76. 'This contextualising is all the more important because Haemstede is the first, indeed the only one of the four major Reformed martyrologists at this stage to present the modern persecutions as part of a complete scheme of church history extending back to the beginnings of the Christian church' (p. 64).

[10] White, *Tudor Books*, pp. 169 ff.

[11] Foxe, *Acts and Monuments* in 'A Protestation to the whole Church of England': 'in this History might appear ... the Image of both Churches ... especially of the poor, oppressed and persecuted Church of Christ ... neglected in the World, not regarded in Histories, and almost scarce visibly or known to wordly eyes ... .' This presents a picture other than what he wrote in his dedication to Queen Elizabeth I.

pursued. And, last but not least, in this period the Protestant govern-
ment of King Edward and his adviser Cranmer was replaced by the
Roman Catholic repression under Queen Mary and the cardinals
Gardiner and Reginald Pole.

In other words, the Protestant martyrologies appeared in a period of
repercussion. The Counter-Reformation became an almost irresistible force
and the Reformation seemed to be retreating. Protestant martyrologies
were published at precisely that moment in history when an armed
struggle seemed no longer, or not yet, possible. In this precarious position, Protestant leaders had no other weapon than an appeal to public
opinion. They tried to furnish as much information about the cruel
repression as they could find, and to disseminate this material on a scale
wider than their own country, for which reason they published these
works in Latin. The martyrologies were meant as propaganda, in the
hope of changing the course of history by telling the truth about the
unbearable suffering of God's own children.

Only in later times were reprints in the vernacular, intended for the
national public, to commemorate the great deeds of the powerful warriors of Christ during the hard days. Only then did these books become,
as Helen White concluded about the work of Foxe, 'the rationalization
of a victory'.[12] The first editions of these martyrologies were guns, the
latter a monument.

To ensure that every shot found its mark, the authors of the first
editions selected their material carefully. In later editions all the names
of martyrs which could be found were assembled. The first editions
functioned similarly to the eyewitness accounts in modern times on
television, smuggled from South Africa or from the occupied parts of
Palestine: faithful but selected. What Foxe wrote, 'God hath opened the
Presse to preach, whose voice the Pope is never able to stop with all the
puissance of his triple crown',[13] applies also for his own book of martyrs. It is not surprising, that the suffering of the martyrs was depicted
with the most shocking details, so that even a gentle character like Foxe
could be named 'master of horror'.[14] Because of this motivation the

---

[12] White, *Tudor Books*, pp. 169 ff.

[13] Quoted by Perez Zagorin, *Rebels and Rulers 1500–1660*, (2 vols (Cambridge,
1982), vol. I. p. 151. See Collinson, *Archbishop Grindal*, p. 79. About the reliability of
the books of martyrs, H. T. Oberman, 'De betrouwbaarheid der martelaarsboeken van
Crespin en Van Haemstede', *Nederlands Archief voor Kerkgeschiedenis*, n.s. 4 (1907),
pp. 74–110; and Léon-E. Halkin, 'Les martyrologes et la critique; Contribution a l'étude
du Martyrologe protestant des Pays-Bas', in *Mélanges Historiques offerts a Mr. J.
Meyhoffer* (Lausanne, 1952), pp. 52–73.

[14] White, *Tudor Books*, p. 159. See P. Hughes, *The Reformation in England*, 3 vols
(London, 1953, 1954), vol. II. p. 258: 'horror is piled on horror ... '. About the kind

authors of these works emphasized the punishment of the persecutors by God himself; the miracle of retribution was the only one which Protestants wished to recognize.[15] Against this background it becomes explicable why confessions of faith, written by the martyrs themselves, were treasured. Everyone in the world had to know that under a Roman Catholic government not only usurpers of the social order but also peaceful believers were persecuted and killed.

This framework determined the selection of martyr stories. In principle, in the works of Foxe, Rabus, Crespin and van Haemstede, there was no place for Anabaptist martyrs. In these books the victims themselves often criticized, even during painful examinations, the peasants revolt in Germany and the behaviour of the Anabaptists in Münster. Despite their own suffering they agreed with the cruel execution of a man like Michael Servetus in Geneva, if we are to believe the authors of these stories. This defensive element we also find in the Mennonite martyrologies. These authors, too, regularly condemned the disturbance of public order, and what they perceived as real heresy.[16]

III

What was the consequence of this motivation behind the martyrologies for the place which could be given to women martyrs and for the way their martyrdom was described? There are two possibilities, as far as I can see. Their suffering could have been accentuated to expose the cruelty of the persecution. In 1559 Thomas Brice published for the first time a Protestant martyrs' calendar, as a replacement for the Roman Catholic saints calendar. In his preface he expressly deplored the killing of the humble and the helpless, women and, in particular, virgins.[17] But he wrote this in the victory phase, to smother all remaining sympathy for the Roman Catholic belief.

---

character of Foxe, see G. R. Elton, 'Persecution and Toleration in the English Reformation', in *Persecution and Toleration*, Studies in Church History, 21, (Oxford, 1984), pp. 163–87.

[15] Jelsma, *Adriaan van Haemstede*, pp. 246–50. In his closing word van Haemstede asks his readers for other examples of executioners who died in an unusual way.

[16] I confine myself to some examples of victims from the book of martyrs by van Haemstede: Peter Spengler, killed in 1525, condemned the peasants' revolution; Petrus Bruly, executed in 1545, rejected the second baptism; some French ministers, killed in 1555, agreed with the execution of Servetus. Mennonite martyrs too rejected the disturbance of public order, as had happened in Münster; see F. Pijper, *Martelaarsboeken* (The Hague, 1924), p. 99.

[17] White, *Tudor Books*, p. 134.

It is more probable that the share and influence of women in the martyrologies has been minimized. There are reasons for this suggestion. In the earliest editions of the works of Rabus, Crespin, Foxe and van Haemstede, women formed a small minority. In his description of the first centuries Rabus mentioned many women, but for his own time he confined himself to a few ladies of noble birth, like Argula von Grunbach and Anne Askewe. His description of the martyrdom of the latter was more curtailed than in the martyrologies of the other authors, and this was contrary to his habit. Typical of his work is that he always copied the complete text of the transmitted material. He made an exception only for one of the few women in his work. He concluded the story of Anne Askewe with the remark that she, in a miraculous way, had overcome the weakness and vanity of her gender. Perhaps his attitude can be explained by his experiences with independent women. As minister of Strasburg he often took offence at the tolerant behaviour of his colleague's wife, Catharine Zell, tolerant even of spiritualists like Caspar Schwenckfeld. In both work and writings the two contested each other.[18]

In his original contributions to the history of Dutch martyrs – in other words the material which he had not borrowed from other martyrologies – Adriaan van Haemstede did not mention any woman.

The same is true of Crespin's book as for the other martyrologists; none of the women he described actively participated in the dissemination of Protestant principles. Yet this last book deserves special attention in our investigation. His women were not involved in the preaching of the Gospel, but they sometimes exhibited a remarkable attribute; in a particular way they could become fascinated by the horrible death by fire. When in 1547 in the French town Langres some people were sentenced to the stake, it was particularly the women who encouraged their husbands and the other men. One of these women, Jeanne Bailly, compared this death with her marriage. She tried to cheer up her husband with these words: 'My love, in our marriage we were only physically joined together. Please, keep in mind that this was nothing more than a prelude of our future union. On the day of our martyrdom we will be really given in marriage to each other by the Lord Jesus Christ.' This prospect seemed to have heartened her husband.[19] Two years later, on a Saturday, in Orléans, the widow Anne Oudeberte was also sentenced to the fire. At the moment one of the guards bound her hands together, she exclaimed: 'What a nice wedding ring my husband

---

[18] Pijper, *Martelaarsboeken*, pp. 121, 122.

[19] Crespin, *Acta Martyrum*, pp. 350, 351; Crespin's *Histoire des vrays Tesmoins*, pp. 170, 171.

is giving me! On a Saturday I married my first husband; now it is again on a Saturday that I may be married with my new bridegroom Jesus Christ.'[20] The comparison of the cord around her wrists with a wedding ring illustrates her appreciation of marriage.

There is another reason why Crespin's book especially demands our attention. In the Latin translation of 1556 the author gives a personal comment when he describes the perseverance of these women. They all went to death with a masculine spirit, 'virilo animo', 'virili constantia', or more masculine than feminine, 'potius virilis quam muliebris'. All these stories were used by van Haemstede. I have already mentioned that he mostly shortened the original material, but to these examples he remained faithful. In his book, too, all these women died 'met mannelijke moed', with a masculine spirit.[21] The later French editions of Crespin's work, on the contrary, did not retain these qualifications. With respect to women the author now at best concluded that they were assisted by a more than human force.[22] Why did the author in the French edition of 1570 suppress the qualifications of the Latin edition from 1556? Because the Latin edition was intended for the intellectual circles of Europe, in other words for men. The French text was intended for people of all ranks, as an encouragement and a comfort for men and women alike. That makes a difference. There is also the possibility that the author in the mean time, between 1556 and 1570, had discovered that his characterization of the masculine spirit of those brave women had been unjustifiable in view of the reality, but this explanation seems to me less probable.

Another point in Crespin's martyrologies deserves our reflection. As we have seen, Protestant books of martyrs made a strict selection of the executed Protestants. Rabus, Crespin, van Haemstede and also Foxe attempted to prove for public opinion that people were killed who had nothing in common with real heretics such as the Anabaptists. Crespin emphasized this view by means of an extensive intermezzo about Anabaptist heresy. It is interesting to see what he considered as the climax, the culmination of this heresy. This was, of course, the behaviour of Anabaptists such as Jan van Leiden at Münster in 1534 and 1535, but he also detected a dominant influence of women. This opinion is not really surprising. Such an outlook on women was not new in Western European history. Not only the authors of the notorious *Malleus Maleficarum*,[23] but also the sixteenth-century Protestant leaders

---

[20] Crespin, *Acta Martyrum*, pp. 361, 362; Crespin, *Histoire*, pp. 178, 179.

[21] Crespin, *Acta Martyrum*, pp. 169, 221, 385.

[22] Crespin, *Histoire des vrays Tesmoins*, pp. 83–85.

[23] An English translation of *Malleus Maleficarum* by Montague Summers (2nd edn, London, 1971). The authors were Heinrich Kramer and Jacobus Sprenger.

were in general convinced that women were easier to mislead than men, that they were more influenced by demonical influence, that they fell more easily into heresy.

Philip Hughes, in his study about the Reformation in England, has even suggested that during the reign of Queen Elizabeth I the persecution of witches worsened. He saw the growing fear of dangerous women as one of the legacies of the returning exiles. While acknowledging that under Queen Mary Protestants were persecuted, in his opinion these 'bold and hard spirits' did not wish anything else, savouring every moment of their defiance.[24] But following the change in government, Hughes maintained, so-called witches had been forced to take the place of suffering. However that may be, Catholic and Protestant leaders were generally unanimous in their opinion that women should never have the opportunity to become involved in theological issues.

Crespin exhibited the heretical character of Anabaptism, not only in the usual way by relating the course of events at Münster, but also with a story about what had occurred at Appenzell, a small town in Switzerland. There a woman had presented herself as the new Christ, the Messiah of women. She had sent out 12 apostles and, as Crespin wrote, all the territories of Switzerland had been threatened with pollution by this plague. But the Protestant magistrats of Bern had rooted out this pestiferous heresy.[25]

What was the source of this story? He did not fabricate it himself. Crespin is usually reliable in his stories. He had to be; his book was intended as a weapon and for that reason attempted to be substantial. We may assume, that Crespin was acquainted with the attack of Ulrich Zwingli on the Anabaptist movement: *In Catabaptistarum Strophas Elenchus* (1527), in which Zwingli had offered a detailed description of the occurrences in the region of St Gallen. Zwingli is, however, not to be totally relied upon, in contrast to Johann Kessler who had written a chronicle about the history of his town during the years 1525–39, and who, in a way as participant, had been deeply moved by the course of events. Everything had seemed possible at that time.[26] For the inhabitants of this region – to quote the singer Paul Simon – 'these were the days of miracle and wonder'. Women especially were drawn to the new ideas. They did not really harm anyone. We may assume that, if Crespin had used this chronicle for his ac-

---

[24] Hughes, *Reformation*, vol. II. p. 286.

[25] Crespin, *Histoire des vrays Tesmoins*, pp. 83–5. For the course of events see Chapter 4 in this volume.

[26] For the history of the Anabaptists, especially in the environment of St Gall and Appenzell: Emil Egli, *Die St. Galler Täufer* (Zurich, 1887). See Chapter 4 in this volume.

count, he would have been more cautious in his comments on the events. Crespin utilized these incidents, however, as a demonstration of the pestiferous character of Anabaptism. His most convincing argument was the disturbance of the political as well as the social order by the adherents of this heresy. Therefore he characterized the radical Reformation with the stories of Jan van Leiden in Münster and the women from St Gallen and Appenzell. In this light it is not surprising that in his book of martyrs women could not play an essential role. They were suited only for suffering.

Rabus, Crespin and van Haemstede wished to prove with their books that Lutheran and Calvinist martyrs had nothing in common with Anabaptist feelings. One of the consequences was that the women of the Reformation had to disappear into the shadows.

If this reasoning is correct, we may expect that Mennonite martyrologies should offer us, in some regards, another picture. And indeed, they do. Instead of the 5 to 10 per cent normally found in other martyrologies, women account for 20 per cent of the martyrs in *The Sacrifice of the Lord* and even 30 per cent in van Braght's *Martyrs' Mirror*.[27]

When van Braght described the martyrdom of three sisters, he commenced his story with these words: 'The host of God, which equipped itself for the struggle and the suffering of Jesus Christ did not only consist in men (who sometimes are considered as the stronger sex) but of women as well.'[28] In Mennonite martyrologies women possess a marvellous knowledge of the Bible. For their relationship with God they did not want to stay dependent any longer upon often uneducated priests or even academically trained scholars. Some of these women did achieve a leading role in the Anabaptist movement. In 1549 soldiers made an investigation in the house of a Beguine, Elizabeth, in the Frisian capital Leeuwarden. They found a Latin New Testament. 'Now we finally have found the teacher of the group,' they exclaimed. Elizabeth was accused of the seduction of a great number of people. She did not deny it. She refused only to mention names.[29]

Claesken was burned at Antwerp in 1559. During the examination her interrogator tried to intimidate her. That theological research had been going on for so many centuries, he asserted, was not without

---

[27] Crespin (1556) described the suffering of 130 men and 8 women, van Haemstede (1559) 220 men and 16 women, van Braght (1685) 611 men and 221 women, Cramer, *Het offer des Heeren* (1904) 20 men and 5 women.

[28] Van Braght, *Het Bloedig Tooneel*, p. 822.

[29] Cramer, *Het offer des Heeren*, p. 91.

reason. How dare she suggest that she would be better informed than the holy fathers in the course of 1500 years! Did not her attitude prove her simplicity? Claesken answered: 'I may be stupid in the eyes of men, I am not stupid in my knowledge of the Lord.' Therefore she could no longer be content with the theology of men. Her husband could not read. She had learned to. Thanks to this lead she had obtained a remarkable self-confidence. By her reading skill she had procured for herself admission to the sources of salvation.[30]

A similar self-consciousness was exhibited by a certain Anneken in the will she had made for her son while in prison in Rotterdam in 1539. The testament began with the words: 'Listen, my son, to the teaching of your mother, open your ears for the words of my mouth. See, I am going the way of the prophets, apostles and martyrs, and will drink the chalice they had to drink.'[31]

In *The Sacrifice of the Lord*, the letters between Jeronymus Segers and his wife Lysken, written from prison in Antwerp in 1551, take up a greater part of the book. Van Braght transcribed this correspondence completely in his *Martyrs' Mirror*. A remarkable detail is that in the later English translation of this work the letters of Lysken were removed. During their separate examination the interrogator had concluded that Lysken belonged to the most important of the heretics in the town. He reproached her because it was by her influence that her husband affirmed his heretical feelings. He also blamed her for her study of the Bible, which in his opinion was not fitting for a woman. Her task was in the kitchen, not in a book. She had to leave the study of the Holy Scripture to the educated priests.[32]

The husband of Claudine le Vette belonged to the spokesmen of the Anabaptist movement. But often when he was studying the Bible he asked his wife for advice; she was much better informed than he.[33]

Comparing the material of Mennonite martyrologies with the books of Rabus, Crespin and Van Haemstede, I must conclude that there is a difference, not only in theological views but also in the place which was assigned to women. How are we, in this regard, to judge the work of John Foxe?

In general there has been appreciation for the way in which he had dealt with women. Comparing John Foxe's *Acts and Monuments* with Bunyan's *Pilgrims Progress* and the Bible, Roland Bainton concluded: 'All three give a high place to women.' In his opinion, Foxe tells us

---

[30] Ibid., p. 327.
[31] Ibid., p. 70.
[32] Ibid., pp. 136–76.
[33] Van Braght, *Het Bloedig Tooneel*, pp. 383, 384.

more about the women of the Reformation in England than does any other source. Ellen Macek affirmed this conclusion regarding Foxe's book: 'His accounts of female Protestants who lacked a voice of their own provide a unique insight into early modern women's religious experience.'[34] I do not want to challenge this appreciation, but I wish to append some notes.

Following his return to England during the reign of Queen Elizabeth I, Foxe did indeed create more space for women in the new editions of his work. He had to do so. The later versions of his work differed from the editions of 1554 and 1559. Under the new circumstances Protestant leaders definitively attempted to persuade the population to accept the Reformation. Foxe's book of martyrs attained a new purpose, as Philip Hughes writes: 'The instinct that demanded a Golden Legend was still active and, all unconsciously, Foxe was supplying the need.'[35] I am not sure whether it really happened so subconsciously. Indeed, he vigorously rejected the suggestion that there was anything in common between his book and the Golden Legend so despised by Protestants. But that Foxe was not entirely unaware of the possibility of making an effective substitution becomes apparent in the calendar, very much in the primer fashion, which he prefixed to his book. He did offer a substitute for the rejected Golden Legend, as Helen White has also affirmed.[36] For each day of the year he supplied martyrs to retain in memory and, as the Golden Legend included many female saints in its calendar, it would have been disgraceful for Protestantism to offer only men in remembrance.

There is another argument to explain why Foxe made more room for women. In the later editions he wanted to describe as completely as possible the atrocities which society had suffered under the Roman Catholic repercussions during the reign of Queen Mary. Therefore, he summed up all the names of martyrs that he could gather. Among them were many women. The vast majority of victims belonged to the working classes as the greater part of academically trained Protestants had left the country. Often Foxe knew little more about the victims than their names and places of execution. The percentage of women in the new editions indeed grew, but the number of pages reserved for them remained minimal. It is not always clear what the women he described actually believed. Not without reason Hughes supposed that some of

---

[34] Bainton, *Women of the Reformation*, p. 211; Macek, 'The Emergency', p. 66. See also A. G. Dickens, *The English Reformation*, 4th edn (London, 1968), p. 26: 'the most informative of our sources, the *Acts and Monuments* of John Foxe'.

[35] Hughes, *Reformation*, vol. II, p. 258.

[36] White, *Tudor Books*, p. 136.

the martyrs under Queen Mary would also have been executed if King Edward had lived.[37] Consider for example the woman from Exeter. Foxe described her in this way: 'She was as simple a woman to see as any man might behold, of a very little and short stature, somewhat thick, about 54 years of age.' During the examinations she brought the bishop to despair. Often he uttered the sigh: 'O foolish woman!' She had left her husband and children and had wandered around in the environment of Exeter. 'Why did you leave them?,' the bishop asked. She appealed to the words of Christ, that when an apostle was persecuted in one town he had to flee to another. 'But who persecuted thee,' the bishop asked. 'My husband and my children,' she answered. They had not listened to her when she had tried to deliver them from their idolatry.[38]

This urge to completeness could, as a consequence, have caused Foxe in the later editions of his work to make room for martyrs who would not have been permitted in the earlier martyrologies of Rabus, Crespin or van Haemstede. This could explain why Foxe, in his description of women's religious experience, retained a position between the previously mentioned martyrologies and the Mennonite works. But in one respect he remained on the same level as his Lutheran and Calvinist colleagues. In his book of martyrs, too, women were not permitted to be equally active in teaching as women sometimes could be in Mennonite martyrologies.

IV

A final question remains. Did the position of Lutheran, Reformed or Anglican women differ from that of Anabaptist women not only in the martyrologies but also in reality? I think not, at least not during the first half of the century. What Claire Cross wrote in her article 'He-goats before the Flocks' about English women in the seventeenth century applies, as far as I can see, even more so a century earlier. She wrote: 'Many of these women at least partially educated themselves; once they could read, by regular attendance at sermons and exercises and by diligent reading of the Bible and contemporary theological and

---

[37] Hughes, *Reformation*, vol. II, p. 262; Horst, *The Radical Brethren*, pp. 155, 156. See also W. Haller, *Foxe's Book of Martyrs and the Elect Nation* (London, 1963), pp. 13 ff. See for an analysis of the Protestant martyrs of Mary's reign: Andrew Pettegree, *Marian Protestantism. Six Studies*, St Andrews Studies in Reformation History (Aldershot and Brookfield, 1996), pp. 4–7.

[38] John Foxe, *Acts and Monuments*, vol. III, pp. 746, 747.

devotional writers they attained to very considerable biblical learning.'[39]

In the diary of a Dutch chaplain, Christiaan Munters, over the years 1529–45, we can find an example which reveals how startling this new possibility for women could become in the eyes of men. He noted what had happened in the town of Maastricht. There a woman had met a stranger who wanted to sell her some books. The woman answered that she could not read. That was no problem, he said. He could teach her. He took her to his home and after some hours she could read. Enriched with this new facility and with some Protestant books she returned to her husband. He asked her where she had stayed so long. 'I have learned to read,' she exclaimed, 'I can read everything now!' Her husband paled. Immediately he warned the priest. She confessed what she had done. After the absolution a miracle took place. Thanks to the mercy of God she could no longer read one letter of the alphabet; she was saved.[40]

This incident not only discloses how stormy the process of learning to read sometimes could be, but also to what extent this new possibility could allow women an advantage over their husbands and how threatening this sometimes was for men. It was a development that must have occurred throughout the whole of Europe during the sixteenth century. People with differing backgrounds learned to read and became involved in the theological issues of their time on a much wider scale than ever before. Many of these self-taught men and women felt the urge to disseminate what they discovered in the Bible. The frontiers between the varying opinions were not always very clear during the first half of the sixteenth century, at least not at the foundation of society. For the magistrates this situation must have been an extremely confusing situation. They tried to apply the correct names to their religious prisoners: Lollards, Lutherans, Sacramentists, Anabaptists, spiritualists. Gradually points of recognition became visible, determining issues being the perception of priesthood, mass and baptism, but also the attitude to the social order, including the relationship between men and women.

During the second half of the century, when Roman Catholicism recovered part of its lost territory, the magisterial Reformation looked for means to maintain its position. Books of martyrs became a weapon in this struggle for survival. Lutheran, Calvinist and Anglican authors

---

[39] Claire Cross, '"He-goats before the Flocks": a Note on the Part Played by Women in the Founding of Some Civil War Churches', in *Popular Belief and Practice*, Studies in Church History, 8 (Cambridge, 1984), pp. 201, 202.

[40] *Dagboek van Gebeurtenissen, opgetekend door Christiaan Munters, 1529–1545*, ed. J. Grauwels (Assen, 1972), p. 26.

tried to prove that in Roman Catholic territories people were persecuted, even though they had no intention of disturbing the political or
social order. Of course, in these books there was no place for women
who were too independent. Thanks to the Anabaptist martyrologies we
know better how intensive the contribution of women, especially in the
lower strata of the society, must have been. It is improbable that only
Mennonite men and women wrote each other letters from prison, but
these were of no interest to the other martyrologies and, therefore, were
not collected, unless in the case of women of noble birth. Women who
were too quick-witted were unprofitable for the image that authors
such as Rabus, Crespin, van Haemstede and Foxe sought to create.

These concluding remarks bring us back to the beginning, the case of
Anne Askewe. I do not think that it has been by accident that her
perceptive remarks were removed from most martyrologies. The meta-
phor she had used in her discussion with Bishop Gardiner had been
nothing less than gunpowder. What she really expressed was that in a
world where unfit men could often hold a bishop's see, women had the
right, even the obligation, to explain the Word of God. When men
defaulted, women should take over their task. If an ass bears a bishop's
mitre, a pig has to be saddled with the Word of God.

CHAPTER SIX

Why the Reformation failed

I

Italian Protestantism

I would not be surprised if people wonder at this title. Is it possible to regard the sixteenth century Reformation as a failure? Is this not, from a historical point of view, a nonsensical supposition, which is refuted merely by my being a Reformed theologian? This conclusion should not be drawn too quickly. The thesis becomes more accessible when a geographical designation is added to the title of this essay. In some areas of Europe Protestantism was indeed able to gain the upper hand, in others it was not. The north of the Netherlands, Scandinavia, England and certain parts of Germany could be Protestantized to some degree, but in Spain and Italy a Protestant Reformation had failed. What were the decisive factors, why did the Reformation fail in some places?

The Italian Reformation history is especially interesting from the point of view of failure.[1] It is undeniable that during the first half of the sixteenth century Protestantism could count on sympathy and approval among large numbers of the population. In certain monasteries the works of Luther, and later also those of Calvin, were studied eagerly. Reading groups of clergy and lay people came into existence, in which the latest Protestant products were put to the test, just as we find them in The Netherlands in that same period. In humanistic circles in particular there was a tendency to regard the Protestant Reformation as the renewal movement to which humanists like Erasmus (1466–1536) had been looking forward for such a long time. Protestantism could certainly not count on fewer adherents here than elsewhere in Europe. And yet, what was a success there, failed here.

---

[1] See for an accurate overview Manfred E. Welti, *Kleine Geschichte der italienischen Reformation* (Gütersloh, 1985). See also the standard work by Delio Cantimori, *Italienische Haeretiker der Spätrenaissance*, German translation by Werner Kaegi (Basle, 1949). Recent essays about the Italian Reformation: Euan Cameron, 'Italy', in Andrew Pettegree (ed.), *The Early Reformation in Europe*, (Cambridge, 1992), pp. 188–214; Ugo Rozzo and Silvana Seidel Menchi, 'Livre et Réforme en Italie', in Jean-François Gilmont (ed.), *La Réforme et le livre; l' Europe de l'imprimé (1517–v.1570)*, (Paris, 1990), pp. 327–74.

In an illuminating essay Philip MacNair described the Italian Reformation as 'the biggest non-event of the century'.[2] This seems a rather debatable characterization. Why would a movement be regarded as a non-event, only for the reason that later on it was violently liquidated? MacNair, however, chose this term for a different reason. Not only was Protestantism in Italy eradicated; all traces of it were destroyed as thoroughly as possible, so that for a long time it was overlooked in historical research. It seemed that there had never been any Reformed groups in these regions.

Now we know better, and in recent years much has been publicized about the Italian Reformation.[3] Gradually the contours of the Spiritualistic, evangelical movement that gathered here around the figure of Juan de Valdès, have become apparent. He was from Spain, but had fled to Italy because of the persecution in his country.[4] It appears that he allowed himself to be inspired by the young Calvin, among others. Certain quotes from a work that gives a good representation of his ideas, are adopted almost verbatim from an early version of Calvin's *Institutes* (1539).[5] And although the Vatican still has not released all the sources from its archives, it has become clear how radically the Inquisition liquidated the movement. The Protestants were left only three possibilities, which MacNair called 'flying', 'dying' or 'lying'.[6] Many went into hiding or assimilated. A considerable number ended their lives on the stake or in prison, and many fled.

---

[2] Philip M. J. MacNair, 'The Reformation of the Sixteenth Century in Renaissance Italy', in *Religion and Humanism*, Studies in Church History, 17, ed. Keith Robins (Oxford, 1981), pp. 149–66: 'In one obvious sense the Reformation in Italy was the biggest non-event of the century. It simply did not happen ... By 1600 there was hardly a Reformation relic left in the country' (p. 151).

[3] See also Barry Collett, *Italian Benedictine Scholars and the Reformation. The Congregation of Santa Giustina of Padua* (Oxford, 1985).

[4] See J. C. Nieto, *Juan de Valdes and the Origins of the Spanish and Italian Reformation* (Geneva, 1971).

[5] The booklet by an anonymous author, written in Italian, bore the title *Trattato utilissimo del beneficio di Giesu Christo crocifisso verso i Christiani*. According to estimates from that time 60 000 copies were sold in Italy during the first six years. It was placed on the Index and burnt. Not until the nineteenth century was a copy discovered in Cambridge. See for details Collett, *Italian Benedictine Scholars*, pp. 157 ff.

[6] MacNair, 'The Reformation ... in Renaissance Italy', p. 163. A fourth category should be added: People who, without being forced to do so, freely returned to Catholicism because of disappointment with the course of events within the Reformation. This too occurred.

Italian refugees

At first the majority of this last category went to Switzerland. This is a result not only of geographical location but also of the religious situation. Most of the Italians felt drawn more to Reformed than to Lutheran Protestantism. That the Waldensians eventually resolved to join Reformed Protestantism is another indication of this.

Not all Italian refugees remained in Switzerland. A number of them sought safety in England, and even founded their own church in London, although certainly not all of them joined this church.[7] Others went eastward and ended up in Poland. The reasons for these migrations were not exclusively, or rather not in the first place, economic. The Italians were not free from self-assertion. Most of them were well-educated. They were not docile. They claimed the right to resolve for themselves the basic principles of Reformed Protestantism. Indeed, it was for this right of freedom of conscience that they had left their native land. Therefore, they developed ideas which the spiritual leaders of Reformed Protestantism regarded as heretical. Calvin especially was irritated by their independence. Ultimately he viewed every Italian a heretic, unless the contrary was proved. Therefore, the statement that an Italian Protestant lurks behind virtually every radical movement within Reformed Protestantism, is correct.[8]

Initially, because of its radical character, the Italians were drawn to Reformed Protestantism, but many withdrew from it later as a result of negative experiences.[9] The conflicts that emerged almost naturally drove them to even more radical movements such as the Unitarianism of

---

[7] O. Boersma, *Vluchtig voorbeeld. De Nederlandse, Franse en Italiaanse vluchtelingenkerken in Londen, 1568–1585* (n.p., 1994). A considerable part of the Italian members were Marranos (that is Jews) by descent. See O. Boersma and A. J. Jelsma (eds), *Unity in Multiformity. The Minutes of the Coetus of London, and the Consistory Minutes of the Italian Church in London* (London and Amsterdam, 1997), pp. 29, 30.

[8] 'Wherever there was trouble, there was an Italian behind it.' This statement is from MacNair, quoted by Patrick Collinson, *Archbishop Grindal, 1519–1563. The Struggle for a Reformed Church* (London, 1979), p. 327, n. 32. See for Calvin's opinion of these 'Italian academic sceptics', as he called them, W. K. Jordan, *The Development of Religious Toleration in England from the Beginning of the English Reformation to the Death of Queen Elizabeth* (London, 1932), p. 306. See also Antonio Rotondo, *Calvin and the Italian Antitrinitarians* (St Louis, MO, 1968).

[9] Cantimori, *Italienische Haeretiker*, p. 318, is right in stating with reference to these Italian emigrants: 'Keiner von ihnen will so weit von den Ideen der protestantischen Reformatoren entfernt sein, wie Calvin sie nun distanzierte.' [None of them wanted to become so alienated from the ideas of the Protestant Reformers as Calvin had forced them to be.]

Michael Servetus (1509/11–53)[10] or the individualistic spiritualism of Hans Denck (*c.* 1500–27).[11] Some returned, disillusioned, to the bosom of the Roman Catholic Church, now with more understanding of the choice which Erasmus had earlier made.[12] Disappointed with the outcome of Protestantism, Erasmus had decided to remain faithful to the original church. Some of the Italians put into words why, in the end, they regarded the Reformed Reformation as a failure.[13]

Forms of failure

Therefore, there are indeed historical reasons to view the sixteenth-century Reformation from the point of view of failure. The concept of 'failure' can be understood in two ways. A movement can be regarded as a failure if it ceases to exist, or if it becomes estranged from its original ideas. Both forms of failure were present in the sixteenth century. In some regions of Europe Protestantism was a fiasco. Besides, in the sixteenth century we meet authors who, despite their original approval, eventually came to the conclusion that the Reformation as a whole had failed or was in danger of failing. In this chapter I hope to

---

[10] A worthwhile summary of his ideas can be found in Jerome Friedman, *Michael Servetus. A Case Study in Total Heresy* (Geneva, 1978). He makes clear that his view is not to be equated with that of the later Unitarians. His view had rather a modalistic character. He believed in the full divinity of Christ, but rejected the doctrine of the Trinity. Since he uses Jewish literature extensively, one can assume that he had been influenced by the Marranos (Jews that had accepted Christianity under pressure). Later Unitarianism strongly emphasized the humanity of Christ.

[11] For his writings see Georg Baring and Walter Fellmann, *Hans Dencks Schriften*, 2 vols (Gütersloh, 1955, 1956).

[12] For example Francesco Pucci, who as a witness of the cruelties against the Protestants during the massacre of St Bartholomew's Day chose the Reformation. He spent a great deal of time in London. Here he put into words the sort of church he dreamt of: a peaceful community of people who grant one another much freedom dogmatically, with just the Apostles' Creed as its basis. Later he returned to Catholicism, settled again in Italy, where eventually he was burnt in 1597 because of remaining heretical ideas. See Welti, *Kleine Geschichte*, pp. 115, 116. See also Cantimori, *Italienische Haeretiker*, p. 497; he assumes that Pucci was killed in an accident in 1593, while travelling to Rome. He does mention that the writing in which Pucci motivated his return to Catholicism was placed on the Index in 1596. Another example was Simone Simoni of Lucca, characterized by his colleague Marcello Squarcialupi as 'at first Catholic, after that Calvinist, in later time Lutheran, finally again Catholic, but always atheist', quoted by J. Tedeschi, 'La Littérature de la Réforme italienne', in *Le Livre dans l' Europe de la Renaissance. Actes du XXVIIIe colloque international d'Etudes humanistes de Tours*, eds P. Aquilon and H.-J. Martin (Promodis, 1988), pp. 405–33.

[13] 'The thesis that the Reformation is a failure is admittedly of longer standing, and reaches as far back as Luther's earliest opponents', as Heiko A. Oberman wrote in *The Impact of the Reformation* (Grand Rapids, MI, 1994), p. 175.

discuss what was the basis for this conclusion, what the accusers regarded as the cause of this failure, and what have been the consequences of their view for the history of the Reformation. I shall begin with the latter.

II

Space needed for growth

Some of these critical writings were translated into Dutch and had much influence on Arminians, the so-called Remonstrants, and adherents of even more radical movements. We even chanced upon a preacher from Kampen, the town where I had the opportunity to teach Church History for almost 30 years in the Theological University of the Reformed Churches in The Netherlands.

In 1604 a certain Jean de la Haye (or Johannes van der Heyden) received a call from a congregation in the town of Kampen. As his original name indicates, he was born in France but, like countless other Huguenots, had fled that country because of the situation there. In view of the positions he had held, it appears that he had received an academic education. In Cologne he was pastor of the 'church under the cross' which had come into existence there. Some years later, in 1601, he was appointed rector of the Latin school in Breda, and three years later received a call to Kampen. There he was responsible for church services not only in the Dutch-speaking congregation, but also for the Walloon community. So, he had a twofold task, which he found onerous.

Therefore he wrote in 1608 to the town council of Kampen (referring to himself in the third person): 'There have been weeks in which he had to preach nine or ten times, which is unbearable.' In this letter he not only complained about his busy schedule. Without there having been an official complaint against him, some church members appeared to be unhappy about his preaching. To them he was not orthodox enough. The latter was the decisive reason for his resignation. It was to him unacceptable that, while he devoted all his energies to the church, some of the church's members did not refrain from discrediting his name, although they had not taken the trouble to discuss their objections with him. In such an atmosphere of insinuations he was not able to work properly. The letter ends with an emotional allusion to his own name: 'Let the heather grow' (his Dutch name 'Heyden' means 'heather').

He asked the civil authorities to find a replacement for him within half a year. He was convinced that elsewhere in The Netherlands there would be congregations, among whom he could work more fruitfully.[14] He appeared to be correct. In 1610 he became pastor in the Hague, and from 1611 he served the Walloon church in that city. Yet, here too problems arose. After a few years he was removed from office. He died in 1618.

What were the grievances against him? It is not totally clear. Judicial documents have not been kept. The battle between Remonstrants and Contra-Remonstrants was raging at that time, but the synod which led to the removal of a number of pastors, had not yet taken place. Perhaps the most appropriate way to gain an understanding of his offensive views, which had already discredited him in Kampen, is to study the writings which he probably translated while living in Kampen, since they were printed as early as 1611.[15]

In his preface, written to all pious Christians, de la Haye states that, despite the reformation which had taken place, the church was still in a poor state: all but dead. In his despair he had been looking for a potent drug, which might bring healing. Eventually he had found it, a work written by a house member of the faith, as he calls him, a sincere lover of the truth and of Christian love. He sums up a series of characterizations of the book: 'an alarming book, a book of Christian love which leads to peace and unity, a book of art, a medicinal book, a treasure book of Christian virtues, a battle book in which Christians are exhorted to fight together against Satan'.[16] So, he has a high regard for this book. It has become Holy Writ to him. In dedicating it to the Dutch Estates General he describes it as 'a godly work', bathing in heavenly light, which shows 'the teachers of the Church how to lead God's Church to a blessed state'. In view of the outcome of the judicial process he suffered, the publication did not answer its purpose. From

---

[14] See J. van Gelderen, 'Kerkelijke Geschiedenis: zeventiende en achttiende eeuw. "Maer het is hier te Campen"' in *Geschiedenis van Kampen; 'maer het is hier te Campen'*, ed. H. J. J. Lenferink (Kampen, 1993), pp. 149, 186. J. P. de Bie and J. Loosjes, *Biografisch Woordenboek van Protestantse Godgeleerden in Nederland* (The Hague, 1903), vol. III. pp. 591, 592. The letter is in the archives of the city of Kampen, Oud-Archief 1608.

[15] He translated more works from Latin, especially writings which urged tolerance; an irenic writing of Franciscus Junius, *Den vreedsamen Christen* ... (Amsterdam, 1612); two writings by P. du Moulin (1615, 1622). He also translated into French the work of E. van Meteren, *Historie der Nederlandsche ende harer Naburen Oorlogen ende Geschiedenissen* (The Hague, 1614). For the latter work he received stipends from the Dutch Parliament, so that he was not without income despite being defrocked.

[16] Johannes de la Haye, *VIII Boecken van de Arglistigheden des Satans, waerin gehandelt wert van de maniere, hoe men de Kerck (dat is de Gemeente Gods) sal reformeren, soo wel in leven als in goede zeden, en versien tegen de lagen des Satans, in 't Latijn uytgegeven ... door Jacobum Aconcium* (2nd edn, Amsterdam, 1660).

his recommendation we learn how much this book had refreshed him. He knows it influenced him. Here he found the heart of his own theology. What type of book was this?

III

Acontius

The book had originally been written in London by an Italian, Giacopo Aconcio (or, to use his Latin name, Jacobus Acontius), and been printed in Basle in 1565 by an Italian, Pietro Perna. Basle was at that time a refuge for dissidents and free-thinkers. David Joris was living there, albeit under a pseudonym. Perna, who had fled from Italy, had succeeded in establishing here one of the largest printing-houses of Switzerland, in which most authors with an unusual or debatable view could have their works published. He printed the works of the alchemist Paracelsus, the fierce antagonist of Castellio against the judicial murder of Servetus, the Bible translation by Castellio which on some points was attacked by Calvin, and all writings of Acontius, including the work that was later translated by Johannes van der Heyden, which bore the title: *Satanae Stratagemata (Satan's Stratagems).*[17]

Who was Giacopo Aconcio? Originally he was from the area of Trent, born *circa* 1500, he studied law and philosophy, learnt to build military defences, became skilled in mathematics, gained prominent positions at different courts, joined the Reformation at an advanced age, when he was in his fifties, fled to Switzerland, and arrived in London in 1558/59. Here he joined the church community which had originally been founded by the Dutch pastor Adriaan van Haemstede.

The latter soon came into conflict with the consistories of the Dutch and French refugee churches, when he wished to accept adherents to the Anabaptist teaching as brothers and sisters in Christ. Acontius acted as his lawyer and following van Haemstede's excommunication and banishment, he too was excommunicated, together with businessman and historian Emanuel van Meteren and other prominent members of the

---

[17] The full title is *Satanae Stratagemata libri octo* (Basle, 1565). A new edition was provided by Walter Köhler (Münster, 1927). The work was translated into all European languages. Köhler provides an overview in the introduction to his work, pp. IX–XIII. See for other works of Acontius: Walter Köhler and Erich Hassinger, *Acontiana. Abhandlungen und Briefe des Jacobus Acontius* (Heidelberg, 1932). About Pietro Perna and other Italians in Basle: Welti, *Kleine Geschichte*, pp. 108 ff. See also Rozzo and Seidel Menchi, 'Livre et Réforme en Italie', p. 339.

Dutch congregation. For Acontius the consequences were less serious than for van Haemstede, because he received a stipend from Queen Elizabeth I and enjoyed enough support in court circles. His sad experience with the way in which Reformed Protestants dealt with conflicts like these were an important reason for his book.[18]

The wiles of Satan

In his book Acontius expresses himself in a very sombre way over the situation of Reformed Protestantism. Satan has more or less gained the upper hand there. In his preface he explains why he has waited so long before writing this book, although he had known for a considerable time how cunningly and with how much success Satan infected the body of the church. It is not without its dangers, he writes, to expose how the spiritual leaders have fallen for the wiles of Satan. Experience teaches what the consequences can be when one becomes an enemy of those with high repute in the church.

Already it becomes apparent what Acontius regards as the main reason for the Reformation's failure: the way in which the great leaders attempted to maintain their authority. Although he writes about the church in general terms, he intends to expose the critical situation of Protantism. He writes in the preface:

> I realize that the papists will chuckle, if this work falls into their hands, now that we lay bare our wounds. But it is better if they laugh at our wounds, which can be healed, than if we would let them deteriorate until they became incurable. For then they could mock us for our downfall.

Of course, it is impossible to discuss all aspects of this book in the short space of this chapter. Elsewhere I have given more extensive attention to this work.[19] There I quoted especially those parts, in which it becomes clear how much the lawsuit against Adriaan van Haemstede inspired Acontius to write this work. In this chapter I wish to go into the causes which according to him had led to the deformation, and therefore to the threatening failure, of the Reformation.[20]

---

[18] For this conflict see Collinson, *Archbishop Grindal*, pp. 134 ff.; Andrew Pettegree, *Foreign Protestant Communities in Sixteenth-Century London* (Oxford, 1986), pp. 140 ff. The latter calls Acontius 'the driving force behind Haemstede's stubborn resistance' (p. 173). See also A. J. Jelsma, *Adriaan van Haemstede en zijn martelaarsboek*, dissertation (The Hague, 1970), pp. 115–205. It is assumed that, despite his excommunication by the Dutch (and therefore also by the French) church, Acontius could later function as an elder in the small Spanish community (Collinson, *Archbishop Grindal*, p. 145).

[19] Jelsma, *Adriaan van Haemstede*, pp. 206–28.

[20] For a description of the contents also see Jordan, *The Development of Religious*

Throughout the book the same complaints recur. The penetration by Satan led to increasing disunity within Protestantism. Protestantism, he writes, has fragmented into a growing number of sects. He enumerates several reasons for this disunity. The second generation of spiritual leaders is undoubtedly less qualified than the first. However much they had erred, the first spokesmen had at least been inspired by an ideal. They wanted to open the dungeon in which the church lay imprisoned. They wanted to return to the Word of God all the authority it deserved. They championed the believers' freedom of conscience.

The men who succeeded them, however, had rather different motives. They were after power; they wanted to strengthen their positions and to restrict freedom of opinion. They could not bear criticism, either of themselves or of the teachings of the first generation of spiritual leaders, they immediately called in the executioners to punish and kill all people with a slightly differing view. They forced their interpretation of Holy Scripture on to the church members, so they adulterated the principle of *sola Scriptura*, and they found it necessary to prove themselves by writing their own institutes or other summaries of what they regarded as the only true teaching. They eradicated the distinction between the heart of the Gospel and what they themselves had deducted from that heart, refused to discuss things openly, chained people's consciences again and similarly imprisoned the church, as a result of which the Reformation threatened to fail altogether.

Acontius tries to be understanding towards their behaviour. He realizes how gradually, almost unnoticed, this corruption can seep in. The *doctores* of the church have, of course, the task to explain the Gospel. Thinking about the heart of the Gospel they draw conclusions which they themselves regard as inescapable and therefore try to force on to others. In the long run they cannot imagine that others find those conclusions less self-evident. So they experience such differing opinions as betrayal of the Gospel itself. Often they express themselves vehemently; in criticizing their opponents they usually show great eloquence. Because they have defended their position so fanatically it is difficult for them to acknowledge that they were wrong, without losing face. Often they sincerely think that the Gospel itself will suffer if their reputation is tarnished. And so they continue. They inflate the differences. As a result of this pugnacity the discrepancy between their teachings and their lives becomes greater. He regards as boundless the ambition of these leaders, who fancy themselves as gods and become furious about any deviations from their teachings.

Toleration, pp. 300–364. He writes about Acontius: 'The lay thought of the century received its finest and fullest expression in the writings of Jacobus Acontius Tridentius.'

His work ends in a 'woe to you!' for the shepherds who by this sort of behaviour continue to call forth new quarrels, who pursue their own honour, who want to be like the gods, who want to have authority over consciences and who bear the papacy, which in the old church was situated in faraway Rome, in their own bosoms. It is their behaviour which causes the Reformation's failure. Because of this countless people lose all sense of religion. They do not want to return to the old church; the new church, however, has removed them even further away from the kingdom of God. It is this degeneration in religion that is to blame for the civil war in France, according to Acontius.

A possible restoration

Is restoration at all possible? Acontius believes it is, and points to the example of ancient Israel. There, too, minor derailments took place on several occasions. Every time restoration appeared to be possible by taking God's law exclusively and literally as the norm, removing all accretions that had been added in the course of time.

Protestantism should really take *sola Scriptura* as its sole point of departure. He warns against the accumulation of creeds. 'I had rather no creed at all than so many of them,' he writes literally in his work.[21] With a growing number of creeds we only play into Satan's hands, is his opinion. If there is to be a creed, than one as short as possible, with as few words as in the Apostles' Creed, but – unlike the Apostles' Creed – exclusively with formulations that are derived from the Gospel itself.

The Dutch translation contains a tentative example of such a creed, which is not to be found in the first Latin edition and was probably added later in order to avoid the risk that Acontius would be charged with Unitarian ideas.[22] Such a minimal creed is all that may be imposed upon the believers.

Acontius advocates freedom of opinion. In no way may the authorities be involved in these discussions. The task of the authorities should be limited to the protection of the free proclamation of the Word of God. If somebody appears not to accept even this very minimal creed, then excommunication is the only sort of pressure which is acceptable. Only if, in love, we are willing to bear all our differences in opinion,

---

[21] 'Malim nullam esse quam tot.' Acontius, *Satanae Stratagemata*, p. 225. In the Dutch translation I have not found this statement in such radical a form. For an elaboration of this theme in the Dutch translation see pp. 577 ff.

[22] In Köhler's edition the changed text including the tentative example of a creed is published in a note (pp. 186 ff.).

what will undoubtedly remain is possible restoration and a chance that the Reformation will succeed.

Compensation for a deficiency

What is remarkable about this book is not its diagnosis nor the remedy it suggests, but the psychological unravelling of the feelings that are hidden behind theological rationalizations and constructions which often precede them. Acontius is aware that theological opinions do not always spring from the heart, but may be compensation for a deficiency. He who speaks about love is not necessarily a loving person. The heart and the tongue are often further removed from one another than their position in the body would suggest. He also realized how much a clash of characters can unnecessarily intensify theological differences, as a result of which people who are comparatively close to one another end up miles apart. Quarrelling they force each other into positions and they draw conclusions which they would not have drawn without such a battle. He especially blames the spokesmen of the church for permitting the congregation to suffer for their conflicts. The believers are forced to ally themselves with, and to accept, beliefs which result more from their theological battle than from the study of the Scriptures.

So, Acontius advocates tolerance, the reduction of doctrine to a minimum, the separation of church and state, diminishing the dominance of incumbents, the personal responsibility of the church members, freedom of opinion, in short, he does exactly what Calvin blames the Italian free-thinkers of doing. Does this mean that he should be reckoned among the Unitarians or the spiritualists? Some authors have drawn this conclusion, but in my opinion this is not justified. What he wants, like his friend Adriaan van Haemstede, is to be able to accept people as brothers and sisters in Christ, who at certain points have a dissident opinion, without being branded a heretic merely for accepting them.

It is not very clear what his personal beliefs are, he does not elaborate on them. In fact, he cannot. For then he would do exactly that which he blames others for doing. He thinks that the Reformation should limit itself to its main principles of *sola Scriptura* and *sola gratia*. Holy Scripture alone should have authority in the church of God. Justification by faith alone should be the basis for life. Consequences which theologians derive from these principles, such as the teachings on predestination and original sin, may have some value, but they are not to be forced on to the church, for then the church is destroyed.

Thus Acontius put into words what the Dutch Reformed theologian Harry Kuitert wrote in his book *I Have my Doubts*:

> There's nothing against systematic thought in theology, but there is something to be said against theological systems, and everything to be said against systems which seek to provide total views of God and God's work. I don't think that we're in a position to do this, and it can only harm the church and Christianity ... We simply know too little of God to be able to make such a rounded structure. A total view disguises the gaps, fills them in, suggests that we never need to stand tongue-tied and never need to pray 'we know not what'. But the gaps are there, indeed there are a great many of them, and they can't be removed. If we take no account of them, we remain stuck in 'doctrine about doctrine'. That may be good for 'questions' and doctrinal differences, but it's no good for searching and finding God.[23]

That was exactly what Acontius had in mind, that was the attitude of faith with which the pastor in Kampen, Johannes van der Heyden, identified himself.

IV

Castellio

Were these views of Acontius new? Not at all. Erasmus and other humanists had on several occasions made a plea for the reduction of what people had to believe in, for example, the Apostles' Creed. Also criticism of the *doctores ecclesiae*, who could boast as if they were seated in heaven itself, had been heard several times previously. With some of these humanists their criticism had indeed led, as Acontius warned, to scepticism and religious indifference.[24]

We find similar thoughts to Acontius's with someone like Sebastian Castellio (1515–63).[25] He, too, wrote very gloomily about the prospects of Reformed Protestantism. It is worth comparing his views with those

---

[23] H. M. Kuitert, *I Have my Doubts. How to Become a Christian without Being a Fundamentalist*, translated from Dutch (London and Valley Forge, PA, 1993), pp. 6, 7.

[24] See for an overview of these ideas and for their development Jordan, *Development of Religious Toleration*, pp. 28 ff. See for Erasmus's view C. Augustijn, *Erasmus* (Baarn, 1967), p. 67: 'The more dogmas there are, the sooner new heresies will come up. "And the Christian faith was never purer and cleaner than when the world was content with this one and very short symbol".'

[25] Jordan, *Development of Religious Toleration*, p. 315, typifies both of them: 'Castellion is the Luther of the literature of toleration; Acontius the Calvin.'

of Acontius, because Castellio mentions other causes for the failure of the Reformation.

As is well known, this intelligent compatriot of Calvin's soon came into conflict with the great reformer during his stay in Geneva. At that time it was still about a minute difference in opinion. Castellio believed that the *Song of Songs* was merely a love song, a view which Calvin found unbearable, and he had to resign his position as rector of the Latin school to find refuge in Basle. Here too, persecution threatened, instigated by Calvin and his co-workers.

In response to the judicial murder of Servetus, Castellio, using a pseudonym for his own protection, wrote his well-known work about the question of whether heretics should be persecuted.[26] The work consists mainly of quotes from earlier church fathers and from authoritative authors from his own time, in which religious persecution is emphatically rejected. Of course, we encounter the names of outspoken defenders of tolerance such as Erasmus and Sebastian Franck (1499–1542/43). Castellio, however, was clever enough to include a quote from Calvin himself, from the first edition of his *Institutes*, in which Calvin opposed the practice of using violence if need be to put pressure on heretics or to kill them. This quote is a direct attack on Calvin's later activities. 'It is plainly criminal,' Calvin wrote in the first edition of the *Institutes*, 'to kill heretics. Liquidating them by the sword or by fire means a denial of every principle of humanity.'[27] In later editions of his *Institutes* he did not repeat these words. So, Castellio's compilation of protests against religious persecution does not contain a systematic discussion, as Acontius offered, but makes a significant enough impression to have infuriated Calvin and Beza.

The right to doubt

In a later study, *De Arte Dubitandi*, which in his own time was never fully published, Castellio put his own views into words much more

---

[26] Sebastian Castellio, *De haereticis an sint persequendi*, facsimile of the edition of 1554 by S. van der Woude (Geneva, 1954). See the English translation of R. H. Bainton, *Concerning Heretics, Whether They Are to be Persecuted and How They Are to be Treated. A Collection of the Opinions of Learned Men, Both Ancient and Modern. An Anonymous Work Attributed to Sebastian Castellio* (New York, 1935). See also the rendering of the conflict between Calvin and Castellio by Stefan Zweig, *Castellio gegen Calvin oder Ein Gewissen gegen die Gewalt* (Vienna, Leipzig, and Zurich, 1936). Zweig also gives the infamous quote from Theodore Beza (1519–1605): 'Libertas conscientiae diabolicum dogma,' or in English; 'Freedom of conscience is the dogma of the devil' (p. 238).

[27] Castellio, *De haereticis*, p. 208 (English translation: p. 203).

thoroughly.[28] He, too, had become aware of the Reformation's failure. Good advice is costly and has even become, as he states, life-threatening. The risk of being branded a heretic is great also within Protestantism. Many therefore keep quiet. Castellio takes the risk.

He makes a comparison with a general who did not know how to cross a river with his army because the river had become too turbulent. Being at a loss, he gathered all his soldiers and gave them permission to come to him at any moment, even in the middle of the night, if they thought they had found a solution to the problem. By thus appealing to the responsibility of his soldiers, he finally found someone who could give the correct advice. Doubt is necessary, Castellio believes. People often accept things uncritically when they should doubt. In this critical phase in the history of the Reformation everybody should be able to speak up. He appeals to the divine gift of reason. Christ may be God's son, reason is God's daughter. Conscience is founded on reason. Therefore doubt is necessary.

The main reason for the failure of the Reformation is, according to him, the way in which *sola Scriptura* is put into practice. He regards the reformers' biblicism as deadly. 'If they continue to cling to the Scriptures in this way,' he writes, 'they will never achieve more than the present results, namely that, biting one another, they will consume each other.'

He mentions as an example the way in which the doctrine of predestination was based by the Protestant theologians on one verse from Romans 9, in which Paul puts the words into God's mouth that He had loved Jacob and hated Esau even before they were born. Castellio regards it as absolute foolishness to deduct from a single statement in the New Testament that God would indeed have harboured such thoughts at the birth of those twins. One should not ascribe more authority to the authors of scripture than they themselves did. The Bible is indeed trustworthy, but in a special way. A new view of the Scriptures is necessary, he believes. He advocates a relational interpretation of the Bible. One should use common sense when reading the Holy Scriptures. Literally he says, 'Reason is God's language, much older and more certain than the Scriptures and religion'.[29]

In this work Castellio also included a fascinating dialogue about the Trinity, ostensibly from an anonymous author – he knows the risks! One of the participants is Athanasius. Castellio repeats verbatim the

---

[28] The text, written in 1563, was not fully published until 1937. A Dutch translation was provided by A. Dirkzwager Czn and A. C. Nielson, *Sebastiaan Castellio 1515–1563. De kunst van twijfelen en geloven, niet weten en weten* (The Hague, 1953).

[29] Dirkzwager Czn and Nielson, *De kunst van het twijfelen*, pp. 24 ff.

contents of the creed which carries Athanasius's name, including all anathemas. The other participant deals with the arguments and states that God would be rather fickle if Athanasius were right. According to Athanasius, after the year 325 Christians would be condemned to eternal hellfire, merely because they rejected ideas which were not held by any of the believers before 325. Although Castellio does not clearly take the position of Unitarianism, but regards this question as one of the open debatable ones, his sympathy for the anonymous participant is undeniable.[30]

Mockingly he also speaks about the doctrine of original sin, as it had been developed in the theological reflection and of liturgy of Reformed Protestantism. There is reason enough for criticism of those church reformers, is his opinion:

> They themselves admit openly that they are wicked. The same people who boast not only that they are Christians but church reformers as well, daily confess openly, solemnly, while the whole congregation affirms it loudly, that they are inclined towards all evil, unfit for any good and that they continually transgress God's holy commandments by their sins. Now I ask you in all conscience: Is it possible to say something about the most criminal people that ever existed which is worse than what these so-called Christians daily proclaim from the housetops? And witnesses to prove the crimes that they continually commit are not necessary, because they confess them openly, unasked for and without compulsion.

Nevertheless, these church reformers cannot bear any criticism.[31]

So Castellio, too, states the failure of Reformed Protestantism. 'Posterity will not be able to understand this,' he writes, 'that once again we have to live in such a thick darkness, while the light had risen.'[32] Just as Acontius he advocates a free open discussion and tolerance. More than Acontius he stresses the value of reason, the gift of God that precedes the gift of the Holy Scriptures and may therefore have the final say. Much more emphatically he distances himself from the teachings in Geneva. Perhaps Acontius would have reckoned him among those who, for the very reason of intolerance of the church leaders, were pushed towards more radical views.

---

[30] Ibid., pp. 52–7.

[31] Ibid., p. 10.

[32] Zweig, *Castellio gegen Calvin*, included this statement as a motto at the beginning of his book.

V

The culprit

We know whom Castellio had in mind, whom he saw as the culprit, by whose actions, according to him, the Reformation threatened to become a failure: John Calvin, whose image watches over the inner court of the building of the Theological University in Kampen. Who did Acontius have in mind when he criticized the spokesmen of the Reformation? In his work he deliberately omits to mention any names. It is his opinion that the theologians of his time already abused one another more than enough, that all too easily people were discredited. At the same time his criticism is undoubtedly called forth by certain events and conflicts. In England he personally experienced how the Bishop of London, whom he had met and learnt to appreciate in Strasburg, and the Dutch consistory, especially by the prompting of Nicholas des Gallars a pastor who had come from Geneva, had been driven to ever more severe measures. He will undoubtedly have known what des Gallars had reported about him to Calvin.[33]

While most other leaders of Reformed Protestantism were still hesitating about the position of the church, Calvin had drawn the lines. That is why it was not without reason that Acontius especially pointed to the writing of institutes, in which theological spokesmen had developed all-inclusive views, which were forced on to all believers. In my opinion Acontius thought, when writing his *Satanae Stratagemata*, as did Castellio, first of Calvin and his disciples Theodore Beza (1519–1605) and des Gallars. It was they above all whom he deemed responsible for the failure of the Reformation.

Disillusionment

In a certain sense he knew a similar disillusionment to Philip C. Holtrop, by whom one of the most remarkable studies on Calvin has been published.[34] As a member of the Christian Reformed Church he felt closely allied to Calvin. Motivated by this relationship Holtrop began his study of Calvin's conflict with Jerome Bolsec, the physician who attacked Calvin because of his teachings on predestination. Holtrop trawled through all the acts, all the letters, all writings and eventually

---

[33] Jelsma, *Adriaan van Haemstede*, pp. 206 ff.

[34] Philip C. Holtrop, *The Bolsec Controversy on Predestination, from 1551 to 1555: the Statements of Jerome Bolsec and the Responses of John Calvin, Theodore Beza, and Other Reformed Theologians*, 2 vols (New York and Ontario, 1993).

came to the shocking discovery how much Calvin reacted with paranoia to all criticism, how much he ascribed divine authority to his theological views, which in the end made a free expression of opinion impossible. This attitude meant disaster for every attempt at reformation.

Of course, Holtrop realized that his own circle would not be pleased with this view of Calvin, and that others could paint a much more positive picture. The reason for this, he wrote, is that most authors base their opinion solely on the ideas which Calvin developed in his best-known writings and on apologetic biographies of Beza and others. Holtrop believes that whoever really studies the sources, cannot arrive at any other picture of Calvin than the one he himself has drawn. Indeed, my predecessor as professor in Church History in Kampen, J. Plomp, similarly discovered this when, for his dissertation, he researched the way in which under Calvin's leadership discipline was exercised in Geneva. People were kept from the Lord's Supper and imprisoned when they dared to sing a song mocking Calvin.[35]

VI

Negative experiences

It was experiences like these which, in the 1550s and 1560s, led independent thinkers like Acontius, Castellio and many others to their critical considerations of the Reformation. Because of their convictions they had broken with the old church. Unlike Erasmus they had risked their lives for an actual renewal of the church. Consciously they had embraced Reformed Protestantism, because they thought that there the Reformation had the best chance to succeed. Characteristic of a real reformation was, to them, the principle of freedom of conscience. Every believer should have the opportunity to read the Scriptures independently and to be inspired by God's Spirit. That freedom, however, was threatened and restricted by growing confessionalism. Besides, as was stated especially by Castellio, the new view of the Scriptures had caused a biblicism which had led more to constraint than to freedom of conscience. It was their conviction that these were the causes why the Reformation had eventually failed.

It is an interesting question as to whether or not they were correct. To a certain extent they were. An ideological edifice such as Calvinism offered, albeit beautiful, is more conducive to doctrinal disputes than to

---

[35] J. Plomp, *De kerkelijke tucht bij Calvijn* (Kampen, 1969).

seeking and finding God. The history of Reformed Protestantism has proved this time and again. There is, however, another side to this. The same force that, due to the clash of personalities and views, drove figures like Castellio to ever more radical ideas, convinced leaders like Calvin and Beza ever more of the need to fence in Protestant theology, to seal it off, to build it into a system. What is most remarkable in the history of the Swiss Reformation is not that somebody like Calvin became too rigid in the end, but that also more moderate leaders like Heinrich Bullinger (1504–75) eventually followed him.

Calvinism and Counter-Reformation

It can be historically demonstrated that precisely this, at times, forced unity of doctrine gave Reformed Protestantism the power to be influential in the history of religion. One can say the same thing of Reformed Protestantism as of Roman Catholicism. Before the Council of Trent (1545) a renewal movement had begun on a large scale, a Catholic Reformation, which had raised high expectations in many people. It was, however, sacrificed in the struggle against Protestantism to build the stronghold of the Counter-Reformation. So, a hardening had taken place. Before 1545 within Catholicism one could state things for which after 1545 one ended up at the stake. Therefore it is correct to state that this Catholic Reformation failed, but because of this the Counter-Reformation succeeded. In a similar way one can say that the Reformed Reformation as many had envisaged it failed, but because of that Calvinism triumphed.

This was the broad picture that the Arminian pastor Geeraert Brandt painted in the seventeenth century in his famous book, *Historie der Reformatie en andere Kerkelijke Geschiedenissen in en ontrent de Nederlanden* (History of the Reformation and other Church Events in and around The Netherlands).[36] In his dedication to one of the regents of Amsterdam Brandt describes what originally had been the intent, the richness and the power of the Reformation: the constraint of conscience taken away, the Scriptures, which the papacy had denied the people, put into the hands of everybody. 'Strangling, burning, slashing has finished.' But soon things changed, he noticed. Piety had to give way to subtle scholarship. The spiritual leaders confirmed their judgements with anathemas. And churches were once again turned into dungeons. As did Acontius and others, he too calls on the believers to look for their unity not in confessions or a catechism, but in

---

[36] Geeraert Brandt, *Historie der Reformatie en andere Kerkelijke Geschiedenissen in en ontrent de Nederlanden* (Amsterdam, 1671).

love, which he calls the mother of tolerance. It was of little avail, although precisely those families of regents – to which Brandt dedicated his book – did ensure, along the lines of Acontius, that constraint of conscience and religious persecution were soon a thing of the past in The Netherlands.[37]

---

[37] The same tolerance was displayed by the English government. In an extensive letter to the Bishop of London Acontius pointed to the remarkable phenomenon that he had been denied the membership of the refugee churches, while the English church was obliged by law to accept him as a member if he wished it. Therefore Collinson states in *Archbishop Grindal*, p. 152:

> What Acontius could not have foreseen (and within two years he was dead, not long after the publication of his *Stratagems of Satan*) was that the tolerant latitudinarianism and advanced adiaphorism of which he was a lonely advocate would have a more secure future in the Church of England than Calvinism.

CHAPTER SEVEN

The attack of Reformed Protestantism on society's mentality in the northern Netherlands during the second half of the sixteenth century

I

A small minority

Since L. J. Rogier introduced and could underpin his thesis that in the northern Netherlands 'the majority of the people were *made* Protestant, did not *become* it',[1] various researchers have tackled the question of in what way those small Reformed nuclei have tried to influence the general mentality, and to what extent they have succeeded. It is not contested that the Reformed (or Calvinist) church was indeed a minority and that it remained such, despite the preferential treatment it received from the government throughout the sixteenth century. In rural areas the situation was even more serious. Here, the Reformed variant often had to be imposed fully from the outside, from above. Rogier summarized the situation tersely and adequately: 'The small groups in the cities became the centres of propaganda, which sent ministers to the deserted churches in the country. The first preachers in the villages were generals without an army.' He even qualifies the Reformed actions as 'evidence of the most impudent terror by a minority'.[2]

---

[1] Italics are L. J. Rogier's.

[2] L. J. Rogier, *Geschiedenis van het Katholicisme in Noord-Nederland in de 16e en de 17e eeuw*, 2 vols and index, 2nd edn (Amsterdam, 1947), vol. I. pp. 439, 442, 513. See, among others, I. Schöffer, 'De opstand in de Nederlanden, 1566–1609', in *De Lage Landen 1500–1780*, eds I. Schöffer, H. van der Wee, and J. A. Bornewasser, 4th edn (Amsterdam, 1988), pp. 103–65: 'However much the Prince of Orange had wanted freedom of religion and striven after it, in the fierce battle the Calvinist minorities had gained the upper hand everywhere, and in every city they had first established the new Church, then extended it, and finally given it a monopoly position.' (p. 126); or P. Geyl, *Geschiedenis van de Nederlandse Stam*, 6 vols (Amsterdam and Antwerp, 1961–62), vol. I. p. 286:

In spite of all the support from the authorities, and despite its identification with the rebellion, the growth of the Reformed church, and thus also its grip on the population, remained limited. This is all the more remarkable since elsewhere in Europe society often complied, without much pressure, with the rule which had been established in Augsburg in 1555: *cuius regio, illius et religio*. And so, the secular authorities, an extremely small minority, determined the particular variant of Christianity to which the population had to belong, and which way of life was in agreement with this. A process of confessionalization and equalization took place. Stakes became rarer. The wandering craftsmen and merchants, of which in France and the German Empire quite a few were Reformed, less often encountered the stench of charred human remains on entering a city. Of course, not everyone was happy with the ecclesiastical policies of his or her authorities, but usually such dissidents had the opportunity to seek out rulers elsewhere in the world who showed more respect for their way of believing, or even demanded it. But most complied. Thus the population of a number of Swiss cities had become Reformed, a series of German principalities or cities had pursued the Lutheran reformation, other regions had remained Roman Catholic, the Scandinavian countries had adopted the Lutheran variant, and there were certain regions assigned to the Antitrinitarian faith. Despite a drawn-out civil war, even in France a certain equilibrium had emerged: some regions had become mainly Reformed, while others had remained faithful to Catholicism. As a result, for some time France was the example *par excellence* of a nation in which two variants of believing could exist side by side.[3]

It was, therefore, in line with the generally accepted approach when the rebellious Dutch provinces, after initial hesitation mainly due to William of Orange's religious policies, chose one 'religion', namely Reformed Protestantism. One may have expected the majority of the population to comply with this choice. Yet throughout the sixteenth

---

Before 1567 Calvinism had been weak in Holland ... Now nothing could stand against the stern organization and the purposefulness of the Reformed. They had taken possession of the positions of power in the provinces; conversely, the authorities recognized them as the state church, which could unite the subjects in the struggle against Spain.

[3] A clear picture of the situation in France is painted by Menna Prestwich, 'Calvinism in France, 1559–1629', in *International Calvinism 1541–1715*, ed. Menna Prestwich, 2nd edn (Oxford, 1986), pp. 71–109. Besides, some imperial cities were exempted from the ruling by the Diet of Augsburg, which meant that there, too, two 'religions' were tolerated side by side. This ruling pertained only to the Catholic and Lutheran traditions. See, among others, H. Tüchle, *Geschiedenis van de Kerk in tien delen*, vol. V, *Reformatie*, trans. H. Wagemans (Hilversum, 1968), pp. 149–51.

century the Reformed church comprised a minority of the population, and it succeeded in shaping life only to a limited degree. This is all the more remarkable if one realizes how much discontent the religious persecution under Philip II's rule had aroused, how much the pope, too, identified rebellion with anti-Catholicism, and to what degree the authorities supported the Reformed church with placards and ordinances.

Alastair Duke gave a number of reasons for the slow growth of Reformed Protestantism in the free provinces. In spite of the stern language of the placards, the city magistrates offered but little support to the process of protestantization. The rural population in particular showed a tenacious attachment to the old 'religion' and the way of life it had tolerated. In addition, the battlefronts were changing regularly. So, it was advisable to be cautious in adopting a divergent ecclesiastical structure. A fourth reason, however, was due to the Reformed's own actions: the way in which they protected access to the Lord's Supper, in other words, the way in which they had made discipline one of the marks of the true church. As a result the church continued to distinguish sharply between those who belonged to the kingdom of God and those who belonged to the world. Another consequence was that the Reformed church could never fully identify the struggle for freedom with the restoration of the true church. In ecclesiastical policies the latter continued to have priority.[4]

II

An area of tension

This last point in particular is worthy of further consideration. Indeed, with respect to the struggle for freedom, an area of tension can be detected between William of Orange (in his function as the highest authority) and the Reformed consistories. Initially, the consistories were

---

[4] Alastair Duke, 'The Ambivalent Face of Calvinism in the Netherlands 1561–1618', in *International Calvinism*, ed. Menna Prestwich, 2nd edn (Oxford, 1986), pp. 109–34:

> An important, and rather neglected, obstacle to the rapid growth of the Reformed churches in the northern Netherlands was self-imposed, for the Dutch Calvinists insisted that access to Communion should be restricted to those who had placed themselves under the 'discipline of Christ'. In this way they drew a distinction between 'those of the Church' and the 'children of the world'. And the patriotism of the diehard Calvinist was tempered by his conviction that the cause of the Gospel should take precedence over 'the restoration of the Netherlands'. (p. 113).

ahead of Orange. P. Geyl characterizes the relations excellently: 'Orange wanted to bridle at least the Calvinists. He was quite irritated by their tendency to take an ell if they were given an inch, and he praised the respect for the authorities which characterized the Lutherans in comparison with their intractability.' He expressly warned his brother Louis 'that he would spoil everything by encouraging the Calvinists'.[5] At this stage, the Reformed consistories, which then played a significant role mainly in the southern Netherlands, made an active contribution to the resistance, inspired by the example of the French Calvinists.

A few years later the situation changed. William of Orange showed himself to be the pre-eminent leader of the revolt. Increasingly, he felt obliged to identify with the Reformed Protestants. 'Orange himself had moved more and more toward the Calvinists. No other helpers, as zealous and faithful, offered themselves.'[6] They alone appeared to possess the resilience and the perseverance that were indispensable for the success of the rebellion. In 1571, through his envoy Marnix of St Aldegonde, Orange hoped that the Reformed that had fled abroad and the Protestants who held their meetings secretly in The Netherlands itself, would openly support battle. In Bedburg, delegates from various regions had come together with the intention of organizing a synod at Emden in that same year, which would represent all Dutch Reformed. Orange hoped that he then would receive the unconditional support of Reformed Protestantism even more manifestly than had happened in Bedburg at Marnix's request. To his disappointment, however, the delegates in Emden refused to take a stand on the rebellion. So the tables had turned. Now Orange was running ahead of the Reformed consistories.[7] The synod was now exclusively aimed at organizing ecclesiastical life according to a typically Reformed model. In Duke's words: 'the cause of the Gospel should take precedence over "the restoration of the Netherlands"'.

---

[5] P. Geyl, *Geschiedenis Nederlandse Stam*, vol. I. pp. 248, 249. See also I. Schöffer, 'De opstand in de Nederlanden', p. 119: 'Calvinists, Sea Beggars and refugees had ... established close links.'

[6] Geyl, *Geschiedenis Nederlandse Stam*, vol. I, p. 265.

[7] See J. J. Woltjer, 'De politieke betekenis van de Emdense synode', in *De synode van Emden 1571–1971*, eds D. Nauta, J. P. van Dooren and Otto J. de Jong (Kampen, 1971), pp. 22–49; W. F. Dankbaar, *Hoogtepunten uit het Nederlandsche Calvinisme in de zestiende eeuw* (Haarlem, 1946), pp. 41–85. The text of the meeting is in Bedburg in J. F. G. Goeters, *400 Jahre Bedburger Synode* (Jülig, 1971), pp. 18, 19. The text of the synod at Emden is in *Die Akten der Synode der Niederländischen Kirchen zu Emden vom 4.–13. Oktober 1571*, ed. J. F. Gerhard Goeters (Neukirchen, 1571). See on the complex relations also Auke Jelsma, 'The 'Weakness of Conscience' in the Reformed Movement in the Netherlands: the Attitude of the Dutch Reformation to the Use of Violence between 1562 and 1574' in *The Church and War*, Studies in Church History, 20, ed. W. J. Sheils (Oxford, 1983), p. 217–29.

At the Provincial Synod of Holland and Zeeland, held at Dordrecht in 1574, those present decided to remain faithful to this policy. They did not wish to make statements on political or secular matters, as, for example, the war or the way in which the States made their policies: 'The ministers and elders will see to it that in the consistories, classes and synods, they will not deal with other than ecclesiastical matters.'[8] That this principle was maintained is all the more remarkable since such an ordinance is missing in the Scottish and French church orders. It is not easy to ascertain what was the exact motivation of the Reformed churches in The Netherlands to introduce such a strict separation between ecclesiastical and secular matters. This regulation looks more Lutheran or Anabaptist than specifically Calvinistic. It is possible that precisely because of the tense relations in a war situation, the consistories did not wish to be a hindrance to the authorities. Thus there was no need to worry about the often ruthless manner in which the war was waged. It seems likely to me, however, that the motive Duke mentioned also played a role. The consistories had priorities other than the authorities. It was difficult enough, being in a minority position, to rectify the ecclesiastical life in general and to purify people's way of life from all that, from a Calvinistic point of view, was sinful, idolatrous or superstitious.

This orientation toward ecclesiastical matters shows itself in a special way in a letter that the Dordrecht minister Bartholdus Wilhelmi sent on 23 October 1573 to the Dutch refugee church in London, where he was minister until 1572. He could report some good news. After an extremely critical phase in the battle, there had been a welcome development on three fronts. Two of these concerned the war. Alkmaar had been able to resist 'Don Frederik's army of executioners'[9] and had now been relieved. In addition, the Sea Beggars had succeeded in virtually destroying the Spanish fleet which was financed by Amsterdam. During this action, the Count of Bossu, Alva's governor for Holland, Zeeland and Utrecht, had been taken prisoner. As a result the Sea Beggars controlled the Zuider Zee and could execute their raids on the coasts of Holland and Friesland unhindered. The most important news was mentioned first. William of Orange had become a member of the Reformed church and had celebrated the

---

[8] 'De dienaers ende ouderlinghen sullen wel voor hen sien datse niet en handelen inden consistorien, classen ende synoden, dan 't ghene dat kerckelick is', F. L. Rutgers, *Acta van de Nederlandsche Synoden der zestiende eeuw* (The Hague, 1889), p. 149. Later, this regulation became part of the church order, as it was established at the National Synod of Dordrecht in 1578, ibid., p. 240.

[9] P. Geyl, *Geschiedenis Nederlandse Stam*, vol. I. p. 281.

Lord's Supper in this church.[10] This message was the first item on the list.

One could say that at that moment the two, William of Orange and the Reformed consistories, finally kept pace with one another. On their part, the Reformed consistories acknowledged Orange as the highest authority, also with respect to the struggle for freedom, while Orange in turn accepted that the Reformed consistories would refrain from statements on the revolt,[11] not because they denied its legitimacy, but because their tasks pertained to a different area. Just as the consistories refused to make explicit statements on the rebellion, although they supported it, so Orange refused to fulfil the Reformed's wish to facilitate the persecution of dissenters, although he himself had joined the Reformed church. Based on this equilibrium, the Reformed church could now attempt to purify Dutch society from all the unrighteousness that it thought to encounter there.

In practice, this equilibrium appeared to be precarious enough. The central authorities were, in general and to a certain degree, prepared to

---

[10] J. H. Hessels, *Epistulae et Tractatus cum Reformationis tum Ecclesiae Londino-Batavae Historiam Illustrantes (1542–1622)*, 4 vols (Canterbury, 1887–89), vol. II. p. 469:

> And finally, brothers, I could not hide from you the grace that God has bestowed on us, first, that the Prince of Orange, our devout stadholder, has come to the church, has broken the bread of the Lord with the congregation, and has subjected himself to its discipline, which is not to be regarded a small thing. Secondly, that the army of the godless tyrant had to break up from Alkmaar and had to leave in shame. Thirdly, that our ships on the Zuiderzee have put to shame all the warships of Amsterdam.

(Ten laesten broeders en hebbe ick ulieden niet konnen verbergen die genade die ons Godt bewesen heeft, voereerst dat die Prince van Orangien onse godtsalige stadthouder hem tot der gemeinte begeven, het broot des Heeren metter gemeinte gebroken, ende hem de discipline onderworpen heeft, het welcke niet kleijn te achten en is. Ten tweden, dat het legher des godtlosen Tijrans van Alcmaer heeft moeten opbreken ende met scande heeft moeten ruijmen. Ten derden dat onse Schepen op die Zuijzerzee alle die oirloch schepen van Amsterdam te scande gemaect hebben.)

[11] This does not mean that the consistories did not also inform one another concerning military matters. So an elder of the Dutch church in London writes a letter to his London brothers from Flushing on 2 October 1572, in which he accurately mentions all the reports he has received. Once in a while, something of a moral judgement shines through in his reporting. When he has described how William of Orange 'has taken all their money and goods' ('alle haerlieder ghelt ende goet berooft') from the priests, monasteries and burghers in a certain place, he adds: 'which is a piteous start, but it needs a good end' ('dwelck een compasselick begin es, maer het strecke tot eenen goeden fine'). Without any comment he passes on how Orange has taken possession of Venlo: by killing the inhabitants. From a large part of the troops of van Batenburg encamped there, he had the right hand cut off. See J. H. Hessels, *Epistulae et Tractatus*, pp. 430–36.

enforce ecclesiastical ordinances. However, one of the problems was that the motivation to participate in the rebellion varied in The Netherlands. For some it was a matter of religious freedom, others wished to restore the legal status of the Dutch nobility, while city magistrates mainly hoped to regain their privileges. What the central authorities deemed necessary, was to the local or provincial authorities sometimes a matter of minor importance. Regulations by the States General were not automatically adopted by all the provinces.[12] Measures which the church wished to introduce with the aid of the highest authority, were often boycotted at the local level. It may be that, finally, Orange having become Reformed, this was no guarantee that the local regents wished to follow his example. This resulted in the situation, exceptional for the religious relations at that time, that only a minority of the population was willing to join the church which was the only one publicly acknowledged. Against this background, investigation of the way in which the Reformed church tried to launch a campaign of protestantization by means of its 'major assemblies' is necessary.[13]

III

The disciplinary offensive of a small élite

According to Duke, the exercise of discipline as was common in the Reformed church in The Netherlands was an important reason why, here in particular, Calvinism gained ground only gradually. Ten per cent of the population at most joined the church. Membership was only available to those who were willing to publicly pronounce their agreement with Reformed teachings. This included acceptance of the supervision the consistory wished to exercise over their beliefs and lives. The percentage of those who sympathized with Protestantism in general must have been higher. In the first half of the sixteenth century, under the influence of writings like those of Erasmus and Luther, and because they abhorred the way in which the old church tried to maintain its position of power, many had moved toward a freer view

---

[12] See for the way in which the various provinces were prepared to grant special privileges to the Reformed, O. J. de Jong, 'Unie en religie', in *De Unie van Utrecht. Wording en werking van een verbond en een verbondsacte*, eds S. Groenveld and H. L. P. Leeuwenberg (The Hague, 1979), pp. 155–81.

[13] In Reformed ecclesiastical law 'major assemblies' are understood to be all regional, provincial or national ecclesiastical gatherings at which delegates from the churches meet: classis, provincial synod and national synod.

of the church.[14] It was precisely the religious freedom which they had appropriated that created a reluctance to subject themselves anew to a similar yoke. Thus they wanted to become Protestants, but not Reformed. To them, the Reformed variant had come too late. Besides, soon it became obvious that the Reformed ecclesiastical model would mould their lives to a much higher degree than had ever been possible under Catholicism. And so this church remained in a minority. 'A consistory, supported by classis and synod, as an instrument with which militant Calvinists wanted to impose their views on the congregation, met with the resistance of many.'[15]

And yet, this explanation is not fully satisfactory. The Reformed consistories in The Netherlands had only in mind what Reformed Protestantism as a 'Second Reformation' wished to achieve elsewhere in Europe, namely to realize now, in the wake of the *reformatio doctrinae* as it had been started by the Lutheran Reformation, a *reformatio vitae*.[16] Elsewhere the population had conformed to such a denomination to a much larger extent, if, that is, the authorities had chosen this particular variant, even if the initiative had originally been taken by a small minority. The practice of discipline, which was part of the Reformed ecclesiastical model, was to a number of the authorities a decisive reason for choosing it. As Robert M. Kingdon wrote, precisely 'its tradition of consistorial discipline' was attractive to governments. 'It gave them a new effective and efficient way to control their populations. Calvinism thus appealed to these governments as a way to secure social control.'[17]

---

[14] This is obvious from the tempestuous growth of the Anabaptist movement in the 1530s, and from the impetuosity of the 'breaking of the images', but also from the lists of people who, in the 1560s, presented themselves in various places to the magistrates with requests for a church building; a large number of those names are not to be found among the first groups of communicants in the Reformed church. See, for example, F. van der Pol, *De reformatie te Kampen*, dissertation (Kampen, 1990), p. 256. See also A. C. F. Koch, 'The Reformation at Deventer in 1579–1580. Size and Social Structure of the Catholic Section of the Population during the Religious Peace', in *Acta Historiae Neerlandicae*, eds B. H. Slicher van Bath, J. A. Kossman, H. Balthazar, A. Th. van Deursen, W. Prevenier and J. J. Woltjer (The Hague, 1973), vol. VI, pp. 27–66.

[15] J. J. Woltjer, *'Een niew ende onghesien dingh'. Verkenningen naar de positie van de kerkeraad in twee Hollandse steden in de zestiende eeuw* (Leiden, 1985), p. 4.

[16] See for an introduction to this subject Paul Münch, 'Volkskultur und Calvinismus. Zu Theorie und Praxis der "Reformatio Vitae" während der "Zweiten Reformation"', in *Die reformierte Konfessionalisierung in Deutschland – Das Problem der 'Zweiten Reformation'*, ed. Heinz Schilling (Gütersloh, 1986), pp. 291–307. It seems to me that the term 'Second Reformation' is only acceptable if it includes both the Anabaptist and the Reformed reformations.

[17] Robert M. Kingdon, 'Calvin and the Establishment of Consistory Discipline in Geneva: the Institution and the Men Who Directed It', *Nederlands Archief voor Kerkgeschiedenis*, 70 (1990), pp. 158–72, quote p. 168.

In the second half of the sixteenth century there must have been a general feeling that something was lacking in life, that society had serious shortcomings, that there were symptoms of disease and that the Christianization of the population had failed. This was not just people's experience in regions where governments had chosen the Reformed ecclesiastical model: 'The early modern era is characterized by a disciplinary offensive of élite groups, people in authority of various inclinations, who attempt to impose several codes of conduct on "others" by (sometimes subtle) coercive measures.'[18]

Thanks to research into social history, it has become more obvious how much society before the invention of the printing-press was determined by popular culture, and only superficially Christianized. Until late into the fifteenth century, the written word remained mainly the domain of the clergy. The people, the majority of whom were illiterate, lived by the traditions handed down from generation to generation. The clergy did, to some degree, try to influence popular culture by means of sermons and miracle plays, but in general they left it unhindered as long as their authority was not undermined.

Since the eleventh century, a second 'writing élite' was added to the clergy, men who had received their education at universities and Latin schools and who managed to achieve important positions at courts and city tribunals. This resulted in a gradual shift in the later Middle Ages. More often the church was confronted by people who could not only experience but also understand what happened in the Latin liturgy. An increasing number of people began to distance themselves from what they experienced as superstition and idolatry. Against this background one should also view the revival of the Modern Devotion, which strove for moderation of the Christian life, without the trappings of popular culture. Only the invention of the printing-press and the unfolding of the languages of the people that came with it, made it possible to really develop the Christianizing offensive on a large scale. Despite all the attachment to the traditional culture, the desire among the people for more education, for active involvement in the ecclesiastical life, for knowledge of the Bible which made it possible for them to bring their lives in line with biblical norms, must have become greater and greater. Only in this way can the effect of the Reformation and the vehemence of a phenomenon like the 'breaking of the images' be understood. This way of believing can

---

[18] This is how Willem Frijthof summarizes this point of view; 'Vraagtekens bij het vroegmoderne kersteningsoffensief', in *Religieuze Volkscultuur. De spanning tussen de voorgeschreven orde en de geleefde praktijk*, eds Gerard Rooijakkers and Theo van der Zee (Nijmegen, 1986), pp. 71–98, quote p. 72.

only become more general after it has become possible to distribute books at a large scale. Churches can only start to function in this way after the invention of the printing-press, and after this invention's consequences have had a chance to result in a wider offer of education ... Therefore, only in the course of the sixteenth century does this development become possible at all.[19]

So, the fact that a small élite tried to impose its norms and values on the rest of society was not a specific characteristic of Reformed Protestantism in The Netherlands. That situation could be found everywhere in Europe. The population appeared to be willing to be guided by this élite to a large extent. Usually this led to the general acceptance of the ecclesiastical model which the élite preferred. Thanks to the invention of the 'elder' and the exercise of discipline, the Reformed model appeared to offer special opportunities for disciplining people's conduct.[20]

In the liberated provinces of The Netherlands a specific situation existed. The national and provincial authorities recognized the opportunities the Reformed ecclesiastical model in particular offered toward 'a new and effective and efficient way to control their populations'. Therefore, they usually appeared to be willing to hinder the expressions of other religious variants and to propagate the Reformed model by means of placards. But precisely this intertwining of the interests of the Reformed church with those of the authorities created problems. Local and regional authorities often sought to prevent all too effective control by central government. As a consequence they were prepared only to a limited degree to look energetically after the interests of the Reformed 'religion'. Of course, the central authorities' grip on society did increase steadily. That is why in the Republic of the Netherlands also, major assemblies like classis and synod could eventually continue their Christianizing offensive with a reasonable measure of success. This, however, did not lead to a situation in which the majority of the population was prepared to join. Despite the area of tension between local and na-

---

[19] A. T. van Deursen, 'Volkscultuur in wisselwerking met de elitecultuur in de vroegmoderne tijd', in *Religieuze Volkscultuur. De spanning tussen de voorgeschreven orde en de geleefde praktijk*, eds Gerard Rooijkkers and Theo van der Zee (Nijmegen, 1986), p. 60. See for a comparison with the development in other parts of Europe the several contributions in the second part of *Histoire vécue du peuple chrétien*, ed. Jean Delumeau, 2 vols (Toulouse, 1979), vol. I. 2e partie: 'L'offensive chrétienne'. The contributions of Aleksander Gieysztor, Francis Rapp and Bernard Vogler in particular contain valuable material for comparisons.

[20] See the above mentioned articles of Robert M. Kingdon and Paul Münch in notes 17 and 16 respectively. Not only in The Netherlands but also in Scotland the process of Protestantization did not proceed as smoothly as was generally assumed, as is obvious from Michael Lynch's essay, 'Calvinism in Scotland, 1559–1638', in *International Calvinism 1541–1715*, ed. M. Prestwich, 2nd edn (Oxford, 1986), pp. 225–56.

tional/provincial authorities and despite religious differences, here too, one did become aware, as at this stage of history one did everywhere else in Europe, that the way of life of most of the population had to change to some degree. Popular culture had to make way for the ethics which the emerging bourgeoisie regarded as necessary for a well-functioning society. The Reformed church actively co-operated in this. Therefore it is worth analysing this policy in more detail.

An important aid for this is the model that German scholars have developed to analyse and compare the Christianizing offensive as it took place in the sixteenth century. They distinguish seven aspects:

1. Establishing clear-cut principles.
2. Spreading and implementing new norms.
3. Propaganda and the prevention of counter-propaganda.
4. Education.
5. Disciplining the adherents in a stricter sense.
6. Influencing the language.
7. The use of rites.[21]

I think it is worth analysing in more detail the classical and synodal acts, as far as they have now appeared in print, applying these seven stages.

IV

The policies of major assemblies

Establishing clear-cut principles   In The Netherlands, it appeared to be far from easy to find one common denominator for the various Reformed groups which regarded themselves more or less akin to the Swiss Reformation. For Reformed Protestantism was the last of the reforming waves that had flowed into the Low Countries from Germany, Switzerland and France (if they did not spring from Dutch soil).

---

[21] O. Mörke, '"Konfessionalisierung" als politisch-soziales Strukturprinzip?', *Tijdschrift voor sociale geschiedenis*, 16/1, February (1990), pp. 31–60. He investigated this process of confessionalization mainly on the basis of some recent studies on the history of local reformation. This has a drawback in the sense that it was precisely the local authorities who often tried to obstruct the civilizing offensive that the central governments wanted to encourage. In this connection, see also J. J. Woltjer, 'Stadt und Reformation in den Niederlanden', in *Kirche und Gesellschaftlicher Wandel in Deutschen und Niederländischen Städten der Werdenden Neuzeit*, ed. Franz Petri (Cologne and Vienna, 1980), pp. 155–68.

Apparently, the spiritual leaders of the Dutch reformation were aware of the threat this plurality posed to the survival of Protestantism. While Orange saw the importance of all the Protestants coming together mainly in the united support of the right to rebel, the ministers who met in Emden valued especially the common acceptance of a church order and the signing of a confession of faith. It is not known in what way one succeeded in overcoming the resistance some had against such uniformity. It may be assumed that the power that comes with unity was most persuasive. This, at least, was the motivation that one of the signatories at Emden, Jan Arendsz, advanced two years later, when he urged all ministers at the Provincial Synod of Alkmaar to sign the Belgic Confession.[22]

In the ecclesiastical regulations of Emden it was agreed in what way the local church community would henceforth be structured. In line with the Reformed model from Switzerland and France, one chose the structure of a consistory, a form which made it possible for a small élite to organize and influence a whole community.[23]

The later synods, which were organized after 1572 in the liberated provinces, also, saw the importance of such a tight structure. From classical and synodal acts it is clear that in some places local resistance arose against this tight framework. Ministers who regarded it as much too compulsive often received support for this view from their magistrates. So in the acts of the Classis of Dordrecht there are several complaints about 'illegal ministers' who had not been called according to the regulations in the church order, about congregations who still had no 'legal consistory', about places where one adhered to a 'false doctrine' (namely the Lutheran one). Time and again it is decided in such cases to appeal to the highest authority, that is, William of Orange, to bridle the local ecclesiastical and secular authorities.[24]

---

[22] *Acta der Provinciale en Particuliere Synoden, gehouden in de Noordelijke Nederlanden gedurende de jaren 1572–1620*, eds J. Reitsma and S. D. van Veen, 8 vols (Groningen, 1892–98), vol. I. p. 7.

[23] For the text of the acts of Emden see F. L. Rutgers, *Acta zestiende eeuw*, pp. 42–119. Besides the Belgic (or Netherlands) Confession, the French Confession, which for a large part had been copied verbally, was accepted as a witness to an even wider fellowship. For instruction in the new teachings, the Heidelberg Catechism was prescribed for the Dutch situation. See the various contributions in *De Synode van Emden 1571–1971*, eds D. Nauta, J. P. van Dooren and Otto J. de Jong (Kampen, 1971).

[24] *Classicale Acta 1573–1620; Particuliere Synodes Zuid-Holland I: Classis Dordrecht 1573–1600*, ed. J. P. van Dooren (The Hague, 1980), *passim*. For an analysis of these acts see C. A. Tukker, *De classis Dordrecht van 1573 tot 1609*, dissertation (Leiden, 1965). An accurate overview of the most important issues that were discussed at the provincial and national synods is offered by R. H. Bremmer, *Reformatie en Rebellie* (Franeker, 1984), albeit in a somewhat apologetic way.

At the Provincial Synod of Dordrecht, 1574, the case of the Gorcum minister Henricus Rolandus was discussed; despite the magistrate's support for the preacher, the synod insisted on his being deposed, although the minister promised to behave better in the future. Besides this, the synod appealed to Orange to urge his officers to allow, also in rural areas, only those ministers who had a written declaration of approval from the classis.[25] The Caspar Coolhaes affair, which was discussed at several synods and classes, became notorious.[26]

Precisely with a view to uniformity, important additions were made to the existing church order at the National Synod of Middelburg (1581). Here it was stated that elders or deacons (or doctors) who administered the sacraments without being authorized to do so, would be treated as schismatics. Once more, it was decided that ministers should be linked with a certain congregation. Unattached, wandering ministers of the Word, free-wheelers (who were uncontrollable) were no longer accepted. A regulation was laid down, which was already being applied, that the consistory had to be subject to the classis, the classis to the particular synod, and the latter to the general synod. It was also decided to present this church order to the government in order that it would 'be confirmed by the authority of the same'.[27] So a network of churches came into existence, which were all placed under a central power, whose authority was enforced with the assistance of the central government. It seems that none of the ministers protested when Orange's lieutenant for North Holland, the Lord of Sonoy, 'who was little less insolent in North Holland than Lumey was in South Holland',[28] appeared in person at the Particular Synod of Alkmaar on 11 April 1575, arguing that it was his duty, just as previously at the great councils it had been the task of the emperors to maintain pure doctrine and to prevent discord.[29]

This Protestantizing offensive can best be compared with the way in which someone like Wynfrith-Boniface tried to combat both ecclesiastical plurality and pagan popular culture in the eighth century. As soon as he had the opportunity, he imposed a structure on the church which was characterized by centralization (each priest was tied to a place and subject to the bishop's authority; the bishops were subject to a national

[25] Rutgers, *Acta zestiende eeuw*, pp. 131 ff.

[26] See for the way in which the Caspar Coolhaes affair was discussed at several synods and classes, Bremmer, *Reformatie en Rebellie, passim*; and Woltjer, '*Een niew ende onghesien dingh*'. For the acts see Rutgers, *Acta zestiende eeuw, passim*.

[27] 'Ende doer de autoriteyt der selver befesticht te werden', Rutgers, *Acta zestiende eeuw*, pp. 376–412.

[28] Geyl, *Geschiedenis Nederlandse Stam*, vol. I. p. 278.

[29] *Acta Provinciale en Particuliere Synoden*, vol. I, p. 30.

synod, and the latter bound by the instructions of the pope), by the banishment of wandering clergy, by unity in the liturgy and by the prohibition of all expressions of what was judged to be superstition and idolatry.[30] In a similar way, by establishing general principles, in The Netherlands too, the first condition was met which was necessary for a small élite to be able to impose a set of norms on society.

Spreading and implementing new norms Whoever wants to introduce new morals and norms must possess a large measure of inflexibility. Boniface did not hesitate to make wandering bishops suspect before the highest ecclesiastical authority in Rome, where they could scarcely check his information, even if they had the support of secular authorities and were generally respected. This did not increase his popularity, but he had to pay that price if he was to influence and Christianize popular culture with a small élite of co-workers (who usually had come from England, like himself). Priests who did not follow the new rules were punished severely.

Sometimes, the Reformed churches, too, remained intransigent where the implementation of the new principles was concerned. As we have seen, the classis and the particular synod appealed to the highest authority if somewhere in a town or village a 'free-wheeler' tried to persevere with the help of local government. Earlier on, at the beginning of the 1560s, under pressure from the French refugee church in particular, Adriaan van Haemstede had been obliged to leave England with his pregnant wife and three children in winter, although the Dutch and French consistories knew that on the Continent a price had been set on his head. The only cogent reason was his opinion that Anabaptist refugees should have the same right as the Reformed to find shelter in

---

[30] See *Bonifatii Epistulae; Willibaldi Vita Bonifatii*, ed. Reinhold Rau (Darmstadt, 1968), pp. 376–89. See also Auke Jelsma, *De blaffende hond; aspecten uit het leven van Wynfreth Bonifatius* (The Hague, 1973), pp. 115–46:

> Thus the principle of this structure is that by obedience to one institution one gains freedom *vis-à-vis* another. The priest is free *vis-à-vis* his congregation and his lord thanks to his obedience to the bishop. The latter is able to really lead the priests within his jurisdiction and the ecclesiastical life in his region thanks to his obedience to the synodical consultations. The synod is free to regulate the ecclesiastical life in a national church, because it complies with the highest authority, canonical law, by which the entire ecclesiastical life is judged and which in this way becomes very dominant – an inevitable consequence of this structure (pp. 124, 125).

If we substitute several words (priest for minister, bishop for classis), this passage is applicable to the development of the church structure within Reformed Protestantism as well.

England.[31] Ultimately, independent personalities like Coolhaes could not persevere in the liberated provinces either. Skilfully they were manoeuvred out of the way, even though everybody in the Reformed churches was convinced that Coolhaes qualitatively excelled the majority of the first-generation ministers.

A striking aspect of this introduction of norms is the attention given to the ethics of marriage. Since the Roman Catholic legal procedures fell away, this is understandable, 'because the spiritual courts cease to exist, and for the ordinary magistrate marriage cases are quite new, especially in small towns and villages, so that they are often insufficiently considered, and separation from bed and board is easily permitted'.[32] As for the clandestine marriages, that is, marriages that had not been concluded officially by state or church, the Reformed church continued the policy that had been developed in the pre-Reformation period. The bishops from the early sixteenth century had already 'made the rules surrounding clandestine marriages ... more severe',[33] and, yet, these rules became even stricter in Reformed law, at least in principle. Secret promises of marriage were no longer acknowledged as binding, as had been customary, even if the marriage had been consummated. Rather than sexual intercourse, the promise uttered in public before state or church, with the consent of parents or guardians, was regarded as the actual conclusion of the marriage. This fits the Reformed tradition in which the word and not the (sacramental) act constitutes the heart of the matter. What the ministers combated above all was 'really every giving-in to the senses'.[34]

Also with respect to the prohibited degrees of blood relationship, the Reformed church continued the earlier tradition but, as in the case of

---

[31] For him and the way in which the refugee churches tried to exercise social control over their members, see Owe Boersma, *Vluchtig Voorbeeld; de Nederlandse, Franse en Italiaanse vluchtelingenkerken in Londen, 1568–1585*, dissertation (n.p., 1994), *passim*; Andrew Pettegree, *Foreign Protestant Communities in Sixteenth-Century London* (Oxford, 1986), pp. 149–214; A. J. Jelsma, *Adriaan van Haemstede en zijn martelaarsboek*, dissertation (The Hague, 1970), pp. 143–205.

[32] 'Overmits de gheestelicke hoven cesseren ende de houwelicxsaecken byde ordinaire magistraet besonder in cleyne stedekens ende dorpen seer nyew syn, dicwils niet genoech bewogen, ende lichtelick die echtscheydinge ter tafel ende te bedde toegelaten wort', Rutgers, *Acta zestiende eeuw*, p. 422 (National Synod of Middelburg, 1581).

[33] See P. Bange and A. G. Weiler, 'De problematiek van het clandestiene huwelijk in het middeleeuwse bisdom Utrecht', in *De Nederlanden in de late middeleeuwen*, eds D. E. H. de Boer and J. W. Marsilje (Utrecht, 1987), pp. 393–409.

[34] Herman Roodenburg, *Onder censuur: De kerkelijke tucht in de gereformeerde gemeente van Amsterdam, 1578–1700*, dissertation (Hilversum, 1990), p. 36. In the introduction he discusses the relationship between élite and popular culture. He too notes 'an increasing disciplining of society' in connection with ecclesiastical discipline in the northern Netherlands (p. 27).

the promises of marriage, it was much less prepared to grant dispensation than the previous spiritual courts had been. In 1581, for example, four reasons were enumerated why a nephew and a niece could not be allowed to marry: because of the offence it creates; it is not honourable; because it is contrary to the practice of most Reformed churches; and 'so that friendship may be better spread to other families'![35]

Poignant examples can be given of these prohibitions to marry. In 1581, Adriaan Simons from Benthuizen attempted to have the ecclesiastical condemnation of his second marriage annulled by means of an extensive letter. Thirty years previously his wife had died, leaving him with several small children. Her half-sister had helped him raise the children. After some time he had married her. He had been summoned before the pope for this. In the end he had received absolution. During the religious persecution, several times he had taken refugees into his home. He himself, as well as his second wife, had become Reformed through contacts with the refugees. However, the Reformed church had made it clear that his marriage was unlawful and had to be dissolved. But he considered it inhuman to leave his partner. They were old now and no longer had sexual intercourse, 'so that there is no coming together except for mutual love, help, comfort and advice'. He would like 'to keep the confession of my faith and the fellowship of the brothers and of the Lord's Supper'. But the synod was inexorable and decided: 'It has been judged that the marriage of Adriaen Symonss., living at Benthuysen on the hill, with the sister of his previous wife may not exist, and that, as a sign of his repentance, he must separate from her.'[36] As far as the synod was concerned, from now on the aged couple had to live without this mutual love, help, comfort and advice.

The marriage of a man with a woman who had previously been raped by his brother was declared unlawful because of incest. The couple was excommunicated. In the light of such cases it becomes understandable why the majority of the population hesitated to join the Reformed church.

Many regulations regarding the way of life concerned typical elements of popular culture, like dancing, acting, excessive baptismal and funeral meals, bell-ringing, fun-fairs and Saints' days. Begging and 'idling'

---

[35] 'Opdat de vriendtscap te beter tot andere geslachten mach uutghespreijdt werden', Rutgers, *Acta zestiende eeuw*, pp. 446, 447.

[36] Rutgers, *Acta zestiende eeuw*, pp. 370, 476–9. The original quotes are respectively: 'zoe datter gheen byeencoemste meer en is dan sonderlinghe lyefdde hulpe troost ende raet'; 'in die belydenisse myns geloofs ende gemeenschap der broederen ende avondmaels blyven'; 'Het houwelick van Adriaen Symonss. woonende by Benthuysen opden hil, met syner voriger huysfr. suster is geoordeelt nyet te mogen bestaen, ende dat hy tot teecken der boetveerdicheyt hem daer aff scheyden sal.'

had to be combated. It cannot be denied that, where the Reformed church gained the upper hand, life became more virtuous, more severe, duller, more bourgeois and more ordered, modelled after the Decalogue. Magical practices were rejected. These corrections were deemed desirable by other Protestant traditions and sometimes even by Catholicism as well, but it seems unmistakable 'dass der Calvinismus auf Grund seines spezifischen Anliegens der "re-formatio vitae" am schärfsten gegen die traditionellen Formen der Volkskultur vorging' [that Calvinism was the most vigorous opponent of traditional expressions of the old popular religion, because of its specific emphasis on the 'reformatio vitae'].[37]

In The Netherlands, the consistories could only apply these corrections to the actual members. Yet, they also tried to exert influence outside this sphere by appealing to the major assemblies and to the secular authorities. The ideals were often shared by the central government, so it was by no means only the mentality of the church members that was influenced, although the effect at the local level was considerably less than the Reformed ministers deemed desirable.

Propaganda and the prevention of counter-propaganda   In view of the irritation the placards with lists of forbidden books must have aroused in the 1550s, the major assemblies in the liberated provinces were remarkably quick in urging a renewed censure of books.

At the Provincial Synod of Dordrecht, 1574, a startling increase of 'heretical' groups was observed. Several measures were announced to 'eradicate the false teachings and errors which increase more and more as a result of the reading of heretical books'.[38] From the pulpit, the Reformed pastors would call on the churchgoers to restrict their reading mainly to Holy Scripture. They also had to point to the corrupting influence of unsound books, although not many titles were mentioned; the synod was well aware that this could be counterproductive. Moreover, the Reformed booksellers and printers would be exhorted not to publish and distribute such books anymore. When visiting houses the elders had to check whether there was any harmful literature present.[39]

Such ordinances did not have much success. Twelve years later, at the National Synod of The Hague in 1586, it was again pointed out that 'the sects continue to increase and multiply daily so that the course of the Gospel and civil peace are being hindered'. Once more, measures

---

[37] Münch, 'Volkskultur und Calvinismus', pp. 291–307.

[38] 'Uutroeijnghe der valscher leeringhe ende dwalingen die door het lesen der ketterischen boecken meer ende meer toenemen.'

[39] Rutgers, *Acta zestiende eeuw*, p. 140.

were pressed to prevent writings from being printed which propagated another doctrine and therefore could cause social unrest.[40]

The synod also deemed self-censure among the ministers necessary. They should only proceed to publish their writings after they had secured permission from the classis or from the University of Leiden, which had been founded in 1575.[41] At the National Synod of Middelburg in 1581, minister Nicasius van der Schueren confessed his guilt because he had dared to have his booklet *De corte onderwysinge* printed without seeking permission. The booklet was judged to be unedifying. He promised to track down the printed copies and the Classis of Ghent was instructed to oversee him more carefully.[42] Even the catechism which had been drawn up by one of the most important leaders of this period, Gaspar van der Heyden, was regarded as unsuitable by the synod. He would be reprimanded concerning this publication.[43]

Of course, there was a need for good information. At the Synod of Dordrecht of 1578, it was declared desirable that the standard work of Reformed theology, Calvin's *Institutes*, would at last appear in Dutch translation. Petrus Dathenus was commissioned to do this. Several particular synods requested the Synod of Middelburg, 1581, to consider the publication of a booklet in which the four most important opponents of Reformed Protestantism would be combated: the 'papists'; the libertines, who were unwilling to be subject to any yoke; the spiritualists, who, because of their lack of interest in the ecclesiastical institute, were so difficult to grasp, and whose presence in society was ghostly; and, finally, the Anabaptists who, with their strict discipline and their faithfulness to Scripture, were perhaps most akin to the Reformed. It was decided to ask Marnix of St Aldegonde to draft such a booklet.[44]

Thus the Reformed churches were fully aware of the persuasiveness of propaganda and one-sided information.[45]

Education From the outset, the Reformed church recognized that the control of education is an essential condition for influencing people's consciousness. In all classical and synodal acts of the 1570s and 1580s we encounter this theme. In various ways the church strove to gain

---

[40] 'De secten dagelicx meer ende meer toeneemen ende vermenichvuldigen waerdoor den loop des Evangelii ende de gerustheyt der politije belet worden', ibid., pp. 543, 544.

[41] National Synod of Dordrecht, 1578, ibid., pp. 247, 248.

[42] Ibid., p. 364.

[43] Ibid., p. 370.

[44] Ibid., pp. 371, 415.

[45] See in reference to the way in which the different parties made use of pamphlets P. A. M. Geurts, *De Nederlandse Opstand in de pamfletten 1566–1584*, dissertation, 3rd edn (Utrecht, 1983).

control over education. Local and national authorities were requested to shut down private schools, which were mainly under the control of the Roman Catholic Church. As for Catholic, Anabaptist or libertine teachers who were active in city schools, they had to convert or resign. In all schools, besides Holy Scripture, the Heidelberg Catechism was also to be taught. It was urged that schools be founded in villages as well. The Reformed church unmistakably strove to combat illiteracy.

One of the motives to stimulate education at all strata of the population was the need for trained workers in the church itself. Each church had to have a consistory. Elders and deacons must be able to read the Scriptures, keep the books of poor relief, take down the minutes of consistory meetings and assess their value. Numerous teachers had to be trained in a short period of time if the schools were not to remain under the control of libertines and 'papists'. And there appeared to be a great shortage of ministers. Therefore the congregations were urged at several synods to look out for young men who might be eligible for such a position. They should then be given the financial possibilities to receive a theological education.[46]

During the initial stage, as a result of the shortage of ministers, the church had not been able to prevent men sometimes being admitted to the ministry all too easily, men who were chatterboxes rather than having a thorough knowledge of Scripture, who often had treated a congregation in an insolent way, whose views were at times not very Reformed and who in their walk of life were certainly no examples. Therefore, from now on, those who were newly called to the ministry had to meet the following requirements: they did not appropriate this office themselves but were called by a congregation; they accepted Holy Scripture as the sole Word of God (and did not act on prompting by the Spirit!); and in the case of conflict, they would submit to ecclesiastical discipline.[47]

Among the candidates were many ex-priests. They belonged to the few among the first generation of ministers in the Reformed church who were really trained, unless they had followed the Reformation precisely because they could not satisfy the new requirements that priests had to meet since the Council of Trent. In any event, they more than others were judged critically. If previously they had been guilty of persecution of Protestants or had taken a libertine stance, they were permanently ineligible for the ministry; this was agreed at the Synod of North Holland in 1572.[48]

---

[46] See, for example, Rutgers, *Acta zestiende eeuw*, pp. 246, 247.

[47] National Synod of Middelburg, 1581, ibid., pp. 403, 404.

[48] Reitsma and van Veen, *Acta Provinciale en Particuliere Synoden*, vol. I, p. 1.

The church had a sieve to separate the wheat from the chaff, but in the initial period the holes appeared to be too wide. There were some uncouth folk among the first-generation ministers. 'It is obvious that these people were breakers rather than builders.'[49] Before 1600, out of 67 ministers who worked in the Classis of Sneek since 1583, 24 were disciplined. Nearly half of all ministers in this period were not academically trained, a situation which rarely occurred after 1600.

Thus the value of education at all levels was rather quickly recognized in the Dutch Reformed church.

Disciplining the adherents in a stricter sense In view of the aspects that have already been dealt with, this point needs no further explanation. In the Reformed tradition, contrary to other Reformation churches, discipline applied to the members had been elevated to the status of one of the three marks of the true church, as it is expressly formulated in the Belgic Confession, which all ministers, and later all consistory members, had to sign.[50]

Influencing the language From a liturgical point of view, replacement of Latin and attention to the value of the vernacular, even in religious services, has been one of the most important aspects of the Reformation. However, that which was no longer allowed in worship, remained common practice in the academic world. Earlier it was discussed how from the eleventh century onwards, independent of the religious writing élite, a university literary élite emerged. At the time of the Reformation, the latter even supplanted the first. In Protestant religious services only the vernacular was used; Latin belonged exclusively to the lecture halls and, because of the international function of science, in academic disputes.

The main reason to make religious texts accessible in the vernacular was, of course, to facilitate the active involvement of the people in the religious life. Everybody should be able to read Holy Scripture in his or her own language. In this way the Spirit could blow wherever He wills.

But another element may have played a role too. The old church was intertwined with popular culture to such a degree that ritual texts in Latin, however deformed they sometimes were, functioned as magic. The Reformation wanted to rid itself of all mysteriousness. As with the breaking of the images, the banishment of Latin from the services too

---

[49] J. J. Kalma, *Een kerk in opbouw. Classisboek Sneek 1583–1624* (Leeuwarden, 1978), p. XIV.

[50] *Confessio Belgica*, Art. 29; one of the three confessions of the Dutch Reformed Church, written by Guido de Brès in 1559, after the example of a French confession.

was part of the struggle against that which was experienced as idolatry. We may assume it to be common knowledge that the translation of the Bible, which was also urged at synods in the northern Netherlands, forged the Dutch language and thus advanced the unity between the provinces and a national consciousness.

As far as the Reformed church was concerned, from now on only the spoken and written word was to function in the church buildings. It was not just Saints' images which were removed. Not a single representation was allowed to remain. Even if signs with texts were placed in a church building for adornment, one had to guard against adding illustrations; this was expressly stipulated at the National Synod of Middelburg in 1581. From now on, language, the word, had to be the operative force.[51]

The use of rites   The aim of all classical and synodical regulations with respect to religious customs was especially to clean up all characteristics of the old popular culture which was drenched with Roman Catholicism. Earlier we summed up what was abolished. Preaching was what remained. It received a central position.

It is all the more remarkable that the Reformed church in The Netherlands went to so much trouble – if in vain – to abolish at funerals not just bell-ringing but also the 'funeral sermon'.[52] Elsewhere in this volume I have attempted to find out what the motivation for this was. Apparently, the Reformed tradition was no longer interested in the dead. They were finished. They were either in heaven or in hell. This fanatical break with the dead can only be understood as part of the radical demolition of all that was experienced as idolatry, in short, of all those characteristics typical of popular culture. For the dead played an important role in it. Saints could intercede. Miraculous stories about their intervention abounded. The influence of the dead on the well-being of the living was the keynote of all pilgrimages. The living could, in turn, aid the deceased during their passage through purgatory by certain actions. I think that for this reason the Reformed church wished to devote as little attention to the dead as possible.[53]

Remarkable, too, in this new 'religion' is the special place given to the father of a household; in a sense, he replaced the priest. Time and again it was urged in the major assemblies that a father should have his child baptized as soon as it was born. He should be present. He had to take

---

[51] Rutgers, *Acta zestiende eeuw*, p. 370.

[52] See, among others, van Dooren, *Classicale Acta Dordrecht*, p. 6; Rutgers, *Acta zestiende eeuw*, pp. 248, 501.

[53] See Chapter 12 in this volume.

the initiative. The mother's presence was not appreciated. If at all possible, the father had to answer the baptismal questions. Even if he was excommunicated, for whatever reason, he was still welcome when his child was baptized. If need be, unmarried mothers had to be forced by the authorities to disclose the name of the father.[54]

So, in a curious way, women moved to the background. As part of the present research into the history of women, the significance of the Reformation for the position of women has been investigated several times. It is noted that in general this position did not improve.[55] The classical and synodal acts confirm this picture. Every now and then the question arose as to under what conditions a baptism that had not been administered in the Reformed church could still be recognized. In this respect the Reformed church took a generous stand. If at all possible, the baptism was acknowledged as legal. Only if in an emergency the baptism had been administered by a midwife, did it have to be redone in an orderly way, 'since a woman's baptism is not a baptism'.[56]

It was explicitly stated that there was no reason to reintroduce the office of deaconess. It was realized that sick women were sometimes in need of care that was inappropriate for a man to give but in such cases the wife of the so-called 'ziekentrooster', the comforter of the sick, had to be called in.[57] It can be noted that, because popular culture was pushed aside, certain opportunities that had come women's way in the past, were destroyed.

It is unmistakable that, besides the theological contribution of Calvinism, the struggle against 'idolatry' and 'superstition' has given the Reformed rites and customs their peculiar character, which was aimed at deeply influencing the mentality of the people.

---

[54] Van Dooren, *Classicale Acta Dordrecht*, p. 12. See also Rutgers, *Acta zestiende eeuw*, p. 249.

[55] Els Kloek, 'De Reformatie als thema van vrouwengeschiedenis. Een histories debat over goed en kwaad', in *Vrouwen in de geschiedenis van het christendom (Jaarboek voor vrouwengeschiedenis)*, eds E. Kloek, T. van Loosbroek, J. Reijs and Y. Scherf (Nijmegen, 1983), pp. 106–50; Auke Jelsma, *Tussen heilige en helleveeg*, 2nd edn (The Hague, 1981), pp. 101–13.

[56] 'Overmidts dat vrouwendoop gheen doop en is', Rutgers, *Acta zestiende eeuw*, p. 159. See also ibid., pp. 270, 545; Reitsma and van Veen, *Acta Provinciale en Particuliere Synoden*, vol. I, p. 17.

[57] Rutgers, *Acta zestiende eeuw*, p. 437.

V

Conclusion

In research concerning the sixteenth century, it has been noted several times how much continuity there was despite the breach of the Reformation. This does not alter the fact that in the sixteenth century Western Europe experienced a far-reaching shift. A great amount of pressure was exerted on popular culture. The invention of the printing-press began a development which had previously been impossible. There is a tendency toward centralization. Local rights and liberties are exchanged for centrally established rules. At this stage, each government, irrespective of its religious conviction, strives to make education generally accessible and to improve it. Illiteracy is combated. Morals and customs are changing. Begging and idling are opposed. There is a need for a new business-like approach. In an intensive way the Reformed tradition co-operated in this process by means of its discipline and by continually influencing the authorities and society at large. The decisions taken within this framework at main assemblies contributed considerably to this change of attitude.

Of course, much more can be said about the Protestantization of the northern Netherlands: the inner strength of this typically Reformed spirituality; the autonomy of the people which this church encouraged by training elders and deacons; the theological discussions within this variant – none of this has been dealt with. The emphasis was on the contribution this church has made by means of its major assemblies to combat popular culture, to change society's attitude. By looking at it from this perspective, certain aspects have been made visible which otherwise would have remained in the shadows.

CHAPTER EIGHT

'What man and woman are meant for': on marriage and family at the time of the Reformation

I

> I do not fear for marriage either,
> it's a command of God.
> And if one does what He commands
> one always does what's right.
> (from *De zingende werkmeid* by Betje Wolff and Aagje Deken)[1]

At the time of the Reformation there were changes in all areas of human life. Everything was reviewed and checked for its value: the authority of the church, the relationship between clergy and congregation, the significance of good works, the meaning of this earthly existence, the place of the state, the relation between Christianity and other religions, the influence of angels and demons, the power of rituals, the expectation for the future, the value of tradition, the function attributed to God, and many others. So much became unstable that the ecclesiastical and secular authorities – that is, the people who prefer a certain order, clear-cut relations and a regulated existence – did their utmost to proscribe life, so that sacred cows were instituted again, albeit smaller and less secure than before. But this almost feverish ordaining in the second half of the sixteenth century could not prevent this temporary chaos from having lasting consequences. The various lines which were drawn then, stayed and have remained visible until today. It is good to gain a clear picture of these lines, especially now that we are again going through a time of reorientation.

Between two women

In our search for what the Reformation has achieved and what it has eliminated, it may be useful to pay attention to someone whose own life at that time became entangled because of the social and religious changes.

---

[1] From the collection poems *De vrouw over de vrouw*, ed. Inge Lievaart (Kampen, 1974), pp. 85 ff.

His name was Antoenys de Reus and he came from Kortrijk. As a consequence of the religious disputes he had ended up in London. I do not know in what year he crossed the Channel but it will have been soon after 1559, the year in which Queen Elizabeth I of England began to grant asylum again to Protestant refugees from Italy, France and The Netherlands. Special refugee churches came into being, particularly in London.[2]

Not all refugees, however, were allowed in. Those with Anabaptist ideas were refused entry. When Adriaan van Haemstede, one of the ministers of the Dutch refugee church, pleaded for a more lenient policy of admittance because of the dangers the returned Anabaptists faced in The Netherlands, he himself was banned from England with his family. But Antoenys de Reus and his wife, Lijsken, were accepted. On their arrival they joined the Dutch refugee church of their own accord, which was certainly not done by all the foreigners in England. They really felt at home in this ecclesiastical climate, more than, for example, in the Church of England. It was not hard for them to convince the consistory of their thoroughly Reformed views. As far as we know from the minutes of the consistory, there were never any problems with them. They were not even involved in the affair of Adriaan van Haemstede, which at that time caused great disturbance and almost a schism in the church. In the minutes of the consistory we do not encounter their names except when they themselves went to see the council because of a personal matter of conscience.

Thursday 22 April 1563 was such an occasion. According to the minutes:

> Around fifteen years ago, in Kortrijk, Antoenys had for some time lived, slept and shared a home with a woman called Jan. He had promised to marry her and she gave birth to two daughters by him. When he was later asked about his promise, he denied it and married another woman, Lijsken, here present. From her he also has two children. During the past eleven years he has been able to relieve his conscience because he had promised to marry the other woman outside the faith. But a sermon of Petrus Delenus,[3] stressing the seriousness of the sin not to fulfil a promise to be married, has disturbed his conscience. He now asks advice from the minis-

---

[2] See for the situation in London mainly O. Boersma, *Vluchtig voorbeeld; de Nederlandse, Franse en Italiaanse vluchtelingenkerken in Londen, 1568–1585*, dissertation (n.p., 1994); A. J. Jelsma, *Adriaan van Haemstede en zijn martelaarsboek*, dissertation (The Hague, 1970); Andrew Pettegree, *Foreign Protestant Communities in Sixteenth-Century London* (Oxford, 1986).

[3] Petrus Delenus was from 1559 till 1563 one of the most influential ministers of the Dutch refugee church in London.

ters. Lijsken, his wife, too is troubled, wondering whether she has committed adultery ... .[4]

The problem is clear. Antoenys is a victim of differing views on the ethics of marriage. He seems to be sincere. In contrast with others of his time he does not want to take advantage of the changed views. He wants to live responsibly, as is pleasing to the Lord. When in Kortrijk he left his first wife and two children and later, probably only after his arrival in London, started a relationship with Lijsken, he thought he had a perfect right to do so. It often happened that only at a late stage did couples go to church to have their marriage blessed. Often it did not happen at all, as a result of which the wife in particular was more vulnerable. The breaking of a semi-official pledge to be married was simply easier than the discontinuance of a marriage that was recognized by the church. But apparently, Antoenys had gained the impression that a promise before one's conversion to Protestantism was not valid.

This was not really extraordinary. Many a Protestant minister had suggested it. For priests and monks it had been self-evident that they were no longer bound by their promise of celibacy after they had crossed over to the Reformation. In a similar way Antoenys no longer felt bound by his pledge to marry Jan. The breach with the Roman Catholic past was experienced as such a deep one that nothing remained the same. Those who crossed over became different people. Probably his first wife was not willing to follow him when he changed his religious convictions. And so he deemed himself justified in breaking the bond with her.

Thus it is not the case that after crossing over to the Reformation Antoenys no longer recognized the value of marriage. Although marriage was not a sacrament any more it remained something holy, so much so that a personal pledge had the same validity as an official ceremony in the church, but it had to remain subordinate to the imitation of Christ. If someone was called by God he had to go, even if this meant a breach with his relatives, family and wife. To be in the service of God was of the highest value.

To his dismay, however, Antoenys hears in London that he has misinterpreted the Gospel. God's ordinances are holy in all circumstances. Clergymen may break their promise of celibacy because the obligation to remain celibate is not a divine ordinance but a human invention.

---

[4] *Kerkeraadsprotocollen der Nederduitse Vluchtelingenkerk te Londen 1560–1563*, ed. A. A. van Schelven (Amsterdam, 1921), pp. 406 ff. Although Jan is nowadays a man's name in The Netherlands, it is not surprising that Antoenys's first wife was called by that name. There was not such a clear distinction between names for men and women as there is in our own time. Adriaan van Haemstede's wife was called Peter.

This, however, does not apply to marriage. Marriages are contracted in heaven. Even a change in beliefs cannot justify a divorce. Only if the other partner has committed adultery is divorce acceptable, because we live in a sinful world in which not all keep the commandments. Faithfulness in marriage, the care of the family and following Jesus, all belong together.

According to this view Antoenys is still bound to his first wife. So he is advised to return to Kortrijk in the company of a trustworthy brother 'to encourage him and as an assurance for Lijsken'. The two men have to tell Jan that she is the only person who can renounce a further relationship, for it was really Antoenys who committed adultery by entering into a relationship with Lijsken. If Jan demands him back, he is still bound to her.

This advice could have far-reaching consequences: for Lijsken who would have to wait for the decision of her predecessor, and for Antoenys himself, if only because of the risk a journey to The Netherlands would entail. Later the consistory becomes more cautious. When Antoenys and Lijsken are present at another meeting on 11 May they hear that the consistory has decided to send a letter to the city council of Kortrijk to ask for information about Jan and the two girls. They now discourage Antoenys from travelling himself. He could send a messenger. Strangely enough, he finds this decision difficult to accept.

'In the end he said that he would travel to Bruges and send a messenger from there to Kortrijk,' the minutes tell us. Apparently, his curiosity about his previous partner has increased. Perhaps he longed to see his first wife and his two daughters. Besides, it is an open question whether his relationship with Lijsken could survive these tensions. The matter clearly developed in a direction which was detrimental to her. Whether he indeed made the trip and what were the results, we do not know.

There appear to be two views in this Reformed refugee church. Originally, Antoenys was convinced that there were values that transcended conjugal fidelity. Under certain circumstances, living according to the will of God could imply that it was permissible to dissolve a marriage. But according to Petrus Delenus and the consistory, the bond between husband and wife was so holy that nothing but adultery legitimated a divorce. This difference struck me, because I had gained the impression that with respect to the ethics of marriage the most important Reformers were to a large extent in agreement. What Luther wrote about marriage and family seems to me to be normative and characteristic of the entire Reformation.

II

Luther on marriage and family

It is not easy to do justice to a man like Luther, whose thinking was heavily influenced by his emotions and by practical problems, and who was therefore not always consistent in his views, but on this issue in particular there is a high degree of continuity in his work. He deemed it absolutely incontrovertible to think that it is possible to serve God by going against nature. This he more or less regarded to be the fall of the Roman Catholic Church. For example, in an exhortation 'An die Herren Deutschen Ordens, dass sie falsche Keuschheit meiden und zur ehelichen Keuschheit greifen' he writes:

> We have all been created to act in exactly the same way as our parents did. So, begetting and rearing children – this has been charged, ordered and implanted in us by God; this is proved by the way our body is built, by our daily feelings, and by the example of the whole world. If not, God himself works a miracle in you and yet you remain single, your sin is comparable to adultery or something else which God has forbidden.[5]

When he defends several nuns who, after fleeing from a convent, have been helped by him to find a husband, he explicitly points out a woman's obligation to use her natural possibilities.

> A female has not been created to remain a virgin but to have children, as is also proved by the way a woman's body is built. God himself will make certain exceptions, not based on our vows or free will but in a powerful way in accordance with his own counsel and will. Where He does not work in this way a female must remain a woman and be fruitful, which is what God created her for.[6]

Also with respect to other relations Luther defends the same argument, for example with reference to the relationship of parents with children. God has given each of us specific parents. That is determined by the natural order, and therefore has God's backing. 'So if I want to do good and holy works I cannot think of better ones than to fully honour and obey my parents,' he writes in his *Der grosze Katechismus*. He pities the monastics who despite all their abstinence and exertion cannot manage to do one work which is so pleasing to God as the natural obedience of a child to its parents.[7]

---

[5] *Martin Luthers Werke*, vol. XII (Weimar, 1891; reprint 1966), 'An die Herren deutschen Ordens' (1523), pp. 232–44.

[6] *Martin Luthers Werke*, vol. XI (Weimar, 1900; reprint 1966), 'Ursach und Antwort, dass Jungfrauen Kloster göttlich verlassen mögen' (1523), pp. 394–400.

[7] *Martin Luthers Werke*, vol. XXX (Weimar, 1910; reprint 1964), 'Der grosse Katechismus' (1529), pp. 123 ff.

These words are all the more striking if one has some knowledge of Luther's inner struggle. It was not easy for him to enter the monastery against the will of his father. He did his best to convince his father that this was a good decision. With hindsight he had to acknowledge that in this respect his father had a better insight than he himself, that it had not been God but rather the Devil who had driven him to the monastery. Only after an inner struggle which lasted for years did he understand that God does not ask the impossible from us. We need not go against our own nature to be able to be his children. On the contrary, it is his intention that we start living in accordance with our nature in a new way, from grace.

Of course, Luther also was aware of sin. More powerfully than others he taught of the total depravity of man, but man cannot combat this degeneration by withdrawing from the natural life. On the contrary! According to him, sinful tendencies only increase when one does this. People therefore must be restrained. So they need the state to keep them within bounds. Thus the Christian life is to conform as well as possible to the God-given order, to marry, to have children and to properly fulfil the task set to us in society.

This view had significant consequences for the position of women.[8] It became important for a woman to find a husband as soon as possible. Married women gained considerable esteem. If they became widows while they were still young, that is, in their fruitful period, they had better marry again. Women who remained single or childless were regarded as unnatural. Perhaps this is part of the reason why also in Protestantism the witch-hunt continued unabated; it was directed especially at single women and widows who for whatever reason were offensive and showed unadapted behaviour.

For Luther nature had to be done justice. He even went so far as to give a woman the right to break up her marriage if her husband appeared to be impotent, for in such a case the natural possibilities of her body were in danger of remaining unused. If the secular law then prohibited a divorce, in his view the woman could appeal to the divine law. 'She may not be compelled to live in abstinence.' In a case such as this Luther himself would not hesitate 'to marry someone else and to flee to an unknown place'.[9] Thus divorce is not allowed when the beliefs of the partners differ, but it is when justice cannot be done to nature!

---

[8] A. J. Jelsma, *Tussen Heilige en Helleveeg; de vrouw in het christendom*, 2nd edn (The Hague, 1981), pp. 101 ff.

[9] *Martin Luthers Werke*, vol. VI (Weimar, 1888; reprint 1966), 'De Captivitate Babylonica ecclesiae praeludium' (1520), pp. 557–60; also cited by J. O'Faolain and L. Martines in *Not in God's Image*, 2nd edn (Glasgow, 1974), pp. 207, 208.

There were also consequences for others. Every disturbance of the God-given order was regarded as a sin. Children who disengaged themselves from their parental milieu to go their own way, quite a common theme in saints' lives, behaved according to this view in an unnatural way and therefore opposed God himself. They who were not prepared to accept the place in the natural order which was assigned them by nature, God would oppose, and so would Christian society.

To deviate from the natural and the normal was a sin. Eccentrics were to be viewed with suspicion, unless it was very clear that it was God himself who had created them differently. So there are exceptions to the rules, Luther admits.

III

A bourgeois way of life

The motive for these ethics was, namely, the protest against the devaluation of the common, earthly life, against the idea that a holy life is a life in abstinence. Another way of putting it is that the protest was first directed against Gnostic elements which the ancient church had accreted in the course of time, as viruses which had nestled themselves in the organism without being noted, as the accretions a ship attracts during a voyage. The church was not the only place where they could be found.

Outside the official church there were also Christian groups in which these tendencies were even less concealed. In the Christian Gnosticism of the second century, in Marcion's church, but also among the Cathars of the twelfth and thirteenth centuries, life with Christ was regarded as a total break with the natural existence. All the 'ordinary' things like intercourse between a husband and wife, pregnancy, birth, food and drink, tilling the earth, planting a tree, building a house, belonged to the material world and, therefore, to the realm of darkness. They who awoke from the nightmare of this common life and chose the real, spiritual life, could only turn away from that natural order in disdain. Truly pious people did not marry and combated the secret longings of their body, if need be with flagellation. A true bride of Christ only wanted to produce spiritual fruit. True children of the Lord sought spiritual parents.

The official church which was usually linked with the state continually wished to rid itself of this web of Gnosticism, but it never fully succeeded. Certain elements clung to it like cobwebs. But I think that the Reformation meant the most forceful breakthrough which Christianity had known up to that time. At last the natural life received the rights it deserved. This breakthrough was attended and made possible by the emergence of the bourgeois lifestyle.[10] The commoners benefited from the abolition of celibacy, holy days and fasts. They benefited from a wife who bore them children and cared for them. They benefited from a church which blessed the natural life instead of draining it. And, of course, they benefited from ascertaining what exactly could be regarded as normal and natural.

In this connection it is important to note that at this time belief in God's providence began to play a dominant role. As a result, not only the way our bodies are built, but also the class in which we are born became a 'natural' given, assigned to us by God, and therefore normative.

This identification of the imitation of Christ with a natural life in accordance with the norms of bourgeois ethics had some negative consequences. The opportunities women had always had, even in the traditional Catholic Church, to form groups, to influence public opinion, to self-realization, to develop its own leadership, to cultivate their own spirituality, were in a sense reduced. Youth, too, had less of a chance to go their own way. It was the end of vagabonding along the paths of the Lord. Instead of noble knights and saints, decent commoners were held up as examples.

Although the new Protestant ethics freed a large part of Western Europe from the power of the clergy and the monasteries, which was in many respects oppressive, it also robbed it of people like Francis of Assisi and Teresa of Avila, or at least of the appreciation of such people. It should be added, however, that the Catholic world was also turning more bourgeois. Here, too, the appreciation of a married woman rose.

IV

Deviations within the Reformation

It is time to return briefly to Antoenys de Reus, who after all prompted us to reflect on these matters. It seems clear to me that the consistory in London followed the general view as was voiced by the most important Reformers. Marriage, instituted in order to guide man's natural inclinations along proper paths, was so important that even a change in beliefs was no cause to break off the relationship.

---

[10] This was strikingly put into words by C. W. Mönnich in *Vreemdelingen en bijwoners, hoofdlijnen uit de geschiedenis van het protestantisme* (Baarn, 1980), p. 87: 'God's Word not only became flesh: it has become a commoner.'

One may ask from where a man like Antoenys gained the view that his conversion to the Reformation gave him the right to leave his first wife. Perhaps the consistory had not been careful enough when it accepted Antoenys. It is possible that the latter had found his way to Calvinism via the Anabaptist movement. He certainly would not have been an exception. The rigorous persecution to which the Anabaptists were exposed, almost naturally led to the fact that many from these circles joined more acceptable forms of Protestantism instead.[11]

In the Anabaptist movement such a view of marriage had been common. When Jan Matthijs, the baker from Haarlem, broke with the Catholic Church this had consequences for his entire existence. He not only changed his beliefs, but also his work and his wife. He now married the much younger and beautiful Dieuwertje, who after his death would play such an important role as Queen Divera in the Anabaptist kingdom of Münster. Matthijs did not believe that he had committed adultery.[12]

In the confession which was drawn up in Münster it was clearly stated that only a marriage in which both partners had joined the new covenant could have been contracted in heaven.[13] Any other marriage simply did not exist in God's eyes. It was not self-evident that God approved of natural relationships. The bond with Jesus was of an infinitely higher value than any other bond. In this respect the Anabaptist movement was not at all in line with the Reformation. We even encounter here the Gnostic idea that Christ, in becoming man on earth, remained totally free from Mary's flesh. One must be suspicious of the natural.[14]

Such ideas can not only be found in the ecstatic group in Münster. When after 1535, under the leadership of Menno Simons, the move-

---

[11] See Auke Jelsma, 'The "Weakness of Conscience" in the Reformed Movement in The Netherlands; the Attitude of the Dutch Reformation to the Use of Violence between 1562 and 1574', in *The Church and War*, Studies in Church History, 20, ed. W. J. Sheils (Oxford, 1983), pp. 217–29. Petrus Delenus's father, Walter Delenus, is an example of this.

[12] See the description of these events in 'Bekentenisse Obbe Philipsz', in *Bibliotheca Reformatoria Neerlandica*, ed. S. Cramer (The Hague, 1910), vol. VII, pp. 121–38. This text is also included in *Der linke Flügel der Reformation. Glaubenszeugnisse der Täufer, Spiritualisten, Schwärmer und Antitrinitarier*, ed. Heinold Fast (Bremen, 1962), pp. 319–40.

[13] *Bekenntnis des Glaubens und Lebens der Gemeinde Christi zu Münster. Die Schriften Bernhard Rothmanns*, ed. R. Stupperich (Münster, 1970), pp. 204–7. See Chapter 4 in this volume.

[14] This thought gained respect within the Anabaptist movement mainly because of Melchior Hoffman. For his ideas see especially Peter Kawerau, *Melchior Hoffman als religiöser Denker* (Haarlem, 1954), pp. 31, 46 ff.

ment began to focus more on the interior and on stillness, this view remained. One of the characteristics of this movement was not only the prohibition of holding public office but also of marriage outside the church. If an adherent to this group married a girl who was not Anabaptist, this demonstrated that to him the bond with Christ was of less value than the natural inclinations of his heart, and he was expelled; a thought which in later centuries would re-emerge in other Protestant groups as well. In these circles a husband sometimes called his wife 'conjugal sister' in order to show that above all he knew and loved her as a child of God, and only secondarily as a wife. And among the Hutterites, who lived together in 'Haushabens', comparable to the earliest kibbutsim in Israel, the leader of the commune sometimes decided who was to marry whom and how the children were to be raised. It was to this degree that marriage and family were subjugated to the service of God.[15]

Thus Antoenys could appeal to others, albeit to those people who had been rejected as heretics by the official reformed leaders. Besides, could he not have appealed to Jesus himself? Remarkable statements can be found in the Gospel, for example the word in Luke 14:26: 'If anyone comes to me and does not hate his father and mother, his wife and children, his brothers and sisters – yes, even his own life – he cannot be my disciple.' It is words like these, this 'hatred' against natural relations, which will probably ensure that Gnostic elements in Christianity are virtually ineradicable.

Undoubtedly there is a certain tension in the Gospel between the imitation of Christ and the life according to our nature. In its resistance to the Catholicism of those days, Protestantism has not given due attention to this tension. The problems are not solved by recognizing God so easily behind the ordinary course of things. In reality this so-called natural life is often so diseased that restoration is not possible. In marriage, husband and wife can complement and enrich each other in a special way, but they can also destroy one another so that neither is able to be human anymore. Does serving Christ in such a situation not mean breaking the bond with one's partner? Does doing the will of the Lord under all circumstances correspond to keeping a marriage intact? It may be true that children develop in an excellent way when they are guided and stimulated by loving parents, but in reality children sometimes suffer such spiritual (and physical) damage that for the rest of their lives

---

[15] Examples of this view of marriage among the Dutch Anabaptists are given in in W. J. Kühler, *Geschiedenis der Nederlandsche Doopsgezinden in de zestiende eeuw*, 2nd edn (Haarlem, 1961), pp. 308–46. See G. H. Williams, *The Radical Reformation*, 3rd edn (Kirksville, MO, 1992), *passim*.

they cannot be free anymore. Does following Christ under all circum-stances mean that children honour and obey their parents?

It may have been valuable that in the Protestant Reformation such a forceful plea was made for the rights of the natural life, but this has not solved all problems. What precisely is this natural life?

CHAPTER NINE

Believing in darkness: a Protestant view of St John of the Cross

> It is certainly necessary that over against this great God we remain silent. The only language He understands is the silence of love.
>
> John of the Cross, letter 22[1]

I

After he was beatified in 1675 (less than a century after his death in 1591), the Roman Catholic Church canonized John of the Cross in 1726. Thus called St John. Protestants did not easily utter such an honorary title. St Nicholas (Santa Claus) was an exception, and strict, orthodox groups wished to have nothing to do with this devotion.

This did not mean that Protestants had no feeling for greatness, or that they could not express admiration for impressive personalities from history, but it had been inculcated in them that 'even the holiest men, while in this life, have only a small beginning of this obedience'.[2] From the choice of words it is obvious that Protestants too had their ranks and classes. Apparently, some were regarded as 'the holiest men'. But it is believed that even they could not progress very far on the road to sanctification. However high Lutherans might regard their Luther, however little criticism of their Calvin hard-core Calvinists could bear, they would never present them as St Luther or St Calvin.

But even if such language was current among Protestants, they could still not have been called saints. However different they may have been, the saints from the Catholic tradition appeared to have attributes that could not be found among Protestants, with the exception of some Quakers. This, of course, could have been an optical illusion. The Catholic believers not only adorned their saints with a halo round their heads, but also placed them on a secure pedestal of legends. The saints' lives which must prove the saints' holiness to posterity were always written according to a certain formula, depicting an image that was not

---

[1] *Joannes van het Kruis; Mystieke Werken* [John of the Cross], trans. Jan Peters and J. A. Jacobs, 2nd edn (Ghent, 1975), p. 103.

[2] *Heidelberg Catechism*, question 114.

fully human. This can be summarized by the following statement: that which is an offensive smell to ordinary people spreads a fragrant odour with saints.

St John could not elude this. Even in the biography of him written by the Carmelite Crisógono de Jesús in the 1940s and which was translated into Dutch as late as 1985 because of its reliability, the typical hagiographic elements are unmistakably present. *In extenso* the greediness with which the nurses kept St John's bandages, drenched with pus, as relics in order to use them for the healing of other sick people is recorded. The prior of the monastery in which St John spent his last days tried to put an end to such a devotion. Whatever the prior's motive may have been, he was correct to do so. But the biographer is very critical of this behaviour. And if we may believe the story, in the end the prior also realized that his behaviour had been scandalous. Humbly he knelt at the saint's deathbed to confess his sins.[3] Such events are absent in the biographies of Protestant spiritual leaders.

It is not just the way in which the authors of such lives depict the saints of the Catholic tradition, which endows them with an aura different from the 'holiest men' in Protestantism but a difference in theology and anthropology. If the theology changes, another sort of man emerges; indeed, that is how important theology is after all. According to the Catholic tradition it is possible for a select group of people to rise above the usual level of the average believer and to come so close to God that their whole existence glows as a result. Generally, this talent is visible at an early age. Apparently, these qualities can best be cultivated in a monastic environment. Ordinary family life with its sexual intercourse, its whining babies, its visiting of neighbours and its conflicts in puberty is not very suitable for this. The saints of the heydays of Roman Catholicism are raised above normal earthly life, and this bestows on them the supernatural appearance which distinguishes them from others. They rarely become excited, are unfamiliar with bouts of anger, always remain amiable, like to withdraw in solitude, and sometimes are so alienated from the normal earthly life that, so their biographers allege, they actually start to float. According to the texts, John of the Cross fulfils all these characteristics. Ordinary people can only look in awe at such figures.

Protestantism does not know such personalities and does not strive to deliver people with such qualities. There is some wisdom in this, if we may believe Wim Zaal. As he writes in his book on several saints, one has to be quite disturbed in order to be eligible for sainthood: 'The

---

[3] Crisógono de Jesús, *Geboren uit Gods adem; Joannes van het Kruis*, translated from Spanish by Ed Herkes (Ghent, 1985), pp. 386–98.

church does not confer this honour on commitment, piety or virtue. Something else is needed, something that blinds the eye.' He characterizes the saints as 'in our eyes impressive enigmas, sympathetic people who are deluded, or patients ready to see a psychiatrist'.[4] He, too, is aware of the typical Roman Catholic character of these saints. He realizes that the writing of saints' lives is 'always done by Catholic authors for Catholic readers'. Only they can really appreciate this genre. In this respect I am apparently an exception among Dutch Protestant church historians with my studies on Willibrord, Boniface, Francis of Assisi, Bridget of Sweden and John of the Cross, although my origin remains visible in that I tend consistently to leave out the addition 'St'.[5]

What is it in such figures that fascinates me? They give me access to a certain time. I am interested in the literary genre of the saint's life. I am especially intrigued by the mental training to which people in a Catholic milieu are exposed from their youth onward. A certain soil is necessary, a sort of humus, if from time to time a society is to produce those individuals that are recognized as saints. Medieval society contained such a humus to a high degree. At a very early age children were handed over to a monastery.[6] When this fell into disuse, Catholicism continued to have access to those specific families in which, mainly thanks to the mothers, family life was determined by a strong devotion. John of the Cross grew up in a family like this. His brother was appreciated as a little less saintly than he himself. His mother was also quite exemplary.

Saints can be compared with the stars of sports and music in our time. The great violinists, tennis stars or soccer players come from a milieu that made them familiar with their particular sport or art. Without such a background it is virtually impossible to reach the top. The Catholic saints can best be described as the stars of the religious life. They do not shine in the concert hall or in the stadium, but in a monastery cell or colony of lepers. Looking at it in this way, it is worth a Protestant also spending time studying those particular saints, even without violating the belief that 'even the holiest men, while in this life, have only a small beginning of this obedience'. They have qualities that

---

[4] Wim Zaal, *De Heiligen; Erflaters van Europa*, 2nd edn (Baarn, 1982), pp. 7–9.

[5] Besides several articles, the following books: *Met het oog op de kerk van morgen; Willibrord en de kerstening van Nederland* (Bolsward, 1990); *De blaffende hond; aspecten uit het leven van Wynfreth Bonifatius* (The Hague, 1973); (editor of) *De kunst van het loslaten; een confrontatie met het leven van Franciscus van Assisi* (Kampen, 1980); *Dromen onder de druk van de tijd; over Birgitta van Zweden, een verkenning* (Kampen, 1979); *Ballingen* (Kampen, 1985), three short stories, two of which are on Francis of Assisi and Bridget of Sweden.

[6] See especially Mayke de Jong, *Kind en klooster in de vroege middeleeuwen*, dissertation (Amsterdam, 1986).

deserve our attention. If the Catholic milieu sometimes leads to exaggerated religious experiences, the Protestant one is in danger of going down in uninspiring mediocrity.

II

One of the qualities, I noticed, John of the Cross has to a high degree, is his ability to survive mentally in precarious situations. He has taken heed of the exhortations of the apostle Paul in his letter to the Ephesians: 'Be strong in the Lord and in his mighty power.' Paul called on the believers to 'put on the full armour of God, so that when the day of evil comes, you may be able to stand your ground'.[7] It was obvious that John of the Cross could do this. The greatest danger of this 'day of evil' is not to be found in what others do to us, but in the threat that is hidden within ourselves. In the 'ordinary life' all goes well – even elements from our youth and puberty that we have not dealt with hardly burden us – until the ground gives way under our feet. That is the 'day of evil'.

John of the Cross experienced this day when his opponents were able to imprison him and hide him in their monastery. Together with others like Teresa of Avila John of the Cross tried to achieve reform among the Carmelites. I shall not discuss what the purpose of this reform was. I have some sympathy for those Carmelites who had been following a more moderate rule for centuries and were not at all happy with the breach that John of the Cross and the others caused. They did not see the need for such a reform. If some had the ambition to follow a severer rule, they could go to an order like the Carthusians. It is understandable that they experienced the activities of John of the Cross *cum suis* as a relapse. I regard it as an ominous sign that it is figures like King Philip II and the Duke of Alva that were positive about the reforms of Teresa and John of the Cross. Apparently, they viewed it as a support rather than a threat to what they had in mind, namely to conserve the most traditional characteristics of Roman Catholicism.

That does not alter the fact that his opponents behaved in an inhuman way when they laid their hands on John of the Cross. They hid him in a narrow, dark niche in their monastery in Toledo. Not one of his companions knew whether he was still alive. For months he was locked up in this tight space. He could hardly move. A few hours a day a feeble light entered his cell from above. With all possible means they tried to crush him. He was totally isolated. During meals he had to eat the

---

[7] Ephesians 6:10–13.

frugal bits on the floor of the refectory, like a dog. No one was allowed to exchange words with him. Every Friday he was scourged. His health seriously deteriorated. Only after six months did he have a somewhat more humane guard, who at least granted him paper and ink. A few months later he managed to escape.

This imprisonment can be characterized as the 'day of evil' in John of the Cross's life. As he himself indicated later, the greatest threat did not lie in his treatment or in his isolation, but in the confrontation with himself. This 'day of evil' is the moment at which the ghosts that in the clear light of day seem to have no existence anymore, suddenly loom up again. It is no wonder that in such a situation most people go through the barriers, lose their inner coherence, become infantile, beast-like, perish as a result of their nightmares. Thanks to the diaries written in concentration camps, we have become even more familiar with such processes of decay.

John of the Cross appeared to be able to resist this 'day of evil'. In the dim light he wrote the most beautiful song I know, the song of the night: 'On a night of darkness, in love's anxiety of longing kindled ... .' His orientation towards the person of Jesus of Nazareth, his spiritual armour, the intensive training to which he had subjected himself for years, all helped him through this period. 'My only light and guide the one that in my heart was burning', not a human being who looked after him and not a God who was comfortingly near. He was totally dependent on himself, and that appeared to be enough.

It was this poem in particular through which John of the Cross won my heart permanently.[8] As far as I am concerned, such people may be called saints. They persevere, even in a situation in which the last sparks of humanity are in danger of being extinguished. They bear the future of the human race in themselves as a seed. As for myself, a man does not need to do greater miracles than these in order to be appreciated as a saint. I have no need for all those legends about cloths with pus, or elevation or ecstasy, but if they are necessary to receive the official ecclesiastical permission, then the Carmelites are correct to ornament his life with such details.

---

[8] See the Spanish text with an English translation by Gerald Brenan, *St John of the Cross: his Life and Poetry*, with a translation of his poetry by Linda Nicholson (London and New York, 1973), pp. 144–7. The Spanish text with a Dutch translation is in Peters and Jacobs, *Joannes van het Kruis; Mystieke Werken*, pp. 199–202. There are various translations in *Nacht die gelukkig maakt; ervaringen met de mystiek van Johannes van het Kruis*, ed. Marjolein Schuurmans (Zoetermeer, 1991). See also the artistic edition *Fuente; Juan de la Cruz 1591–1991*, eds J. Brand and P. Deiters (Amsterdam, 1991), pp. 36–9.

III

What I also find fascinating in work of John of the Cross is the way in which he is then able, in the exposition of his mystical teaching, to provide this poem with several layers of meanings. He continues to find new layers. In carefully weighing the various parts of the poem he releases his whole spiritual baggage, his past, his academic education, his knowledge of the Bible, the ecclesiastical tradition all play their part. It is, therefore, not a matter of arbitrary exegesis when later, in the two works he wrote as a commentary on this poem, *The Ascent of Mount Carmel* and *The Dark Night*, he interprets this night both as a night of the senses and as a night of the spirit.[9]

At first sight it appears strange that someone would write a commentary on a poem of himself, as if it concerns a passage from Holy Scripture. He must have been convinced that in his poems he had put into words in a condensed way all that he had received in his life from the Holy Spirit. To that other wonderful poem of his, *The Spiritual Canticle*, he also devoted such a study.[10] In these few poems was hidden all that he had learned in his life with God over the years, and that he wished to pass on to his disciples.

All this testifies to a remarkable ability to concentrate. His spirit was trained to such a degree that he did not let any redundant or superficial lines escape his pen. He was fully in control of himself, his style, his thoughts, his experiences. Precisely because he so carefully weighed all his words it cannot be regarded as accidental that his poem, 'The Dark Night', in particular has become the starting-point for two mystical writings. This poem is the basis, the paradigm, the heart of his theology. It is from here that he reflects. This perspective has become pivotal for his walk with God.

In this respect he also differs from the one whom he regarded as his spiritual mother, Teresa of Avila. Unlike her, he tries to rid himself of all the images of God that Holy Scripture, tradition, his religious experience or his imagination can provide. As quickly as possible he leads his disciples beyond the point at which during their contemplation they still have to use certain representations to direct their attention and imagination. As quickly as possible he leads them into the night of the senses.

In Toledo he had discovered that this is God's very characteristic that, when it really matters, He is nowhere to be found. 'Having wounded me you fled like the hart; I followed on behind you, crying out, calling –

---

[9] For the text of all his works see Peters and Jacobs, *Joannes van het Kruis; Mystieke Werken*.

[10] Peters and Jacobs, *Joannes van het Kruis; Mystieke Werken*, pp. 186–98.

and you were gone,' he writes at the beginning of *The Spiritual Canticle*. At the crucial moment, on this 'day of evil', it is obvious that all aids, all representations that people have made in their need for comfort, for a hold, for divine protection, are nothing more than appearances, a temporary base at the most, more often a temptation and a delusion. There is nothing in this world or in the human soul that, even in the least extent, could be a vehicle for the divine presence. More radically than Karl Barth ever did, John of the Cross exposes religion as sham, as self-gratification, as self-satisfaction. Nothing of what our senses teach us, nothing of what our mind can think of, nothing of what human experience has presented us with, really takes us closer to God. Man must get rid of all this, if God is to come near him. Only if we dare to enter this night, if we are willing to rid ourselves of all aids and representations, only if we want to trust ourselves to this 'black hole' in which all is devoured, however terrible this may be, only then the union with God takes place. But then the human spirit undergoes a liberation which transcends all understanding.

It is precisely this aspect that makes John of the Cross's mystical way so fascinating and so terrifying. In the spiritual ascent of Mount Carmel he leads his disciples past the tree line as quickly as possible. That is why his mysticism is so modern. John of the Cross eradicates all the beautiful and pious feelings which are usually connected so closely with religion. Nowhere in the surrounding world, nowhere in history, in none of the religious ceremonies, is God to be found. At most, all the suggestions in this direction are no more than temporary aids for beginners in the faith. In fact, God nowhere has revealed himself better than in the God-forsakenness of his Son on the cross. Only after Christ had entered that night, could he say, 'Father, into your hands I commit my spirit'.[11]

> By dark of blessed night,
> In secrecy, for no one saw me
> And I regarded nothing,
> My only light and guide
> The one that in my heart was burning.
>
> This guided, led me on
> More surely than the radiance of noon
> To where there waited one
> Who was to me well-known,
> And in a place where no one came in view.
>
> O night, you were the guide!
> O night more desirable than dawn!

---

[11] Luke 23:46.

O dark of night you joined
Belovèd with belov'd one,
Belov'd one in Belovèd now transformed!

What fascinates me in his works on this poem, of which I cited only a few verses, is the radical way in which John of the Cross takes his Toledo experience as the starting-point for his faith in God. He did not take the line of least resistance. When the image of the Almighty One who remains close to his children under all circumstances was shattered in the grim situation, he did not exchange it for the surrogate of a powerless God who is very sorry that we have to experience so many things but who cannot do anything about it. He accepted the absence, the emptiness: 'On a night of darkness, in love's anxiety of longing kindled'. He is able to turn the negation into an affirmation. The quotation that Jan Peters and J. A. Jacobs used as a title for their anthology of John of the Cross's works expresses the heart of his theology: *Het donker is mij licht genoeg* (Darkness is light enough for me).[12] Perhaps only in this way is a theology after Auschwitz possible!

The deep insight into human nature which, in view of his works, he must have had is also remarkable. He sees through the human heart with all its caprices, its smallness, ways of escape, fears and hidden recesses. He describes and analyses all man's attempts to stay sane, to distinguish himself from others. Whoever is regularly engaged with his work – and over the years I have been many times – achieves greater self-knowledge. And yet, despite these analyses of all human qualities and weaknesses, he is remarkably mild in his judgement. He rarely criticizes others. He has also outgrown the stage of embitterment, of anger about what they did to him. He never expresses himself negatively about his tormentors and persecutors.

It is an inevitable corollary of 'The Dark Night' starting-point that ecclesiastical ceremonies or offices have hardly any function in his theological reflections. When his work is compared with that of other mystics, it is soon clear that his theology is not ecclesiastical. In their sobriety his views sometimes look almost Protestant. Albeit in a very special way, his theology too can be summarized by the Protestant motto *sola fide* ('by faith alone'). And yet in his writings and letters there is not a trace of support for or sympathy with the Reformed currents, which could also be found in Spain, and which he undoubtedly encountered during his studies at the university of Salamanca. This, however, is understandable. John of the Cross was more a monk than a Christian (if my meaning is taken correctly). He regarded the

---

[12] Jan Peters and J. A. Jacobs, *Het donker is mij licht genoeg. Bloemlezing uit de werken van Joannes van het Kruis* (Bilthoven, 1974).

training in self-emptying, which he encountered only in the severest monastic orders, as indispensable to attain this intimate union with the hidden God. He must have regarded the rejection of the monastic life by the Protestant Reformation as a heresy. However many things he may have disliked in the Roman Catholic Church, at least it offered him an opportunity to realize the spiritual ascent of Mount Carmel.

Within the framework of his mysticism it is understandable that John of the Cross never attempted to excel as a preacher. He did not have a message for the large crowd of seekers after religious comfort and pleasure, collectors of indulgences, pilgrims, venerators of saints and relics, who abounded in his time. He used all his capacities for the pastoral guidance of individuals who entrusted themselves to his spiritual leadership. It was they whom he tried to lead through the night to union with the Beloved. He was no maker of proselytes, no demagogue, no heresy hunter, no diplomat. He was one of the quiet ones in the land. While his country was engaged in an 80 years' war with the Dutch provinces, the Turks invaded the Mediterranean area and a civil war ravaged France, he analysed very accurately the deepest stirrings of the human soul. Nothing of what was happening in the world touched him to such a degree that it entered into his reflections.

It is on this point that he sometimes irritates me to such a degree that I break off my dealings with his work for several months. In this respect I prefer the Jesuits, about whom he himself was not very enthusiastic.[13] At least they cared for what happened on earth. They tried to change the policies of the Inquisition in order that people with dissident religious opinions would no longer end up on the stake, they championed the American Indians, they studied the religions of India and China to investigate whether, here, too, there was space for the proclamation of Jesus of Nazareth and they cared about the fate of prisoners. In short, although they did not shrink from manipulation, and therefore often made an unreliable impression, at least they did something.

John of the Cross surrendered to the 'black hole'. He seems hardly touched by what happened round him. Otherwise, he would never have written that other song, 'The Living Flame of Love', with the commentary linked to it.[14] In terms of themes this song is related to 'The Dark Night' and 'The Spiritual Canticle'. But now he uses the image of fire,

---

[13] See his judgement on the Jesuits in Letter 18: 'I regret that they have not immediately put things in writing with these fathers of the Society of Jesus. As far as I can see, they are not people who keep their word', Peters and Jacobs, *Joannes van het Kruis; Mystieke Werken*, p. 95.

[14] Brenan, *St John of the Cross*, pp. 162–3; Peters and Jacobs, *Joannes van het Kruis; Mystieke Werken*, pp. 972, 973.

which burns away all that can hinder the union with God. 'O cautery that heals! O consummating wound!' One must realize that the burning of heretics, still alive, was part of the public entertainment in the Spain of his time. During his journeys he must have smelled the stench of scorched flesh many times. Therefore I cannot tolerate that writing. Such an image should not have been used in that period. Imagine a German mystic who in 1944 would have used the figure of gas chambers in a song to praise God's healing presence. 'O blessed gas chamber that takes away my breath ... .' Would not that have been revolting?

The use of images in this song reveals to what degree John of the Cross must have isolated himself from the world. Philip II and Alva, therefore, were not at all troubled by him. He was utterly harmless for those in power in his day. He never alarmed public opinion with his revelations. He had already virtually withdrawn from our universe to be swallowed up by that 'black hole'. It is good, therefore, that John of the Cross was not the only theologian of the sixteenth century.

However, one needs to bear in mind how little space there was for Reformed ideas especially in Spain, how carefully the Spanish Inquisition followed all publications and statements of religious leaders, how suspicious the authorities were, how easily they initiated a persecution. Freedom of speech had been smothered in blood long before. Anyone with the slightest sympathy for Protestant ideas had been imprisoned or had left the country circumspectly. He who held Protestant ideals in a world such as this had to conceal them in a theology of silence.[15] John of the Cross's attitude shows some resemblance to that of spiritualists who were found elsewhere in Europe. It is no coincidence that Spanish quietism, as it was prepared and given a foundation by John of the Cross and others, later had many adherents among radical currents within Protestantism, and was combated persistently by the Jesuits in the seventeenth century.

---

[15] See A. Gordon Kinder, 'Le livre et les idées réformées en Espagne', in *La Réforme et le livre; l'Europe de l'imprimé (1517–v. 1570)*, ed. Jean-François Gilmont (Paris, 1990), pp. 301–26.

CHAPTER TEN

The reception of John of the Cross within Protestantism

I

In the previous chapter Spanish mysticism as it was practised and developed by John of the Cross and others was called a secret form of Protestantizing. There was good reason for this. One of the reasons so far omitted was the Jewish background of both Teresa of Avila and John of the Cross.[1] They had this in common with many Spanish Christians, but from the history of the Reformation in Italy we know that in these Jewish–Christian circles there was much sympathy for Protestantism. The Italian refugee church in London consisted to a large extent of Christian Jews.[2] Many of these Italian Protestants chose Protestantism because they expected to find there at least some sympathy for their opposition to the doctrine of the Trinity. There was little difference between the mystical teachings of someone like John of the Cross and Jewish mysticism. His rejection of a religion which was mainly based on visual images, his preference for a silent walk with a hidden God corresponded more with certain forms of Protestant–Christian or Jewish spirituality than with the extravagant visualization that became current within Catholicism under the influence of the Jesuits or Inquisitors. There are also similarities between his work and that of the Spiritualists who were fiercely persecuted during the Inquisition and who were known as 'Alumbrados'.[3] And yet it seems that Protestantism in particular was not very positive towards this quietistic approach. The silence that John of the Cross propagated seems to have settled over his inheritance as well.

If one goes through the indices of the most important reference books on the history of Christian thought, one rarely encounters his name. Restricting myself to Karl Barth's imposing work *Church Dogmatics*, he

---

[1] See Gerald Brenan, *St John of the Cross: his Life and Poetry*, with a translation of his poetry by Linda Nicholson (London and New York, 1973), pp. 91–5.

[2] See for the history of this church O. Boersma, *Vluchtig voorbeeld; de Nederlandse, Franse en Italiaanse vluchtelingenkerken in Londen, 1568–1585*, dissertation (n.p., 1994); see also O. Boersma and A. J. Jelsma, *Unity in Multiformity. The Minutes of the Coetus of London, and the Consistory Minutes of the Italian Church in London* (London and Amsterdam, 1997).

[3] Brenan, *St John of the Cross*, pp. 96–8.

does mention Teresa of Avila's name,[4] albeit in passing and without dwelling on her work and spirituality, but the name of her companion John of the Cross (or in the Spanish version: Juan de la Cruz) is lacking. I have the impression that Barth never looked into the latter's writings. Perhaps his judgement on mysticism would then have been different, less negative?

What can be the cause of this deep silence? The most obvious explanation is the language barrier. Spanish is read by few Protestant theologians and, unlike his contemporaries, John of the Cross had not written his works in Latin but in the vernacular. Other formidable Spanish thinkers are also missing in the usual works of reference. I came across him thanks to the anthology from and the introduction to his work by J. Peters and J. A. Jacobs in *Het donker is mij licht genoeg*.[5] My interest grew into fascination and into a proper study of this thinking when the Dutch translation of his complete works was republished.[6] Precisely because of this fascination I continue to regard it a handicap that I cannot read his works in his own language.

A second reason lies in the experiences the Spanish mysticism of the sixteenth century underwent within the Roman Catholic tradition itself. In the course of the seventeenth century Spain moved into the shadows not only politically and economically, but also religiously. In Italy the pious who had been inspired by Spanish mystics like Teresa, John of the Cross and Miguel de Molinos (1628–96) were deterred by the negative reaction of the Jesuits. In France the famous pulpit orator and at times heresy hunter Jacques-Bénigne Bossuet (1627–1704) discredited this mysticism or at least deflected it. L. Cognet is right in stating in an article on 'Quietismus' that Miguel de Molinos's condemnation in Rome in 1689 and Bossuet's slanderous pamphlet in 1689, *Relation sur le Quiétisme*, were the cause of the fact that for several centuries the attention to mystical writings such as those of John of the Cross disappeared in these two countries.[7] As a result of these complications,

---

[4] Karl Barth, *Kirchliche Dogmatik* (Zollikon, 1959), IV-2. p. 11. He regards her as one of the few within the monastic tradition who understood at least something 'von dem, was wir besser zu wissen meinen', may even possess something which gives us cause to reflect.

[5] J. Peters and J. A. Jacobs, *Het donker is mij licht genoeg. Bloemlezing uit de werken van Joannes van het Kruis* (Bilthoven, 1974). A second edition has been published (Baarn, 1991).

[6] *Joannes van het Kruis. Mystieke Werken*, eds J. Peters and J. A. Jacobs, 2nd edn (Ghent, 1975).

[7] L. Cognet, 'Quietismus', in *Lexikon für Theologie und Kirche*, eds J. Höfer and K. Rahner (Freiburg, 1963), vol.VIII, cols 939–41. For the trials in Italy and France and for the role of the Jesuits and of Bossuet on these see H. Heppe, *Geschichte der quietistischen Mystik in der katholischen Kirche* (Berlin, 1875).

writings previously highly valued no longer received the attention they deserved and finally fell into oblivion. Because the voice of these mystics had become scarcely audible in the Roman Catholic tradition, Protestant reflection also paid little attention to it.

Moreover, even if John of the Cross's work had been cited by various Reformed authors, could that be called a reception of his mysticism in Protestantism? Being mentioned is in itself not reception. His name, with the addition of a few data and some references, is found in several encyclopaedias,[8] but this cannot be called reception. One can only speak of reception, it seems to me, when there has been a degree of influence, or at least a positive recognition of kinship. In view of the general attitude of Protestant theologians towards mysticism, it can be assumed beforehand that a search for the reception of John of the Cross in Protestantism will yield little result.

II

There is an issue which is important enough to pay attention to in a volume such as this on the frontiers between Rome and the Reformation. The very condemnation of quietism in the seventeenth century – as a result of which impressive personalities like Miguel de Molinos, Jeanne Marie de Guyon (1648–1717) and Bishop Fénelon (1651–1715) were, if not condemned as heretics, at least pushed to the periphery of the church – came to the attention of some Protestant circles. Whoever in the seventeenth century brought down the anger of the Jesuits on himself, should at least be able to count on the sympathy of Reformed onlookers.

It is a strange phenomenon that the seventeenth-century Jesuits reacted so spitefully to quietism. 'Jesuitismus und Quietismus waren Gegensätze, zwischen denen es keine Vermittlung gab' [Jesuitism and Quietism were contrary to each other: there was no bridge between them], H. Heppe states in his study on quietistic mysticism.[9] And about this quietism he had earlier written, 'Man hätte den Quietismus geradezu die spanische Mystik nennen können' [It is even possible to typify Quietism as the Spanish form of mysticism].[10] Of course, it is a matter of debate whether this is correct. Even if people like de Molinos and Madame Guyon appealed to writings like those of John of the Cross, it

---

[8] Although it is remarkable that he is absent from the six-volume Protestant *Christelijke Encyclopedie*, eds F. W. Grosheide and G. P. van Itterzon, 2nd edn (Kampen, 1956).

[9] Heppe, *Geschichte quietistischen Mystik*, p. 260.

[10] Ibid., p. 110.

is still possible that what with him remained balanced with the quietists became lopsided; in other words, they not only borrowed certain aspects from this Spanish mysticism but they overaccentuated them. To be able to judge this, one would have to compare the writings of these authors carefully, but this is beyond the framework of this chapter.

The aspects with which in 1687 the Roman Inquisition, under pressure from the Jesuits, reproached quietism concern especially the biased preference of the interior way, its passivity, the total surrender, the self-annihilation, wordless prayer, the giving-up of all images, figures and representations in prayer so that even the Madonna was no longer allowed to be enthroned in our hearts because God will only come and dwell there if our hearts have become a completely empty space. Not only the saints must abandon the field, theological considerations are also said to have been regarded as hindrances by the quietists. Academic theology merely stimulates the imagination; views and speculations only block the penetration of the true light into the human heart.[11] In short, to undergo union with God, the soul must become fully passive and deedless; every effort by man himself is regarded as detrimental.

Once more, to my mind, it is arguable whether the Spanish mysticism of the sixteenth century recommended passivity in such a biased way as that of which quietism was accused, although one can find an abundance of quotes to suggest this. It is also debatable whether the so-called quietists were really as biased in their teachings as the Jesuits alleged. During the polemics certain statements were taken out of context to be used as evidence of heretical views.

I am more interested, however, in the question of why the Jesuits reacted in such a negative way to this unmistakably passive, introverted and therefore totally harmless piety. Remarkably enough, there is little attention given to this in theological writings. This is owing to, I would suggest, the unsavoury character of this battle. People were suspected on improper grounds. Evidence was distorted. As a result authors have either emphasized the evil practices of the Jesuits[12] or they somehow swept the conflict under the carpet. Therefore, the question of why there was such an area of tension between this Carmelite spirituality and the Jesuit spirituality was not discussed in detail. This issue deserves our attention because it highlights another reason why the reception of Spanish mysticism has been so minute in Protestantism.

As mentioned earlier, the Jesuits are the only ones whom John of the Cross ever criticized. Even the tortures to which his fellow Carmelites

---

[11] See for a description of the 68 theses condemned by the Inquisition, ibid., pp. 272–82.

[12] Ibid.

subjected him during his imprisonment could not tempt him to utter even one negative remark about his brothers. But in his view the Jesuits were no good.[13] Why was there from the outset this area of tension which later, in the seventeenth century, led to such a fierce persecution? I accord this with a deep concern hidden under the manoeuvres, the machinations, the insinuations that the Jesuits allowed themselves in this matter. They must have been sincere in their view that the church would be seriously damaged if this spiritualistic mysticism was not blocked.

Their resistance was not fully developed in the Spain of Philip II. On his territory the ecclesiastical institute was not in danger; he would rather destroy his kingdom than the church. Besides, the movement of the 'Alumbrados' had been eradicated so radically in the sixteenth century that mystics who were inclined in this direction had by now adapted to the regulations and limitations of the church.

In the Rome of Pope Innocent XI (pope 1676–89) a century later, however, the situation had totally changed. It was soon clear that this modest and meek pope was greatly influenced by the Spanish mystic de Molinos. He allowed de Molinos to live in the papal palace. One should realize what could have been the consequences of this for the history of Christianity. A pope who recommended wordless prayer as the highest form of devotion, who experienced theological positions only as hindrances for the coming of the Almighty in our souls, who presented the entire ecclesiastical institute which he represented as merely a defective aid, who explicitly bestowed decorations on those French bishops who had opposed the increasing persecution of the Huguenots in France, such a pope could have had fatal consequences for the effectiveness of the Counter-Reformation. The theological stand against the Reformed ideas, as it had been developed at the Council of Trent, could on no condition be rationalized in such a quietistic way. The significance of the ecclesiastical institute had to be strengthened, not weakened, if the church were to prevent new waves of Protestantism. Not only the interior world of the human soul had to be conquered, there was a whole world outside lying fallow. God was not to be sought in the totally emptied recesses of the soul, but in the outside reality that was filled by Catholicism. It goes without saying that the Jesuits of the seventeenth century in particular experienced the piety of these spiritualistic mystics as harmful for the Christianization and Catholicization of the world and, therefore, it was to be expected that in certain Protestant circles such mystics would have been met with a kind reception.

---

[13] See Chapter 9 in this volume.

There was indeed some Protestant reception. The line can easily be traced. The following people must be mentioned in this connection: the ex-Jesuit Jean de Labadie (1610–74) who after fleeing France founded his own community in the northern Netherlands;[14] the ex-minister Peter Poiret (1646–1719) who personally corresponded with Madame Guyon and who spent the last years of his life with the Collegiants in Rijnsburg;[15] the radical pietist Gottfried Arnold (1666–1714) who in his famous *Unparteiische Kirchen- und Ketzerhistorie* emphatically distanced himself from the institutional church and thought he could find the true faith only with the persecuted Christians;[16] and finally Gerhard Tersteegen (1697–1769) whose songs can still be found in Protestant hymnals. I will return to the latter in particular. It is known that all of them were familiar with the writings of Teresa and John of the Cross. Familiarity of the works passed from one to another so, in their circle, one can speak of reception.

What is most remarkable about this list is not that it concerns only individuals who, moreover, had relations with one another, but that it contains exclusively dissidents. Protestantism appears to have had the same reasons to keep a more or less quietistic mysticism at a distance as we found with the Jesuits. Seventeenth-century Protestantism simply could not bear a rationalization of church dogmas or of the ecclesiastical institute either. Of course, they had to fight in order to secure the positions they had gained against the pressing Counter-Reformation. And for Protestantism, too, there was a whole world to be conquered. The true God was to be found not in the soul purged from all self-conceit and from all images, pretensions and representations, but in the warriors clad with an armour of dogmas. Thus the reception of mystical authors like Juan de la Cruz within Protestantism remained minimal.

As late as the twentieth century the opportunity arose again within a variety of churches to properly appreciate the Spanish mysticism of the sixteenth century. Only now can John of the Cross's mysticism, and in his wake that of Gerhard Tersteegen, be fully developed, is the view of Giovanna delle Croce's in her study about the dependence of the latter on the former, to which study she therefore gave the subtitle 'Neubelebung der Mystik als Ansatz einer kommenden Spiritualität' [Revival of mysti-

---

[14] For him see H. Heppe, *Geschichte des Pietismus und der Mystik in der Reformirten Kirche* (Leiden, 1879), pp. 240–374; J. Lindeboom, *Stiefkinderen van het christendom* (The Hague, 1929), pp. 362–84.

[15] Heppe, *Geschichte des Pietismus*, pp. 388–94.

[16] G. Arnold, *Unparteiische Kirchen- und Ketzerhistorie* (photographic reprint of the edition of Frankfurt am Main, 1729; Hildesheim, 1967).

cism as the start of a new spirituality].[17] In this connection it is therefore important to assess to what extent the individuals within Protestantism who had appropriated this mysticism, as early as the seventeenth century, really understood it. Then the figure of Gerhard Tersteegen deserves our special attention. He more than anyone else, C. P. van Andel states in his study on Tersteegen, closely followed quietism.[18] He left behind an extensive description of John of the Cross's life and ideas, so that we can examine whether he really understood his great model.

III

Gerhard Tersteegen

Gerhard Tersteegen lived from 1697 till 1769 in the Ruhr, just to the east of The Netherlands, and was born into a pietistic Reformed milieu. Under the influence of quietistic circles he increasingly withdrew from society. He learned the craft of weaving, because this simple handicraft offered him more opportunities for silence and meditation. His health was weak, a phenomenon that seems almost characteristic of adherents of this type of mysticism. Gradually a group of companions grew round him, for whom, as was usual in quietism, he became the 'Seelenführer', the coach on the narrow path, the guide to life, although it was never his ambition to achieve such authority. In his immediate environment a small commune was founded of men who wanted to be moulded by him. Thus he resembled the desert fathers of early Christianity who had distanced themselves from society and who nevertheless attracted people by their charisma.

On behalf of his spiritual companions he translated the books which had appeared useful for his own inner life. Thus he also provided a translation of Thomas a Kempis's volume of tracts, *The Imitation of Christ*, from which, however, he left out the essay on 'the devout incitement to Holy Communion'.[19] He refused to partake of the Lord's Supper, although he never formally broke with his church. He had an extensive correspondence with many people in his native country and abroad. A number of letters of his in Dutch are extant.[20]

---

[17] Giovanna delle Croce, *Gerhard Tersteegen: Neubelebung der Mystik als Ansatz einer kommenden Spiritualität* (Berne, Frankfurt am Main and Las Vegas, 1979).

[18] C. P. van Andel, *Gerhard Tersteegen*, dissertation (Wageningen, 1961), p. 145.

[19] He replaced it by a translation of the *Soliloquium* of Gerlach Peters; van Andel, *Gerhard Tersteegen*, p. 35.

[20] *Gerhard Tersteegen: Briefe in Niederländischer Sprache* (part VIII of his collected works), ed. C. P. van Andel (Göttingen, 1982).

A rapid acquaintance with his views is best achieved by reading his short treatise about the knowledge of God which he wrote at the request of his followers. In this he distinguishes several types of knowledge. Natural knowledge, however thoroughly and expertly thought through, is of little use. Thus he clearly opposes the Enlightenment. This natural knowledge only leads to a waste of time, to vanity, criticism of the Bible, unhealthy curiosity and an unhealthy pleasure in fine discoveries and turns of phrases.

He also criticizes the way in which the Dutch Second Reformation ('de Nadere Reformatie') believers tend to study themselves, their miserable state and the question of whether God has mercy on them. This soul-searching, too, he regards as a misuse of the natural mind. He pleads in favour of iconoclasts who dare to destroy all self-made images and insights. According to him, people invest too much in their heads and too little in their hearts. They therefore make an unnecessarily large detour, and life is short enough as it is.

Real knowledge of God is to be given to man; the only thing man can do is prepare himself to receive such a gift. As part of the preparations he considers 'the way of inner denial and interior prayer'. Above this true knowledge soars the higher knowledge that God gives to only a few. One should not even strive to receive it. These few enlightened spirits themselves are also very reticent to speak about the things that were revealed to them. It is difficult for them to find the appropriate words in their heads for what was revealed to them in their hearts. All too easily those images of the truth in one's head become insipid, dry, fruitless and, finally, deceptive.

> Therefore truly enlightened and pious people will never walk of their
> own accord to serve their neighbours in spiritual things ... The Lord
> must as it were push them out to work in the vineyard ... They don't
> like to remain too long in their head; the essence in their heart has a
> better taste to them than the picture in their head.[21]

Teersteegen's most important publication was, in his own view, his three-volume collection of biographies of those individuals from history who undeniably had received this higher knowledge of God. It includes a biography of John of the Cross.[22] This work evoked fierce resistance in Protestant circles because it described exclusively Catholic personalities. I will return to this writing.

---

[21] Gerhard Tersteegen, *Eenige belangrijke vragen wegens de kennis van ons zelven, de kennis van God, en wel voornamelijk wegens het natuurlijk verstand, beantwoord in eenen brief aan eenen vriend* (Rotterdam, 1828), pp. 16–35.

[22] Gerhard Tersteegen, *Auserlesene Lebensbeschreibungen Heiliger Seelen*, 3 vols, 3rd edn (Essen, 1784–86).

Undoubtedly, however, he has executed his greatest influence through his poems, a considerable part of which were, several decades after his death, accepted as church hymns.[23] The *Anglican Hymn Book*, first published in 1965, includes three of his songs. A few quotations will suffice to demonstrate the kinship with John of the Cross's mysticism. In a song for Ascension Day he sings about the victory of Christ over the resistance which is still hidden in his own heart:

> Lo! Thy presence now is filling
> All Thy church in every place;
> Fill my heart too; make me willing
> In this season of Thy grace;
> Come, Thou King of glory, come,
> Deign to make my heart Thy home,
> There abide and rule alone,
> As upon Thy heavenly throne.[24]

Teersteegen's best-known song is undoubtedly 'Gott ist gegenwärtig'. In the *Anglican Hymn Book* the first verse is rendered as:

> God reveals His presence;
> Let us now adore Him,
> And with awe appear before Him;
> God is in His temple;
> All within keep silence,
> Prostrate lie with deepest reverence;
> Him alone
> God we own,
> Him our God and Saviour:
> Praise His name for ever.[25]

The fifth verse shows a clear resemblance with John of the Cross's poetry:

> Air that fills everything,
> In which we always hover,
> Ground and life of all things;
> Sea without ground or end,
> Wonder of all wonders,
> I drown myself in You.
> I in You,
> You in me,
> Let me fully disappear,
> To see and find only You.

---

[23] W. Nelle, *Gerhard Tersteegens Geistliche Lieder* (Gütersloh, 1897). Volumes of his songs are still being published. See, for example, *Gerhard Tersteegen: Geistliche Lieder*, ed. Albert Löschhorn (Zurich, 1945).

[24] *Anglican Hymn Book* (Oxford, 1965), hymn 199, verse 4 (translation by Catherine Winkworth).

[25] Ibid., hymn 5, verse 1 (translation by F. W. Foster, J. Miller and W. Mercer).

In the next verse wordless prayer is recommended too:

> You penetrate everything.
> Let your most beautiful light,
> Lord, touch my face.
> Just as the tender flowers
> Willingly open up
> And keep still before the sun:
> Let me like this,
> Still and joyfully,
> Receive Your rays
> And let You work.[26]

And in the song 'Kommt, Kinder, lasst uns gehen' one can even hear an echo of John of the Cross's song of the night:

> We walk introverted,
> Despised, unknown,
> One hardly sees, knows and hears
> Us in this foreign land.
> And if they do hear us,
> Then they hear us sing
> Of our great things,
> Which await us there.[27]

And so this Spanish mysticism, the mysticism of quiet introversion, of wordless prayer, of the inner giving-up of all the riches of knowledge and experience that man has accumulated within himself, of the divine

---

[26] Literal translation. The German original can be found in Löschhorn, *Gerhard Tersteegen*, p. 20:

> Luft, die alles füllet,   Du durchdringest alles.
> Drin wir immer schweben,   Lass dein schönstes Lichte,
> Aller Dinge Grund und Leben;   Herr, berühren mein Gesichte.
> Meer ohn' Grund und Ende,   Wie die zarten Blumen
> Wunder aller Wunder,   Willig sich entfalten
> Ich senk' mich in dich hinunter.   Und der Sonne stille halten:
> Ich in dir,   Lass mich so
> Du in mir,   Still und froh
> Lass mich ganz verschwinden,   Deine Strahlen fassen
> Dich nur sehn und finden.   Und dich wirken lassen.

[27] Literal translation. The German original in Löschhorn, *Gerhard Tersteegen*, p. 147:

> Wir wandeln eingekehret,
> Verachtet, unbekannt,
> Man siehet, kennt und höret
> Uns kaum im fremden Land.
> Und höret man uns ja,
> So höret man uns singen
> Von unsern grossen Dingen,
> Die auf uns warten da.

illumination, of the full and for that reason joyful surrender, weekly trickles into the Protestant religious services through the songs of Gerhard Tersteegen.

IV

Gerhard Tersteegen on John of the Cross

In the second volume of Tersteegen's most important writing, *Auserlesene Lebensbeschreibungen*, which according to Walter Nigg best expresses the soul of Gerhard Tersteegen,[28] he provided a first brief biography of John of the Cross. In this volume Teersteegen characterizes him as 'eine reine und tief-erleuchtete Seele' [a pure and deep enlightened soul]. His writings are full of 'Göttlicher Salbung' [godly devotion]. They have 'der wahren Gottesgelehrtheit ein sonderbares Licht gegeben' [given the true Theology a very special light]. He who reads these works discovers, according to Tersteegen, how much they are based on John of the Cross's experience with God himself. The aim of his teachings was the union of the soul with God up to the level at which the divine silence is experienced. Only if the human spirit remains at the centre of humility will it find this rest.[29]

Tersteegen treated this mysticism much more extensively in the third volume of his work.[30] In it he briefly but accurately renders John of the Cross's development, his relationship with Teresa, his imprisonment in Toledo and the treatment to which he was subjected there. Through all this John developed his 'Liebe zum abgeschiedenen geheimen Wandel mit Gott' [love for a secluded, hidden spiritual relationship with God].[31] As prior of the remote monastery near Ubeda he reintroduced the practice of 'innere Gebetsübung' [interior praying]. As Tersteegen expressed it, the Spanish mystic lived in the wounds of Christ.[32] As much as possible he kept his great erudition a secret. Once he was given a statuette as a point of orientation for his contemplation, but he did not want to keep it; such images would only stimulate the soul and block the freedom of the spirit. Tersteegen stressed John's sincere compassion for the poor and the sick in his surroundings. Although the Spanish

---

[28] W. Nigg, *Grosse Heilige*, 9th edn (Zurich, 1974), p. 400.

[29] Gerhard Tersteegen, *Auserlesene Lebensbeschreibungen Heiliger Seelen* (Essen, 1785), vol. II. pp. x, xi.

[30] Tersteegen, *Lebensbeschreibungen*, vol. III, pp. 277–332.

[31] Ibid., p. 292.

[32] Ibid., p. 296.

Carmelite did not like travelling, visiting or speaking in public, he did develop into a capable 'Seelenführer' [spiritual guide]. He understood better than the people themselves what was going on in them. In his letters he opposed scrupulous soul-searching, of which some nuns were guilty. He regarded this as a waste of time.[33]

Tersteegen sang the praises of the writings John of the Cross had left behind. He characterized them as a delightful garden in which he walked with joy and from which he wanted to pick some flowers for his readers.[34] After this he summarized John of the Cross's mysticism carefully. He distinguished between the two dark nights the soul has to live through, as we know them from John of the Cross's work. In the first night the soul is robbed of all the desires directed at things outside; the second night falls when the soul is robbed of all the activities, considerations, representations and expressions of prayer, which initially were experienced as aids in the spiritual life. Tersteegen emphasizes that this entails an 'entsetzliche Reinigung' [fearful purifying] which can last for years and which makes the soul utter a 'heftiges geistliches Geheul' [an intense mental crying].[35]

He then quotes no less than 104 aphorisms from the work of the Spanish mystic. It is interesting to see which he has chosen and which he has not. He has a preference for those statements in which John of the Cross calls to humility and inner silence. His probably most bold and fascinating aphorism is also included: 'The Father speaks but one word, namely his Son. He speaks it continually in an eternal silence and therefore has to be heard by the soul in silence.'[36]

What has struck me in John of the Cross's aphorisms are the striking images he uses – a bird that lights on to a sticky mistletoe, a fly that sticks to honey, flowers and fruits. But it is these aphorisms that are missing in Gerhard Tersteegen's anthology. Also the daring statement 'God happens to be inaccessible' is not there.[37]

Finally, Tersteegen describes the man's last years and his death. He is remarkably modest in this, not quoting the passages from the oldest texts that speak of the way in which the women who cared for him kept and cherished the cloths with pus.

From this description it is obvious how much fruit Tersteegen has absorbed from John of the Cross's work. Here indeed we can speak of

---

[33] Ibid., pp. 300–303.

[34] Ibid., p. 305.

[35] Ibid., pp. 306–15.

[36] Ibid., p. 318. See also Peters and Jacobs, *Joannes van het Kruis: Mystieke Werken*, p. 1097.

[37] Ibid., pp. 1089–93.

reception. In the introduction to Teresa of Avila's biography Tersteegen wrote:

> This is sure that the holy Teresa and her helper John of the Cross were not among the least who at that time contributed something through their life, their work and their writings to a thorough reformation of the church ... They led the souls by word and example ... into the pure love for God along the route of interior prayer ... Thanks to these two saints in particular, the light has broken through again on the inner roads of Christianity.[38]

Thus he explicitly experienced the work of these Spanish mystics as part of the Reformation. On the basis of such statements Giovanna delle Croce therefore notes 'dass Tersteegens Spiritualität dem Karmel viel zu verdanken hat' [that the mysticism of Tersteegen owed a lot to the Carmelite].[39] This statement has been criticized by another author, who perceives a certain monotony in the German mystic's choice of words which is allegedly absent in John of the Cross's writings.[40]

Undoubtedly, Tersteegen has learnt much from Spanish mysticism, first through people like Peter Poiret and Madame Guyon, later through his own studies. But differences remain. Unlike John of the Cross, Tersteegen fully distanced himself from the sacraments of the church. The way in which he and his companions withdrew to conventicles at the edge of the church differs from the function the Carmelite monasteries had in sixteenth-century Spain. Tersteegen *cum suis* experienced themselves as God's chosen ones in a different way from the Spanish mystics. As a Reformed Protestant he remained faithful to Calvin's doctrine of election, even in his mysticism. In his thought the profession of justification by faith alone remained central. This may be the reason why his mystical expressions lack something of the variation, the optimism, also the joyfulness, which we find with figures like Teresa and John of the Cross. The climate differs. Tersteegen's mystical landscape is less sunny, less weathered, also more misty. With him we find more the mysticism of the inner room than that of the bare rocks in the rough country, in the crevices of which again and again the most surprising flowers are to be found.

---

[38] *Lebensbeschreibungen*, vol. II, p. 2.

[39] delle Croce, *Gerhard Tersteegen*, p. 57.

[40] Hansgünter Ludewig, *Gebet und Gotteserfahrung bei Gerhard Tersteegen*, dissertation (Göttingen, 1985), p. 311.

V

Recognition and kinship

There was, nevertheless, some reception within Protestantism, some recognition and kinship. Something trickles through, but not a big stream. The deepest cause of this hesitant attitude does not lie in Protestant teaching itself. Protestant leaders distanced themselves from this mysticism for the same reason the Jesuits in the seventeenth century tried to ban it from the church. This is not incomprehensible. Whoever wants to conquer the world for God must be sure of his ground, should not doubt himself and may not modify his views, he must use all possible means to convince others that he is right, he cannot deal with the giving-up of his own power and his own views in the dark night of the spirit; he does not dare to take the leap of faith that only in such total darkness God can be found. Perhaps this is why in our time the work of John of the Cross has again evoked recognition? Is it now that this mysticism has a future?

Freer than in the seventeenth century, we can now wander through various traditions. We are no longer so convinced that we are right. From figures like John of the Cross and Gerhard Tersteegen we can learn how limited our theological representations are, how much damage they have done in history, how little recognition they are able to evoke in new generations and in people of other cultures, how much they have hindered people in their spiritual growth by marking themselves above the views of others, and how dangerous it may be for theologizing – in Gerhard Tersteegen's words – to remain in the head while the heart is not involved.

That God can be found only in the dark night of God-forsakenness in which all spiritual hold recedes, is experienced even now in our time by people who are no longer comforted by the religious concepts with which they were raised. Besides, flooded with noise we once more learn to appreciate the value of silence. Thanks to developments in psychology we can also show more appreciation for the knowledge that men like John of the Cross possessed. It has become clear that sometimes people are helped more by a good counsellor, an inspiring 'Seelenführer', than by the official incumbents of the church. It is not for nothing that at various theological institutes in The Netherlands a change to this direction is taking place. So there is good reason for the renewed attention given to the mysticism of such a cross-roads figure as John of the Cross in the frontiers between Rome and the Reformation.

Even so, the criticism the church leaders of the seventeenth century had of quietism still has some validity today. It may be fully justified if people, because of their exhaustion, withdraw into their little circle of like-minded companions, but there still remains much to do on this earth. He who can find God only in the deepest core of his own soul overlooks much of God. But thanks to currents like the Quakers and figures such as Dag Hammerskjöld we also know that this mysticism of silence and surrender is pre-eminently appropriate to activate people without leaving a trail of wreckage.

CHAPTER ELEVEN

Without a roof over one's head: Stephen Gardiner (1483?–1555) and some characteristics of Protestant spirituality

I

There is no doubt that Protestant Christians live in a different climate from their Roman Catholic fellow believers. This is not a problem, but it is a factor to be reckoned with. For each the atmosphere in the church services has its own character, however much they may have borrowed from other traditions and however much they may differ from one another.

The main characteristic of a Protestant religious service is probably the importance of the sermon. Not without reason are Protestant ministers often called 'preachers'. In Dutch they are called 'dominee', from the Latin *dominus*. In several respects they are more a continuation of the preacher friars of the Middle Ages – as the Dominican monks were called – than of the pastors in local parishes. Until recently, their qualities as preachers were the deciding factor for their career. Whether people leave the church 'blessed' is less dependent on the blessing than on the sermon. Ministers who are excellent preachers can take many liberties in their other duties. It is obvious that preachers are often weighed down by this burden. Some of them have therefore strained for effect rather than depend on their imitation of Christ, and have developed into demagogues. How far this may go is shown by the TV preachers in the United States. The 'electronic church' is a typical product of Protestant spirituality, although some Roman Catholic pastors have also dared to enter this scene.

Another characteristic of the Protestant religious service is congregational singing. The words in the Psalm that God is 'enthroned on the praises of Israel'[1] are taken very seriously in these circles, while the question of whether a Christian community may in its devotion identify itself in this way with the people of Israel, is seldom asked. For many

---

[1] Psalms 22:3.

generations of Protestants rhymed versions of the Psalms were the heart of their spirituality. The church-goers were furious when a minister dared to let them sing only unknown hymns. The introduction of a new rhymed version of the Psalms or of a new hymn book in the Roman Catholic Church never led to a quarrel, but within Protestantism it did, even leading to schisms. This does not mean that attention was always given to the quality of the singing. In contrast with the Roman Catholic Church, Dutch Protestantism does not have schools where choral singing is taught. But this lack of schooling has not diminished the zeal with which people sing.

The special character of Protestant spirituality is not only expressed in church services. Family life has been determined by it for centuries. Until recently, a Reformed family in particular could be recognized by the place Bible-reading was given during meals. This reminds one of the custom still practised in monasteries to eat in silence while a devotional book is being read. Also, significant numbers of Protestant families used to end a meal or a day by singing a hymn. For a long time a harmonium was in many Reformed households a loved, albeit maltreated, instrument.

Thus, there undoubtedly exists (or, at least, existed) a Protestant spirituality, however diverse the expressions in the varied modalities may have been. Something such as this is not without its consequences. Religious education creates an aroma which is difficult to expunge. Some even suffer from it and, like people who work all day in a cheese factory or a fish shop, try almost fanatically to rid themselves of the smell. They seldom fully succeed.

The question is whether this special climate can be described. Of course, the differences between the Roman Catholic and the Protestant traditions are also theological. Yet, with a description of the doctrinal differences we have not really uncovered the special character of each tradition. If one investigates the theological views which underlie the church services, one happens more on similarities than on differences. Both the Roman Catholic and the Protestant services are a composition of readings from Scripture, prayers, doxologies and liturgical acts. The texts used at the Eucharist or the Lord's Supper betray their common origin. But there is a difference. Protestants have their own spirituality. Although certain ingredients are obvious, it is difficult to put a name to the whole. I have earlier described spirituality as 'the river bed which develops when people attune their behaviour to one another and to common ideals and norms'. 'Spirituality is for a community what the soul is for the body.'[2] Try to convey something like this in words.

---

[2] *Ruimte om op adem te komen: bezinning over spiritualiteit*, eds Auke Jelsma and Harry Juch (Kampen, 1987), p. 10.

A Roman Catholic attempt

With regard to spirituality, an attempt was made on the Roman Catholic side to track down the difference between Rome and the Reformation, and therefore also the typical characteristics of Protestantism. This was done in a written work, namely *De nieuwe Katechismus: Geloofsverkondiging voor volwassenen* (The new Catechism: Proclamation of the faith for adults), published in 1966,[3] which was produced by order of the Dutch bishops. It is worth citing this fragment in full:

> The differences have been exaggerated on both sides. We both adhere to the same Bible, to the same Twelve Articles of the faith. Both are involved in the present ecumenical movement. Therefore we mention the differences reluctantly. Yet, we need to give some attention to them.
>
> Maybe the deepest distinction can be described in this way. Catholic Christianity believes more strongly that salvation is tied even to the most ordinary things: the bread on the altar, the voice of a meeting in Rome, the words of forgiveness. To such a degree God becomes man, also in the church today ... This belief in God's tangibility is linked with the conviction that worldly reality, man included, is ultimately good. It is good in such a way that, despite all our darkness as a result of sin and corruption, God can let himself be met in it.
>
> In the Reformation, on the other hand, from the outset there has been the conviction that God cannot be reached in such a tangible way in the sacraments and in the authoritative word of the church today. Salvation is more spiritual. Earthly things are not such that they can really absorb salvation. To them Holy Scripture and the confessions of the first great councils are the main points of contact with God. Added to this is a special attention for personal inner experience.

This text needs to be analysed further. To begin with, it is important to keep in mind the year of its publication: 1966, a few years after the Second Vatican Council. The 1960s, when in Europe it was still generally believed that we could make our own good society, when one seriously thought that despite their great differences people could grow towards one another, when 'ecumenism' was understood to be a literal melting together, a unification of churches, when Protestant and Roman Catholic pastors happily blessed marriages together and when combined church services were held on a large scale, those were wonderful times. God nodded gracefully towards us. Mary beamed. And we, who participated in all this in those years, enjoyed the feeling of

---

[3] *De nieuwe Katechismus: Geloofsverkondiging voor volwassenen* (Hilversum, Antwerp, 's-Hertogenbosch, Roermond, and Maaseik, 1966), pp. 265–6.

closeness and harmony. We believed this promised much for the future. Like a magnet we were drawn towards one another. Differences were mentioned only 'reluctantly'.

The way in which the difference in spirituality is worded also deserves our attention. 'Catholic Christianity believes more strongly that salvation is tied even to the most ordinary things.' This is true. It has to do with our origins. That Protestant churches have another spirituality, another structure, that have bred a different type of man, not because they listened more carefully to the Bible, but because they came into existence in a different time.

II

A difference in origin

The Roman Catholic Church only developed its specific features after the fall of the Western Roman Empire. It was characteristic of the young people who settled in Europe after their wanderings over the earth that they felt a need for a tangible gospel. They believed in animated matter. Therefore, they ascribed to blessed water a special power, they believed in the real presence of Christ in the signs of bread and wine once the appointed person had uttered the correct magic formula, they were convinced that a special power was concentrated in the relics of the saints, and they were not surprised when images started to weep. Even if the medieval church had not wished it, the pressure from below would still have created this belief in the tangibility of God's grace.

One of the consequences of the feudal structure that in Western Europe regulated the mutual relations between the three classes – the knightly, clerical and working classes – was that the spiritual class, not unjustly, regarded itself as the church proper. It therefore claimed the sole right to the art of reading and writing, and that there was no need for the common people to interfere with theology or the spiritual life. The working class had to make sure that there was enough food for everybody. The women had to ensure posterity. The knights trained themselves for battle, to protect society against the enemies of flesh and blood. In the monasteries, through incessant prayer the evil spirits who operated from the heavenly realms were resisted. The priests baptized children, blessed marriages, gave absolution, with the extreme unction they helped the people to cross the last threshold of this earthly existence, and so they provided the entire society with a roof over its head. By this the clergy actually created a middle area between the divine and the human, visible to all, in which not only the clergy but also angels and the spirits of deceased saints helped the human community.[4] It goes without saying that the culture of a society which comprised mainly illiterate people, was more visual than verbal. God was indeed present visibly and tangibly. The church unmistakably fulfilled the needs of the people.

However, this changed when, due to the pressures of social and economic changes, a type of man emerged with which the feudal structure and therefore also the old church was unable to cope. The educated commoner who, like the clergy, learned the art of reading and writing and gained a knowledge of foreign languages, who had to serve society, which grew ever more complex, as lawyer, merchant, teacher, doctor, solicitor or historian, did not fit the scheme of the three classes, nor therefore the church structures as they had developed in Western Europe. And so, from the twelfth century onwards the rumblings began, at first still quite far away so that they could be ignored but increasingly closer until the thunderstorm broke and the Protestant Reformation emerged.[5]

So, *De nieuwe Katechismus* accurately indicated the difference in spirituality: 'Catholic Christianity believes more strongly that salvation is tied even to the most ordinary things'. In Protestantism salvation is less tangible, less visual, more verbal, and therefore more spiritual: 'To them Holy Scripture and the confessions of the first great councils are the main points of contact with God.' The Reformation is indeed dependent on words. For it happened to arise in a later period of history, subsequent to the invention of the printing-press.

The appearance of the printing-press must have had a similar effect then to that of the computer in our own time. Just as now 'virtual

---

[4] The most thorough discussion of the feudal structures can be found in Georges Duby, *Les trois ordres ou l'imaginaire du féodalisme* (Paris, 1978); see also Peter Brown, *The Rise of Western Christendom; Triumph and Diversity AD 200–1000* (Oxford, 1996).

[5] This change from visual culture to verbal culture with all its consequences for religious life has been described in an impressive way by C. W. Mönnich, *Vreemdelingen en bijwoners: hoofdlijnen uit de geschiedenis van het protestantisme* (Baarn, 1980), p. 30. I shall restrict myself to one quotation:

> Man as he enters the scene within the Protestantism of the 16th through the 18th centuries is older than the Reformation. He is born in the stench, the disorder, the disruption of life in medieval towns from the 12th century onwards. Then faith's estrangement starts vis-à-vis the old patterns which derive from a very different society, a primitive agricultural one, in which the military possessed the land, the farmer bent his back to work for all others in the world, and the priest prayed for the indispensable favour of God in Christ. The wild urban world of the 12th and the 13th centuries could no longer cope with this pattern. A number of features that will characterize the Protestant after the Reformation begin to take shape here.

reality' begins to replace real life, so in the fifteenth and sixteenth centuries letters and words took the place that stones, bones, statues and wells had occupied earlier. The people no longer needed to travel to holy sites to come into contact with the supernatural, they began to read the Bible. This caused a different spirituality, and eventually another type of man. Because the Roman Catholic Church came into being in the early Middle Ages it was to a large degree determined by visual elements. Because Protestant churches have the bourgeois culture of the sixteenth century as their origin they were increasingly characterized by a verbal culture.

Owing to this difference in origin it is not easy to pass judgement on these two variants. The dispute between Rome and the Reformation is not about good or evil. If the Roman Catholic Church really wished to serve medieval society it had to conform to the structure that was determinative at the time. Therefore it adopted a strictly hierarchical structure, from the top downwards, with a great chasm between clergy and laity, and with an extensive interplay of magic acts. Protestantism's plea for the priesthood of all believers was caused by the growing influence of commoners on society.

It holds good for both churches that they developed their specific characteristics as a result of the spirit of the time in which they were formed, and that this origin continues to play its part, no matter what developments have followed later. Naturally, the growing influence of the commoners on society had far-reaching consequences for the Roman Catholic behavioural patterns also, but it has not been able to eradicate its feudal character; for Protestant spirituality, however, it was determinative. Just as in modernized cities the original layout of the streets can often still be recognized, so in church life the history of its origin continues to play a part. That is why insight into its history is necessary in order to understand the specific Protestant spirituality.

III

Stephen Gardiner

It seems worth investigating, as part of this analysis of the Protestant experiential world, to what degree these characteristic differences between Catholic and Protestant spirituality already existed in the sixteenth century, for they could have arisen later. During my research I happened across a sermon which provided me with interesting material for this.

The sermon was given in 1548, in the presence of young King Edward VI (king 1547–53) and his most important advisers. After Henry VIII's death these advisers wished to give Protestantism in England a firmer foundation, to align it with the main currents of the Protestant Reformation. Henry VIII's policies had not been consistent. He had severed the church's ties with Rome and he had abolished the monasteries, but after some time he had gone back on earlier decisions, for example married priests. People who had spoken of the mass or the other sacraments in derogatory terms were executed. The oscillating views of the king forced convinced Protestants to flee to the Continent. When Edward VI ascended to the throne the situation changed.

Not everyone could adjust easily to the new situation. One of these was the Bishop of Winchester, Stephen Gardiner (bishop 1531–51, 1553–55), a man of humble descent who had willingly complied with Henry VIII's policies and had influenced them with varying degrees of success.[6] So he was viewed with suspicion by those new in power, even though he had pledged allegiance to the young ruler, as he had to his father. Greater scrutiny of him was necessary and, so, he was ordered to expound his views in a sermon before the king and his advisers.

The sermon was not acceptable. Neither was the way in which he implemented the obligatory changes in his diocese. He was taken into custody and interrogated. The process has been published in full by the martyrologist John Foxe. The sermon too was included in the first great edition of his martyrology. In later editions, however, the sermon was sometimes omitted, possibly because it showed the bishop to be more moderate and more pious than the publishers deemed desirable.[7] After Edward VI's early death a recatholicization of the English people had begun under his half-sister Mary, in which Gardiner, restored to his dignity and appointed Lord Chancellor, played a decisive role. Not unjustly, he is held responsible for the death sentences which were then passed.

Therefore, when after 1559 Protestantization became definitive under Elizabeth I, in Protestant circles nobody was inclined to say anything good about the then deceased Bishop of Winchester. Calvin character-

---

[6] For Gardiner see A. G. Dickens, *The English Reformation*, 4th edn (London, 1968), *passim*; *The Dictionary of National Biography*, new edn (Oxford, 1973), vol. VII, pp. 859–65.

[7] John Foxe, *Actes and Monuments of these latter and perillous dayes, touching matters of the Church ...* (London, 1563), pp. 771–6. The sermon (on Matthew 16:13–20) was – with a reference to the previous edition – omitted in the 2nd editon: *The Ecclesiasticall history contayning the Actes and Monuments of thynges passed in every kynges tyme in this Realme, especially in the Church of England*, 2 vols (London, 1570), vol. II, p. 711. The edition of 1610: *Actes and Monuments of Matters most speciall and memorable, happening in the Church*, 2 vols (London, 1610), however, does contain the sermon (vol. II, pp. 1623–5).

ized him as the villain 'who surpassed all devils in that kingdom'.[8] John
Foxe was scarcely outdone by Calvin. He called Gardiner 'a man hated
of God and all good men'. He thought him obstinate ('of a proud
stomach') and opinionated ('flattering himself too much'), but above all
totally unreliable. 'On the basis of his writings nobody can say exactly
whether he is a Protestant or a Papist.'[9]

This is not altogether fair, I submit. The sermon in particular, but also
the interrogations which followed, show a consistent picture. At least he
swayed less than Henry VIII had done. He was and remained opposed to
a reformation as Luther and Calvin had advocated, but he did not deny
that reforms were needed. That is why he had warmly approved of the
separation from Rome and of the way in which Henry VIII had appropriated authority over the English church. There were two ways to combat
abuses in the church, he maintained in his sermon: to abolish practices
and rituals, or to improve them. He was under the impression that the
advisers of Edward VI wanted to abolish more than he thought desirable.

Gardiner's sermon

In his sermon Gardiner was quite open about this. Remarkably often he
declared that he was totally honest now, that he did not hold back
anything and that he was being transparent. He so lavishly scattered
these statements about his sincerity throughout his sermon that as a
result they did not gain credibility. But perhaps he hoped to influence
the young king in this way.

At any rate, it testifies to his courage that he gave his view on the
mass, although it had been made clear to him that he was not to speak
about this sacrament. He emphasized that he had always been in favour
of communion in both kinds, and that the intention of the mass was
above all to commemorate the suffering of Christ by means of representation. He stood by his opinion that the government had to take action
against people who mocked the sacrament. 'I love the Eucharist,' he
said. 'It makes the people more pious.' He did not like travelling preachers
whom the government had given permission to preach but who abused
their freedom to ridicule the sacrament. And he advocated that aid to
the poor, which was partly paid from the offertory at the Eucharist, was
not to suffer.

---

[8] Cited by Patrick Collinson, *Archbishop Grindal, 1519–1583* (London, 1979), p. 90.
See also Gardiner's part in the trial against Anne Askewe in Chapter 5 of this volume.

[9] John Foxe, *Acts and Monuments of Matters most special and memorable, happening
in the Church, with an Universal History of the same*, 3 vols (London, 1684), vol. III, pp.
447, 448. In this edition the sermon was not included.

He acknowledged that he had opposed the removal of images from the churches. It was indeed his opinion that they could serve as books for the laity. But those customs and ornaments were not really important to him. He did not mind if they disappeared. Ceremonies were instituted in order to stimulate people to serve God. As long as they served this purpose there was no reason to replace them. If people were subordinated to customs, then action was needed. But it was his conviction that the celibacy of the priests had to be upheld. It certainly took courage to pronounce openly such a view before advisers and regents such as Archbishop Cranmer (1489–1556), who had married secretly.

However, he was not attached to the supremacy of the papacy. That the King of England had sometimes asked the pope for advice in ecclesiastical matters, did not amount to an acknowledgement of papal superiority, he found. The king had other advisers too. When he was ill he asked advice from doctors, with regard to military business from soldiers, concerning ecclesiastical matters from clergymen and from the pope among others. This did not mean that they stood above him; on the contrary, at those moments they were serving him. Christ alone was the foundation of the church.

So, in his sermon he remained remarkably faithful to the views he had advocated during Henry VIII's reign. In a sense, he stood in the middle of the various attempts at reform, fearing chaotic developments, prepared to adjust, inclined to fall back on more traditional points of view if, in his opinion, the Protestantization threatened to go too far. Therefore, the heading in Foxe's martyrology above the story of Gardiner's trial characterized the situation tersely: 'Stephen Gardiner varieth from other Papists, and also from himself.'[10] But he was certainly a man with a rich experience of several sorts of reformation and repression, with a thorough insight into canon law, to whom it is worth listening when he tries to pinpoint what he regards as the most essential changes brought about by the Reformation and what he sees as the most decisive factors for the new Protestant frame of mind. These are:

1. The abrogation of the central authority of Rome.
2. The abolition of the monastic life.
3. The cessation of the veneration of saints and relics.

Undoubtedly, reformers like Luther and Calvin would have viewed other elements of Protestant teaching as more important, such as justification by faith alone, or the election which rests exclusively on God's free grace and therefore may not be made dependent on what man may

---

[10] Ibid., vol. III, p. 448.

add. Yet, the three changes which Gardiner pointed out may well have been more determinative for a special Protestant spirituality to come about. At any rate, reflection on these three points deepens our insight into several characteristics of this spirituality.

IV

The abrogation of the central authority

Putting the Bishop of Rome aside resulted in the emergence of national churches. There was no longer an international centre which could regulate things. This is not to say that the national churches were totally on their own. In a sense Wittenberg can be called the Lutheran Rome, and Geneva the Calvinistic one. But however much influence these centres had by means of their dogma and through the theologians who had been trained there, they did not have real authority. They could not lay down any rules. Neither were they supported financially from abroad.

Unhindered by the religious influence Mediterranean Christianity had exerted for centuries, the various regions of Europe could now develop their own mentality. In The Netherlands church life could become not only Reformed, but also typically Dutch. This is noticeable. In certain areas of The Netherlands a melancholic religiosity became characteristic, which expressed itself in an intense fear of eternal judgement, in an often life-long uncertainty as to whether one could regard oneself as elected by God or not, and in a very negative view of man. The 'church of black stockings', as some groups within Dutch Protestantism were characterized, was not only a Protestant but also a Dutch phenomenon. This type of Christianity cannot be found in Switzerland.

Thus the abolition of an international centre with great powers is not without risks. If a local or regional church protects itself against outside influences and is no longer connected with the church of all ages and all places through international contacts, it easily deteriorates into a stagnant pool in which gradually all life is suffocated, thus becoming water which is no longer susceptible to moving by the angel of the Lord. Not only a family, but an ecclesiastical community, too, can degenerate as a result of in-breeding.

That Protestantism wanted to break so radically with the church authorities in Rome, despite the high price it had to pay for this, proves that the rest of Europe experienced the Roman Catholic Church of that time as quite repressive. Protestant reformers were even inclined to revert back to the ancient Germanic ecclesiastical law as it had developed in Europe in the time before Boniface, according to which it fell to the sovereign to determine which religion and which church form he deemed desirable for his territory. The dominion that had previously been overseen by the pope was now entrusted to secular rulers and city councils. Even a moderate man like Gardiner was in favour of this. How sick they were of Rome!

The domination from Rome had resulted in far-reaching consequences for the ecclesiastical and social life of Europe. Rome was the pinnacle of a pyramid. One result of this structure was that only the language of Rome, Latin, was deemed good enough for the realization of salvation. As for Western Europe, God only understood Latin. Therefore, for their relationship with the Almighty the common people had to rely on the mediation by the clergy who had mastered this language. Only this clerical class was allowed to develop an opinion on holy things. Owing to this fixation on Rome, the distance between clergy and laity became unbridgeable. Groups of people in Western Europe had regularly revolted against this duality.

The break with the central authorities in Rome therefore characterizes Protestantism as a liberation movement which, as we saw above, was only possible following the emergence of the new lay intelligentsia in the cities. The abolition of the highest authority was necessary to realize this breakthrough. Emphatically the Protestant reformers called on the people to familiarize themselves with Holy Scripture. The struggle against illiteracy was at the top of the list of wishes which they presented to the sovereigns and city councillors. Each family should have the opportunity to read the Bible in its own language. Through preaching the new views were spread.

The abrogation of the highest authority in Rome also led inevitably to a plea for the priesthood of all believers, just as during the French Revolution the abolition of the monarchy aimed at 'liberty, equality, fraternity' for all. In Protestantism it became normal for active believers to be ordained to an office for only a few years, which was unthinkable in Roman Catholicism.

Admittedly the leaders of the Reformation were shocked by the effect they produced. Gardiner was an example of this. They had a start when they noticed that people without any education were presenting themselves as bearers of God's Spirit and interpreters of God's Word. The most diverse views were propagated. Soon, therefore, the exposition of Scripture was reserved exclusively for the select group of those who had been trained at a university. The one pope, in Rome, was replaced by many small local popes, as the more radical reformers pointed out as early as the sixteenth century. Nevertheless, the abrogation of the authority of the pope was of far-reaching significance for Protestantism.

The abolition of the monastic life

Similarly far-reaching for Protestantism's specific spirituality has been the demise of monastic life. This was the second pillar of European Catholicism.

At first the monasteries recruited their members mainly from children who were received at an early age.[11] Of all persons who played an important ecclesiastical role in Western Europe in the early Middle Ages and of whom we have biographical knowledge, it can be ascertained that they were entrusted to a monastery as an oblate when they were still very young. Apparently, the church already understood in those times what is still realized in the areas of music and sports in our own time, namely that people have to start an adjusted training programme at an early age if they are to rise above a certain level. In the monasteries the children learnt to read and write. This opened up opportunities for them which were unavailable to the rest of the population. And they learnt Latin, the secret language of the mysteries of the church.

Monasteries were the pivot on which Catholicism in the early Middle Ages hinged. They were the centres of experimentation in which new spiritualities were developed and the first attempts were made at science in a Western Europe which had disintegrated after the collapse of the Roman Empire. The monasteries were the church proper, the heart of the church. Here one preached. Here one did penance for the sins of society. In the monasteries the system of confession and penance was developed, before becoming the norm in society at large. In the monasteries they prayed for the souls of the departed, made possible by the generosity of noble families. A more or less accidental by-product of the monastic life was the fact that here women, too, had the opportunity to be trained and to express themselves in religious matters.

Naturally, in the course of time the monastic life underwent significant changes. New models were added to the old ones. Monasteries were also centres of agriculture and care. Due to their number and their possession of land they wielded great economic and political power, and thus they were objects to be desired by landowners, rulers and city councils. They were an essential part of medieval society. Perhaps it is an exaggeration to say that the monastery was the cornerstone of society but, alongside the ecclesiastical hierarchy, it certainly was one of the supporting posts of the spiritual life.

The Reformation swallowed it up. With great enthusiasm and with a religious zeal which was not always pure, wealthy landowners took

---

[11] Concerning this, see in particular Mayke de Jong, *Kind en klooster in de vroege middeleeuwen* (Amsterdam, 1986).

possession of the estates of the monasteries. Innumerable monasteries were plundered in the course of the sixteenth century. Sometimes city councils and rulers allowed the monks and nuns to stay till their death. At any rate, monastic life was no longer a determinative factor in Protestantism.

This had profound consequences. The idea that taking vows, a life of prayer, the imitation of Christ in a narrow sense, meditation, training and discipline could be of value for the spiritual life disappeared. The qualities which were enough to function in society were deemed sufficient also for the religious life. The thought of spiritual record performances was regarded as pride. In Protestantism only two places remained in which to practise spirituality: the church service and the family. So both took over duties which beforehand had belonged to the monastic life. Praising God was now a task of the whole community, on Sundays in the religious service and daily at the meals with the family. Singing the Psalms became common property. The melting monastic life streamed over society at large. The imitation of Christ in a strict sense was no longer reserved for one class of people. In Protestant regions carnival lost ground – indulging in sin *en masse* for a short time was no longer tolerated, which is not to say that one did not sin under Protestant rule.

For women the cessation of the monastic life meant impoverishment. It was no longer regarded as a virtue if a woman wished to remain unmarried and did not want to tie herself to a man. For centuries ecclesiastical office remained closed for her, but neither could she become a nun now; every possibility to develop herself religiously was taken from her. So it is not surprising that it was Protestant churches which first admitted women to the offices. They had little choice; they had no alternative for women with a spiritual calling.

The abolition of the monastic life also meant the cessation of certain forms of relief work. It is true that solutions were found for the poor and the sick. Even before the Reformation gained momentum, cities in Western Europe had taken on important tasks such as education and care of the poor. Yet the character of relief work changed. Protestant society no longer had groups of people at its disposal who were prepared to devote themselves fully to others in distress. It was no longer part of the townscape to see a number of men and women fully available for God and for the needs of society.

Without idealizing the situation as it had been, it must be admitted that the religious life in Protestant areas had less variation to offer. All extreme expressions of piety were banished. There was no longer room for devout women who let themselves be walled up in a cell near the chancel of the church. Life became more severe and more dull.

When in Protestantism the need arose again for meditation tech-
niques and prayer practice, one could not circumvent a return to pre-
Reformation times or excursions outside one's own territory as, for
example, Dietrich Bonhoeffer (1906–1945) noticed when he founded
his seminary at Finkenwalde.[12]

Undoubtedly, the abolition of the monastic life made wealthy landowners and sovereigns richer, but spiritual life poorer.

The cessation of the veneration of saints and relics

It seems as if by the abolition of the veneration of saints and relics
Germanic Christianity wanted to revert to its origins. Before the Ger-
manic peoples came into contact with the Roman Catholic variant the
majority had embraced the Arian faith. Typical of Arianism was the
realization that there is an unbridgeable gulf between God and creation.
God himself could not have become flesh and blood, but only his son,
Christ. As far as the sources that have been preserved tell us this Arian
Christianity was characterized by austerity. It omitted the trappings of
Catholicism. It had no veneration of saints and relics. Depiction of the
divine was unacceptable. In its austerity Arianism was more Jewish. In
their struggle against Catholicism the Muslims emphasized, not without
reason, that they regarded Arianism as a much more acceptable form of
Christianity.[13]

Within Western European Christianity itself the abolition of every
depiction of the divine was repeatedly advocated, especially in areas
where contacts with Jews and Muslims abounded. In Southern France
for some time the Cathars and Waldensians gained great successes by
repelling all visible forms. Protestantism too knew this cleansing fury,
particularly in its Anabaptist and Reformed versions. Even a man like
Gardiner did not mind the abolition of such external features, for
Protestant Christianity austerity was one of the main virtues. So it is not
surprising that Reformed Protestantism, as it developed in The Netherlands in the sixteenth and seventeenth centuries, knew a growing interest in Judaism and Islam. One could even interpret the slogan of the
rebels under the leadership of William, the Prince of Orange – 'rather
Turkish than Papist' – not only politically but also religiously.

Even so, there is no doubt that the Roman Catholic veneration of
saints was never intended to replace or even be an addition to the

---

[12] Auke Jelsma, 'Oefening baart vroomheid: Bonhoeffer en de Moderne devotie', in
Het leven is meer dan ethiek; studies aangeboden aan G.Th. Rothuizen (Kampen, 1987),
pp. 102–17.

[13] Floris Sepmeijer, *Een weerlegging van het christendom uit de 10e eeuw* (Kampen,
1985), p. 35.

adoration which is due to the triune God alone. But it was an expression of the belief that divine salvation could penetrate visible and tangible objects. So, bread could really become the body of Christ and an image of Mary could indeed contain Mary's vitality. It was some sort of channel between the believers on earth and the Mother of God in heaven. The same held true for the relics. The distance between the divine and the human was not unbridgeable. Incarnation remained possible, just as, juxtaposed, deification of man was not excluded, as long as the network of connections was well maintained. And so in the course of time a kind of middle world had come into existence – of church buildings, statues of saints and relics – in which the earthly and the divine had melted together. It was from this that the clerical class received its prestige. This class lived daily in this middle world, in some cases incessantly, and so it participated in the reverence the supernatural evoked in the common people.

In Protestantism this whole middle world was shattered. This was done most consistently in Anabaptist circles. Here the distance between the divine and the human was so strongly emphasized that they did not want to believe anymore that God's Son in becoming man had taken on flesh from Mary. Christ had gone through Mary's womb, so they taught, just as water flows through a pipe. He had manifested himself in her, so taught Melchior Hoffman (d. 1543), just as heavenly dew descends in an oyster shell to grow there into a pearl.[14] But Reformed Protestantism, too, stressed the distance. At the same time Protestants sought to enhance the intimacy between God and man. It was not without significance that Luther had let himself be inspired by German mystics. But they no longer accepted this middle world which had made the common people dependent on the men who were in charge there. As with Islam and Judaism, the Protestant wished to be able to be in contact with God directly – humbly, being aware of the distance, conscious of one's guilt, but at the same time confident and independent.

One of the consequences of such a thorough cleansing was a different spirituality. The whitewashed church buildings were no longer a sacred space in which the light of candles made the shadows move and in which priests, enshrouded by clouds of incense, hurried from the altar to the confessional. In Protestant churches all attention was focused on this one pulpit with the opened book from which the people were

---

[14] See for Melchior Hoffman's monophysitism among others, Klaus Deppermann, *Melchior Hoffman. Soziale Unruhen und apokalyptische Visionen im Zeitalter der Reformation* (Göttingen, 1979), pp. 197–202; Peter Kawerau, *Melchior Hoffman als religiöser Denker* (Haarlem, 1954), pp. 46–50. See also G. H. Williams, *The Radical Reformation*, 3rd edn (Kirksville, MO, 1992), pp. 492–505.

taught. With spirited voices the congregation enthroned God on the praises of his people.

There is another aspect connected with the clearing of relics and saints' images. In Catholic piety the middle world was also the domain of the dead who were still present. Not without reason were they buried in or near the church. The belief that the separation between the bodily cloak and the soul is never absolute in this dispensation, is one of the characteristics of Western European Catholicism. The place where the body, or if need be part of it, had been buried remained the point of contact with the spirit of the deceased. Therefore, that was the best place to call on the saints. People who could afford it preferred to be buried in a monastery which they had founded themselves on the precondition that the monastics would pray for them daily. The assumption was that this did help.

To the Roman Catholic consciousness the dead stayed around. Most of them had not reached their final destiny anyway. In purgatory they had an interest in the intercession and in the masses which were celebrated for them. Saints whom they knew to be in heaven, could be asked for help. The link between the living and the dead remained and added an extra tension to the sacred middle space.

So, through the abolition of the veneration of relics and statues Protestantism also mercilessly severed its ties with its ancestors. This sometimes happened with enormous fanaticism, as in The Netherlands during 'the breaking of the images'. In the course of a few weeks in 1566 hundreds of churches were 'cleansed'. Singing Psalms, the iconoclasts battered down the church doors. They called the statues names and chopped at them with great enthusiasm. So they executed judgement on the dead who for a long time had limited their freedom of movement. 'Breaking of the images: murder of the dead.'[15]

A specific spirituality developed, especially in the more radical movements of Protestantism, which was characterized by the absence of a sacred middle space, did not let itself be hindered by the past, was open to the future, had little sense of the connection between the generations, was autonomous, accountable to God alone, independent and free. Sometimes a shadow of fear fell over this spirituality. It is not always easy to live without a roof over one's head. Belief in a divine election

---

[15] Auke Jelsma, *Fossielen of Vruchten: omgaan met het verleden van de kerk* (The Hague, 1984), p. 12.

which would realize itself despite human failures was able to break through this fear many times, but at other times it was the trap in which it was stuck for ever. The Roman Catholic belief in the possibility of doing penance for one's sins in purgatory offered a space which Protestantism had taken for itself.

V

The three aspects that Bishop Gardiner enumerated in his sermon have indeed enabled us to understand more accurately why in Protestant circles a spirituality could develop which deviated considerably from the Roman Catholic one. The characteristics that we encountered in *De nieuwe Katechismus* can be detected in the sixteenth century too. In all those facets we found a central theme: the abolition of sacred space. The Protestant chose to live without a roof over his head. There is an air of loneliness about him. He can fall back only on himself. No guardian angels protect him. Amulets no longer support him. There are no saints who look down from heaven with concern for his clumsiness. The care of his deceased ancestors no longer ties him to a particular place: 'Let the dead bury their own dead.'[16] Neither are there any communities which have devoted themselves to accompanying the Protestant in all his ways with prayer. Nor can he through confession and on authority of the clergy, who in the sacred middle space administer the means of grace, receive an inner cleansing of his sins. He is on his own, free and independent, but also somewhat pathetic.

It is therefore not surprising that the most well-known ecclesiastical textbook of Reformed Protestantism in The Netherlands, the *Heidelberg Catechism*, starts with the question: 'What is your only comfort in life and death?' The answer expresses the heart of Protestant spirituality:

> That I, with body and soul, both in life and death, am not my own, but belong unto my faithful Saviour Jesus Christ; who, with his precious blood, has fully satisfied for all my sins, and delivered me from all the power of the devil; and so preserves me that without the will of my heavenly Father not a hair can fall from my head; yea, that all things must be subservient to my salvation; and therefore, by his Holy Spirit, he also assures me of eternal life, and makes me sincerely willing and ready henceforth to live unto him.

This is the true picture of a Protestant. Confident and independent. There is no need for a priest anymore. Troublesome penances have become utterly redundant. The Protestant can face the open space. No

---

[16] Matthew 8:22.

dark force can play sinister tricks anymore. Man lives by grace alone, and that is enough, that is, as long as he is not plagued by uncertainty over his election.

This last possibility, the threat of existential uncertainty, was certainly not unthinkable. That is why the need quickly to reduce this open space arose. And so God's Word and God's Spirit were almost fearfully identified with the Bible. According to the Protestant model human history had only two fixed points: the embodiment of God's Son in Jesus of Nazareth and the 'embookment' of God's Spirit in the Bible. The one supported the other. The Bible became the only hold, the direct link with God. In the modern age, orthodox Protestantism becomes very agitated as soon as the authority of Holy Scripture is questioned even slightly. The commotion in the Gereformeerde Kerken in Nederland (the Reformed Churches in The Netherlands) over a synodal report concerning the authority of Scripture, *God met ons* (God with us), was typical of Protestant spirituality.[17] Now that the sacred middle space has been blown away, the Bible is the only shelter left. After throwing off other authorities the Protestants appropriated the Bible with tempestuous zeal. As had previously been said in the sixteenth century, they made it into a paper pope.

Such a polemic expression shows that this shelter was not watertight either. However highly the Scriptures were regarded, however much they were identified with the truth, they had to be interpreted and applied. Now that in principle all other authorities were done away with, man was on his own in understanding the Scriptures and so, in the end, his personal conscience became the only really decisive point of reference. In a fascinating way this becomes obvious from the outset of the Reformation, when Martin Luther has to give account of his writings before the Diet of Worms. He declares that he is prepared to revoke what is contrary to Scripture in his writings, 'provided I will be convinced of error with arguments from Scripture'. But his speech before the young Emperor Charles V and the electors and bishops ended with an appeal to his conscience: 'For to go against conscience is not wholesome, nor is it allowed.'[18]

In the empty space, in which the veneration of deceased saints was no longer tolerated, in which the elements of bread and wine no longer underwent a real and miraculous change into the body and blood of

---

[17] 'God met ons; over de aard van het Schriftgezag', *Kerkinformatie*, 113, February (1981). The report was also translated into English by the Reformed Ecumenical Synod: *God with Us: on the Nature of the Authority of Scripture* (Grand Rapids, MI, n.d.).

[18] Cited (among others) by Heiko A. Oberman, *Die Kirche im Zeitalter der Reformation*, 4th edn (Neukirchen, 1994), pp. 60–61.

Christ, and in which the divine was not tangibly present anymore, all attention was directed to the pulpit with the open Bible. The spirituality which flowered here was sometimes more akin to the Jewish service in the synagogue than to the Roman Catholic mystery cult. The church service and the family became the two centres where this spirituality could thrive.

Of course, in the Protestant theological reflection innumerable other aspects were dealt with, but most characteristics of its spirituality remained as bishop Gardiner of Winchester had already noted: this breaking down of the protective, but also repressive and costly, middle space. If one analyses the stories of the Protestant martyrs, one soon discovers what it was that inspired these most stubborn representatives of Protestantism: abhorrence of what they could only regard as accursed idolatry.

Undoubtedly there is more to be said about Protestant spirituality. People are rarely consistent. Even when intellectually they have rejected certain features of their religious past, they are not necessarily free from them emotionally. Not everybody wanted to go the whole way. Many, Stephen Gardiner for instance, went only halfway, or returned part of the way, shocked by what they had unleashed. It appeared that the inner loneliness that the Protestant had chosen in principle – with his own conscience as his only beacon – was sometimes hard to bear. The new leadership of the various Protestant movements soon feared nothing more than the chaos which threatened to break out if everyone demanded the freedom to live by his own conscience.

As previously mentioned, the exposition of Scripture was soon reserved for people with an academic theological education. Already after one generation most autodidacts, those free spirits who knew Holy Scripture very well but were not educated theologically, the travelling preachers who only spoke their mother tongue and had no knowledge of the ancient languages, had to abandon the field.[19] Because of their exclusive right to interpret the Scriptures, the educated preachers formed once more a middle world on which the common people were dependent. Only they were deemed able, by their preaching, to establish a relation between God's Word and human life.

---

[19] See A. P. F. Wouters, *Nieuw en ongezien. Kerk en samenleving in de classis Delft en Delfland 1572–1621*, vol. I, *De nieuwe kerk* (Delft, 1994), pp. 432–57.

Now, centuries later, we see how this specific dimension of the sermon is slowly ebbing away. People do not believe in it anymore. The pressure of modern culture induces a gradual shift in Protestant spirituality. The influence of the mass media will mean that a verbal culture will lose ground to the need for images and symbols. At the same time, however, within Catholicism the reverence for the clerical class (priests and monastics) is diminishing. They are no longer regarded as *the* bearers of the divine mysteries.

Naturally, this development is deplored on both sides, particularly by those in authority. In Protestant and in Roman Catholic circles an attempt has been made to breathe new life into the function of the sermon in the church service and into the exclusive significance of priestly ordination respectively. It seems to me that both fail to appreciate the changes that have come about in the twentieth century. Man does have a need for a system of ultimate meaning, for fixed points of reference, for shelter against the storms that can ravage life, for new rites, at this time. This need is, however, no longer satisfied by preachers and priests functioning in a church service, but rather in a solidarity of people across all borders. The spirituality which can carry our existence nowadays will be neither typically Roman Catholic nor typically Protestant. Above all, it will be humane. For the survival of humanity, a breakthrough to such a new spirituality seems to me to be of the utmost importance. In mutual solidarity we will be able to recognize the compassion which surrounds us out of eternity. That is the ground under our feet and the roof above our heads.

Index